Parent-Adolescent Relationships

PARENT-
ADOLESCENT
RELATIONSHIPS

Edited by

Brian K. Barber

Department of Child and Family Studies
University of Tennessee
Knoxville, Tennessee

Boyd C. Rollins

Department of Sociology
Brigham Young University
Provo, Utah

UNIVERSITY
PRESS OF
AMERICA

Lanham • New York • London

Copyright © 1990 by
University Press of America®, Inc.
4720 Boston Way
Lanham, Maryland 20706

3 Henrietta Street
London WC2E 8LU England

Library of Congress Cataloging-in-Publication Data

Parent-adolescent relationships / edited by
Brian K. Barber and Boyd C. Rollins.
p.   cm.
"Each of the chapters of this book has been previously
published in issues of Family perspective"—Pref.
Includes bibliographical references.
1. Parent and child—United States.   2. Adolescence.
3. Teenagers—United States—Family relationships.
I. Barber, Brian K., 1954–   . II. Rollins, Boyd C.
HQ755.85.P353   1990   306.874—dc20   89–77236 CIP

ISBN 0–8191–7744–X (alk. paper)

 The paper used in this publication meets the minimum requirements of
American National Standard for Information Sciences—Permanence
of Paper for Printed Library Materials, ANSI Z39.48–1984.

Contents

Preface

In recent decades we have witnessed an increase in the scientific study of adolescence and particularly a growth of interest in adolescent development within the family context. Unfortunately, there are to date few volumes devoted to examining the relationship between family processes and adolescent issues. The recent Leigh and Peterson volume (1986) contributed valuably in this area by providing reviews of key areas of family and adolescent concern. The present volume focus on similar substantive areas but differs by presenting a series of complete studies on parent-adolescent research. This approach allows a more detailed view of the empirical aspects of inquiry in this area.

Each of the chapters of this book has been previously published in issues of *Family Perspective*, a peer reviewed family research journal published by the Family and Demographic Research Institute at Brigham Young University. Seven of the chapters appeared in a special issue on parent-adolescent relationships (Vol. 21, No. 4, 1987). To these were added three articles (Clark and Worthington, Kent, Manscill and Rollins) from previous issues of *Family Perspective*.

The ten chapters that make up this volume not only cover a broad range of key substantive issues in adolescent research (e.g., ego development, identity formation, self-esteem, pubertal development, cognitive development, deviant behavior, religiosity, and academic achievement), but as a whole they illustrate some of the key theoretical and methodological trends occurring in parent-adolescent research. Historically, the social mold perspective has been a guiding theoretical focus of parent-child research (Peterson and Rollins, 1987). That this is still very much the case is evidenced in this volume by the several studies that share this

orientation. However, a growing recognition of the complexity of
family interaction and the relevance of other social contexts to
socialization has resulted in more comprehensive research designs
as well as consideration of other theoretical perspectives. In some
ways this shift in research and theoretical focus can be characterized as an expansion beyond the near-exclusive reliance on the
parent-child dyad as the critical element of socialization (Lewis,
1984). In the present set of studies this expansion is seen through
the inclusion of more complex measures of family processes
(Adams et al. and Hauser et al. chapters) and specifically the marital relationship (Barber and Schneewind chapters). Consistent
with the ecological systems perspective (Bronfenbrenner, 1979),
measures of social contexts outside the family are seen in Barnes
et al.'s inclusion of peer relationships, Dornbusch et al.'s consideration of the academic environment, and Kent's focus on the
joint effects of religiosity and socialization. Finally, the Walters
and Norrell and Manscill and Rollins chapters illustrate the usefulness of considering aspects of the adolescent (cognitive and pubertal development and self-esteem) in understanding family
processes. The theoretical importance of child effects in parent-
child relationships has been recognized in the past decade (Lerner
and Spanier, 1978) and is considered to be an important step to the
development of more complex bidirectional and reciprocal models
of socialization (Bell, 1979).

Methodologically, the set of chapters included in this volume
gives an interesting sampling of the variability in design and data
analysis used in parent-adolescent studies. Designs include both
cross-sectional and longitudinal survey, observation, and case
study. Data analyses range from traditional multivariate to causal
modeling through structural equation analysis.

Substantively, the chapters in this volume address several key
areas of concern in adolescent development. The focus of Adams
et al. and Hauser et al. in their chapters of parental behavior correlates of ego and identity development is on "identity" resolution as
the major developmental task of adolescents (Erikson, 1968). The
concern about identity in adolescent theory emerged in the 1950s
(Weigert, 1986) and has since expanded to include many aspects
of self-evaluation by persons of all age levels (Openshaw and
Thomas, 1986). Much of the literature of adolescent identity
development examines societal contexts of adolescent experience.

The chapters by Adams et al. and Hauser et al. provide conceptual clarity to family interaction processes that help and hinder the attainment of such a developmental task. They suggest that parental control strategies require special attention as the family system adjusts to the increasing self-direction of adolescents.

Like Adams et al. and Hauser et al., who focus on a unique developmental aspect of adolescence to orient their chapters, Walters and Norrell explore the idea that the cognitive development of "formal operations" requires an adjustment in parent-child relationships to accommodate a new perspective on family relationship by adolescent children. This seems like an important link between the literature on individual development and the literature on family development. Similarly, the Manscill and Rollins study highlights an adolescent characteristic, self-esteem, which appears to play an important mediating role in the relationship between parental behaviors and academic achievement. The role of self-esteem in this relationship has been on oft debated issue and this chapter represents a particularly valuable contribution due to its level of analysis (structural equation analysis) and control on relevant variables.

Also using structural equation analysis, the Barber and Barnes et al. chapters assess the effects of multiple social system influences on two key areas of adolescence--one internal (self-evaluation) and one external (deviant behavior). The role of the self in development has received increasing theoretical and empirical attention in recent decades (Gecas, 1982). The Barber chapter emphasizes the complexity of both the adolescent self-esteem construct and its relationship to various family processes, e.g., the parent-adolescent relationship and the marital relationship. It also demonstrates the importance of differentiating the sex of parents and children in such analyses. Adolescent drug use and other forms of deviant behavior are issues of critical social concern. The Barnes et al. chapter contributes to our understanding of the relationship of socialization factors to deviant behavior, particularly by dealing with the central issue of the interface between family and peer factors.

The chapter by Dornbusch and Ritter presents a very interesting interpenetration between the family system and the educational system. It demonstrates how scholarly attainment at school is somewhat at the mercy of particular cultural elements, particular family structures, and particular parent-child relationship qualities. Specifically, the study demonstrates that being an adolescent black male child residing in a single-parent authoritarian home seems to sabotage efforts directed toward educational achievement in school. It raises a very difficult question about the peculiar vulnerability of the adolescent black male in certain circumstances. This research suggests that much more effort needs to be made to understand the whole social ecological environment in which human development takes place (Bronfenbrenner, 1979), and particularly the combined influences of family and other institutions.

The focus of the Kent and Clark and Worthington chapters on religiosity illustrates the current trend in social science research to understand the religion and family connection (Thomas and Henry, 1985). The Kent chapter empirically addresses the unique and joint effects of these two social systems on adolescent behavior. The simultaneous analysis of family and religiosity represents important methodological and theoretical contributions to the literature on adolescent substance use. The Clark and Worthington chapter tackles the central issue of value transmission. Their review of studies on the transmission of religious values from parents to children implicates several key aspects of the socialization environment, e.g., parental behavior, communication, and conflict. The authors issue an important call for greater conceptual clarification and more rigorous research designs.

Finally, the Schneewind chapter raises some methodological and theoretical issues that may have important implications for parent-child research. First, he describes a series of family assessment instruments designed to incorporate family systems issues. Second, by contrasting families matched in several structural and demographic areas, he demonstrates the extent to which such families can vary in internal processes. If such findings are replicated with other families, then these results will have important theoretical implications for the relationship between social context, family process, and individual development.

This volume on parent-adolescent relationships does not provide comprehensive coverage of the growing field of adolescent research in the family context. No single volume can. However, it does contain an interesting sampling of theory and methodology related to several key issues in family and adolescent research. We hope that the volume will serve as a stimulus for future work to include efforts toward conceptual clarity, systems-oriented designs, and more powerful analytical methods. Though no chapters in this volume focused on bidirectional influences in parent-adolescent relationships, we strongly recommend in the future that theoretical formulations explicate social processes that are bidirectional in nature, and that research be designed using structural equation modeling to assess the adequacy of such theoretical formulations. Only when theory becomes more isomorphic with social reality by positing simultaneous effects of multiple variables in reciprocal models, and evidence from the empirical world is used to address the fit of the model, will parent-adolescent research mature into the science that has been anticipated for the past two decades.

Many have contributed significantly to the production of this work. We thank particularly Darwin L. Thomas, editor of *Family Perspective*, and the Family and Demographic Research Institute at Brigham Young University for permission to reprint these articles. We gratefully acknowledge the numerous scholars who anonymously reviewed the studies reported here. Finally, we thank Norene Petersen, Karen Seely, and Melissa Townsend for their editorial and clerical assistance.

BRIAN K. BARBER
BOYD C. ROLLINS

References

Bell, R. Q. Parent, child, and reciprocal influences. *American Psychologist*, 1979, *34*(10), 821-826.

Bronfenbrenner, U. *The ecology of human development*. Cambridge: Harvard University Press, 1979.

Erikson, E. E. Identity: *Youth and crisis*. New York: W. W. Norton, 1968.

Gecas, V. The self-concept. *Annual Review of Sociology*, 1982, *8*, 1-33.

Leigh, G. K., & Peterson, G. W. (Eds.) *Adolescents in families*. Cincinnati: South Western Publishing Co, 1986.

Lerner, R. L., & Spanier, G. B., (Eds.) *Child influences on marital and family interaction: A life-span perspective*. New York: Academic Press, 1978.

Lewis, M. (Ed.). *Beyond the dyad*. New York: Plenum Press, 1984.

Openshaw, D. K., & Thomas, D. L. The adolescent self and the family. In G. K. Leigh & G. W. Peterson (Eds.), *Adolescents in families.* Cincinnati: South-Western Publishing Co, 1986.

Peterson, G. W., & Rollins, B. C. Parent-child socialization. In M. B. Sussman & S. K. Steinmetz (Eds.), *Handbook of marriage and the family.* New York: Plenum Press, 1987.

Thomas, D. L., & Henry, G. C. The religion and family connection: Increasing dialogue in the social sciences. *Journal of Marriage and the Family,* 1985, *47,* 369-380.

Weigert, A. The social production of identity-metatheoretical foundations. *Sociological Quarterly,* 1986, *27,* 165-183.

An analysis of several theoretical perspectives is undertaken to establish the basic dimensions on which the study of parent-adolescent relationships is commonly investigated. Using several basic predictive associations between dimensions of parent-adolescent relationships and psychosocial development of adolescents, an analysis of a series of investigations conducted in the Laboratory for Research on Adolescence was made. Findings appear to generally support the predicted relationships. Suggestions are provided for individuals wishing to enhance the identity development of adolescents from a family relationship perspective.

Parent-Adolescent Relationships and Identity Formation

GERALD R. ADAMS, PATRICIA DYK, AND LAYNE D. BENNION

INTRODUCTION

Recently, family scholars have noted the tendency for developmentalists to study individual development in isolation from the social context in which children live (Leigh and Peterson, 1986). Indeed, in our efforts to write *Adolescent Life Experiences* (Adams and Gullotta, 1983), we found it difficult to find a well-integrated, theoretical based, body of research literature on adolescent development within a family life context. Numerous conceptual and theoretical perspectives have been proposed, but only a few consistently influence the direction of research. Nonetheless, considerable commonalities exist between the various lines of scholarship, although

Gerald R. Adams • Laboratory for Research on Adolescence, College of Family Life; Patricia Dyk and Layne D. Bennion • Department of Family and Human Development, Utah State University, Logan, Utah 84322.

the focus of measurement varies from macro-level through micro-level analyses.

Recognizing these limitations, we shall first examine the focus of several theoretical based research programs and attempt to derive several basic principles or predictions that appear to be emerging across different research programs. Second, we shall examine our own research program on the study of family socialization and adolescent identity development to assess the utility of these "common" principles or assumptions about the effect of the family on adolescent development. Finally, we shall draw some practical implications from our analysis.

SOCIALIZATION FACTORS INFLUENCING ADOLESCENT BEHAVIOR AND DEVELOPMENT

Wesley Becker

Becker's (1964) classic analysis of parenting styles pinpointed the importance of *warmth versus hostility* (defined by some as acceptance-rejection) and *control versus autonomy* (restrictiveness-permissiveness). In a review of published research, Becker found that parental warmth promoted children's acceptance of themselves and the development of self-control. In contrast, hostility and rejection are found to interfere with conscience development and enhance aggressiveness and resistance to authority. Further, restrictive parenting fosters dependency and interferes with the positive effects of independence training (Maccoby and Masters, 1970). Becker (1964), in particular, notes that there are considerable disadvantages for the child if reared in either a restrictive or extensively permissive family environment.

Perhaps the most noteworthy accomplishment of Becker's analysis is his identification of four parenting styles using the two dimensions--warm-restrictive, warm-permissive, hostile-restrictive, and hostile-permissive--and their association with social characteristics in children. He found warm but restrictive parenting associated with politeness, neatness, obedience, and conformity in children, but also with immaturity, dependency, and blind acceptance of authority. Children whose parents combine warmth with democratic procedures were found to be socially competent, resourceful, and appropriately assertive individuals (LaVoie and

Looft, 1973). Hostile and restrictive parenting were associated with the lack of self-identity and a personal sense of adequacy and/or competence in children. Finally, parents that combine hostility with permissiveness were found to have children with delinquency and aggressive behavior tendencies.

It has been observed that warmth and moderate control are facilitative childrearing factors, while hostility and permissiveness are inhibiting or limiting factors. However, to understand each factor, it must be examined juxtaposed with others and not in isolation--a lesson we must contribute to the classic analysis of Becker.

Boyd Rollins and Darwin Thomas

Based upon their review of parental control techniques and parental support--two variables identified as critical in accounting for parental influence in the socialization of children--Rollins and Thomas (1979) suggest that for the sake of conceptual clarity the labels "support" and "control attempts" be adopted for the two variables. Support is defined as behavior manifested by the parent toward the child that makes the child feel comfortable in the parent's presence and confirms in the child's mind that he/she is accepted and approved of by the parent (Thomas et al., 1974). Parental support, a continuous quantitative variable, is evidenced by such parental behaviors toward a child as praising, encouraging, expressing terms of endearment, and physical affection. Hence, high supportive interaction is viewed as facilitative, and high nonsupportive interaction as inhibiting in the development of social competence in children.

Rollins and Thomas define control attempts as parental behavior directed toward the child such as giving directions, suggestions, punishments, and the imposition of and explanation of rules, with the intent of benefitting the child. These researchers also argue for a multidimensional view of the control attempts construct that identifies both "coercive" (less autonomy) and "inductive" (greater autonomy) control attempts. Rollins and Thomas propose that the greater the inductive control attempts of parents, the greater the child's social competence, the greater the coercive control attempts of parents, the less the social competence of the child.

Diana Baumrind

Baumrind's (1978) analysis of parenting styles has provided a "profile" of four common parenting tendencies: *authoritarian, authoritative, permissive,* and *harmonious.* The authoritarian parent attempts to shape, control, and evaluate a child's behavior in accordance with traditional and absolute values and standards of conduct. Such a parent believes in keeping the child in a subordinate role and in restricting the child's autonomy. This strategy discourages verbal interaction, and is thought by the parent to enhance compliance behavior. In contrast, the authoritative parent provides firmness in direction with some freedom to pick and choose by the child--although the limits are usually set for the child by the parent. According to Baumrind, both autonomous self-will and disciplined conformity are valued by such parents. She argues this style most closely approximates the enhancement of social competence in children desired in our society. In further contrast, a permissive parent seeks to provide a nonpunitive, accepting environment in which the child can self-regulate his/her own behavior. Going one step beyond, harmonious parents attempt to cultivate an egalitarian relationship with their children, seldom exercising direct control over them.

Since parental control based on coercion (an authoritarian strategy) is difficult to enforce or legitimate during adolescence, Baumrind (1978) advocates that family control attempts should become more symmetrically distributed during adolescence. She suggests that the optimum magnitude of control should decrease and independence granting increase with the age of the child. As Baumrind (1978) has stated:

While at all ages a control attempt by one person towards another results in psychological forces both to comply and to resist, by adolescence the forces to resist become an important counterforce to compliance because they reflect a stage-appropriate drive toward independence. [p. 260]

Therefore, Baumrind (1978) identifies authoritative and harmonious parenting styles as the most effective in facilitating the development of social competence in adolescents. These parents are inclined to see the rights and duties of parents and children as complementary rather than identical and consider their children's needs and views prior to taking steps to alter the child's actions.

Such parents tend to view control attempts as a vehicle to facilitate competence and, thereby, independence in the child.

Stuart Hauser and Sally Powers

Hauser and associates (1984) and Powers et al. (1983) have constructed a structural-developmental framework utilizing Stierlin's (1974) clinical observations regarding parent-adolescent interactions thought to influence adolescent ego development. Stierlin observed that within disturbed families, parents make numerous attempts to interfere with the autonomous functioning of their adolescent children. Through these *binding* interactions, parents actively resist their child's differentiation. In direct contrast to various types of binding or constraining behaviors (e.g., distracting, devaluing, or withholding), Hauser et al. (1984) have also identified *enabling* interactions of healthy families--ways in which family members encourage or support the expression of more independent perceptions and behaviors from each other (e.g., focusing, explaining, or accepting). Two dimensions of family interaction are recognized as being of particular interest in their theoretical framework--cognitive/attentional and affective/relational (Wynne et al., 1982). Within each of these dimensions there are family interactions that can impede (constrain) as well as facilitate (enable) adolescent development.

Powers et al. (1983) indicate that cognitively stimulating family interactions are not sufficient for ego development; they must be accompanied by an atmosphere of positive affect and support. Additionally, the strongest impact of the family on individual development comes through family interaction that encourages family members to understand one another's viewpoints. Indeed, adolescent ego development was observed by these theorists to be most advanced when families presented high amounts of noncompetitive sharing of perspectives in the absence of low levels of both affectively based conflict and cognitively inhibiting behavior.

David Olson and Hamilton McCubbin

Based on a theoretical framework known as the Circumplex Model of Marital and Family Systems (Olson, McCubbin et al., 1983; Olson, Russell et al., 1983), *cohesion* and *adaptability* are used to assess well-being of families where *communication* serves

a facilitative function enabling families to share with each other
their changing needs and preferences.

Cohesion measures the emotional bonding family members
have with each other. Low cohesion is evidenced by distance between family members. Families with high cohesion are close and
function as a unit rather than as a collective of individuals. Healthy families are theorized to exhibit a more moderate or balanced
blend of bonding and autonomy.

Family adaptability is defined as *the ability of a marital or family system to change its power structure (assertiveness, control, discipline), role relationships, and relationship rules in response to
situational and developmental stress.* [Olson, McCubbin et al.,
1983:48]

The four levels of adaptability range from rigid (very low) to
structured (low to moderate) to flexible (moderate to high) to
chaotic (very high) adaptability. Again, middle levels of adaptability (structured and flexible) are theorized as most conducive
to family functioning.

Since families with adolescents face challenges and stresses unique to this stage of the family life cycle, it is not surprising that
both parents' and adolescents' reports of family adaptability and
cohesion reach a low point during adolescence. However, the
families classified as balanced (midrange on both dimensions
simultaneously) are identified as those best prepared to deal with
the stress and tension of the adolescent years.

David and Linda Bell

David and Linda Bell (1983) have examined parental characteristics as determinants of the family system climate and identified an *individuation* (Bell and Bell, 1982) and a *valuing* process
as having particular importance.

The individuation process associated with parenting behaviors
includes differential self-awareness (healthy and complex self-concept) and a corresponding openness to feedback from others, accurate interpersonal perception, and mutual validation among
family members as central patterns of behavior. In this theory, as
one's self-awareness increases, so does one's understanding of the
complexities of others' personalities and, hence, the enhancement
of openness to others. Further, this leads to more accurate interpersonal perceptions that in turn increase mutual validation (consen-

sual validation). Finally, mutual validation is expected to increase an individual's self-awareness. Indeed, the Bells (1983) have found that female adolescent development of differentiated self-awareness is facilitated by a family system in which people take responsibility for themselves, family members are not overly concerned with one another, and there is little overt conflict. The valuing process focuses on positive self-regard of individual family members and on their ability to support one another. In the Bells' theoretical model, positive self-regard is thought to increase one's openness to others as one generalizes one's self-regard to positive expectations about others. This leads one to show warmth and support in interactions with others that result in mutual support and the experience of being valued by another, which enhances one's own self-esteem. While the individuation process focuses on the development of accurate aspects of awareness (self and others) through mutually validating relationships, the valuating process focuses on the development of positive self-regard through positive support within relationships.

Harold Grotevant and Catherine Cooper

In contrast to the prior conceptualization that conceives of adolescence as a time of breaking down the parent-child bonding relationship, Grotevant and Cooper (1985) view adolescence as a period of gradual renegotiation in relationships that are asymmetrically authority focused to more of a peerlike mutuality between equals. Based on a model of individuation in relationships (Cooper et al., 1983), emphasis is placed on the importance of both *individuality* and *connectedness* within family relationships.

Individuality is reflected by separateness (distinction of self from others) and self-assertion (expressing one's own point of view). Connectedness is reflected by mutuality (sensitivity to and respect for others' views) and permeability (openness and responsiveness to others' views). Grotevant and Cooper's (1985) investigation suggests that families with relatively higher levels of individuality and moderate levels of connectedness have adolescents who develop more advanced forms of identity and self-image.

GENERALIZATIONS FROM AN INTEGRATION OF THEORIES

Using a strategy utilized by Rollins and Thomas (1979), we can delineate several basic theoretical assumptions regarding facilitative and inhibitive parent-adolescent interactions and derive some basic generalizations supported across theoretical frameworks. Our analysis is presented in table 1 and includes major assumptions for both positive and negative features of parental behaviors and delineates both affectional and cognitive factors.

From table 1 we have derived six theoretical generalizations that are suggested by two or more theories. These generalizations read as follows:

Generalization 1. The more emotional facilitative behaviors by parents associated with warmth, companionship, and acceptance, the greater the maturity in adolescent personality development.

Generalization 2. The more cognitive facilitative behavior by parents that is associated with setting reasonable behavioral standards, independence training, acceptance of others' perspectives, disciplined compliance to behavioral expectations, and enabling behaviors that provide explanations and focus on relevant communication issues, the greater the maturity in adolescent personality development.

Generalization 3. The greater the encouragement of self-expression, the acceptance of unique viewpoints, and the degree of respect for, or acceptance of, others' perspectives, the greater the personality maturity of the adolescent.

Generalization 4. The greater the hostility, restrictiveness, emotional distance, or perceived rejection, the less the psychological maturity of the adolescent.

Generalization 5. The greater the frequency of parental binding behaviors, systemic rigidity, or chaos in the family's ability to adjust to the child's growth toward maturity, the less the maturity of the adolescent's personality.

Generalization 6. The greater the maturity of the parents' personality, the greater the maturity of the personality of the adolescent.

As a test of the predictive utility of these generalizations, we have analyzed their usefulness in interpreting the findings from a

Table 1

Factors That Enhance or Impede Adolescent Ego Development

THEORISTS	FACILITATIVE	INHIBITING
Becker (1964)	warmth and independence	hostility/restrictiveness, anxious permissiveness
Rollins and Thomas (1979)	high supportive interaction, inductive control attempts	high nonsupportive interaction, coercive control attempts
Baumrind (1978)	setting reasonable limits, independence training, disciplined conformity, harmonious relations, and egalitarian interactions	restriction-rigidity, permissiveness
Hauser et al. (1984)	enabling support through explaining, focusing, and acceptance	binding through distracting, devaluing, and withholding
Olson, McCubbin et al. (1983)	moderate cohesion with structured/flexible adaptability	emotional distance, overinvolvement (enmeshed), rigid or chaotic adaptability
Bell and Bell (1982, 1983)	self-awareness, openness, positive self-regard associated with positive expectations, warmth and support	
Grotevant and Cooper (1985)	separateness and self-assertion, respect for others and openness	

series of cross-sectional and longitudinal studies we have completed in the Laboratory for Research on Adolescence. These investigations have focused on parent-adolescent relationships and their correlation with or prediction of maturity in identity development. Our relationship measures have included self-perceived measures by adolescents and parents. Identity development has been measured using James Marcia's (1966) conceptualization of identity statuses. In his operationalization of Erikson's (1968) theory of identity formation, Marcia has proposed that identity can be measured along two dimensions--exploration in the search process for a stable and self-defined identity and commitment to relatively stable elements of an identity. By using these two dimensions, he has developed four basic identity statuses. A *dif-*

fused identity status adolescent is one who is neither searching for
a sense of self nor has a clear sense of commitment. This status is
considered the least mature of the four. A *foreclosed* identity
status adolescent has accepted a commitment but without a searching and screening process. Rather, this type of adolescent has
merely accepted what has been given to him or her from parents or
other adults. It is generally thought to be primarily based on
"early childhood identifications" and, while reflecting commitment, is seen as only slightly more mature than that of diffused
youths. A *moratorium* identity status youth, in contrast, has not
found an acceptable commitment, but is searching for the right fit
for that adolescent's self-definition. This youth is more mature
than the others because of the searching process for an identity
that is based on greater self-awareness, complexity, and self-selec-
tion. The hiatus of development is thought to be found in the *identity achievement* status youth. The achieved youth has engaged in
a search process, has experienced an identity crisis, and has
resolved it through self-selected personal commitments that reflect
a self-definition.

Using this distinction with a rank ordering in level of maturity,
we can assess the applicability of aspects of the six generalizations
for their utility in predicting level of maturity in adolescent personality development.

A TEST OF THE GENERALIZATIONS USING IDENTITY DEVELOPMENT AS AN INDICATOR OF MATURITY IN ADOLESCENCE

In three cross-sectional investigations we have examined the
correlation between parents' and adolescents' perceptions of
childrearing behaviors and parent-adolescent relationships
(Adams, 1985; Adams and Jones, 1983; Campbell et al., 1984). A
summary of our major findings (*ps* < .05 or better) are detailed in
figure 1. Further, we have recently completed two longitudinal
studies examining the predictive (or causal) association between
earlier family environment factors and later identity development
(Montemayor et al., in press). In one investigation we assessed
family relationships during the freshman year of college for the
predictiveness of identity development over three years of college.
In another investigation we analyzed family relationships during

EXPLORATION

	Absent	Present
	Diffusion	*Moratorium*
COMMITMENT ABSENT	High perceived maternal and paternal rejection[a] High paternal self-perception of rejection-control[b,c] Paternal perceptions of withdrawn behavior[c] Poor affectionate relationship with mother[a] Maternal perceptions of low affection[b]	Low maternal control/regulation[a] Mother's encouragement of independence[a] Father's fairness in discipline with moderation in praise[a] High perceived companionship, physical affection, and support of parents[a] Maternal reports of low affection[b] High perceived independence in parental perceptions[b,c]
	Foreclosure	*Achievement*
COMMITMENT PRESENT	High maternal perception of companionship[b] Paternal perceptions of withdrawn behavior[c] Perceived affectionate relationship with mother[a] Maternal perceptions of high affection[b]	Low maternal control/regulation[a] Mother's encouragement of independence[a] Father's fairness in discipline with moderation in praise[a] High perceived companionship, physical affection, and support of parents[a] Maternal perceptions of high affection[b] High perceived independence in parental perceptions[b,c]

Note: Conclusions drawn from Adams (1985), Adams and Jones (1983), and Campbell, Adams, and Dobson (1984).
a = adolescent's perceptions; b = mother's perceptions; c = father's perceptions
All associations significant at or better than $p < .05$.

Figure 1. A Summary of Family Correlates Associated with Individual Differences in Identity Formation During Middle and Late Adolescence.

the high school senior year and assessed their predictions for identity development over the course of the freshman year in college. The findings across these four studies can be examined for tentative support of the generalizations derived from the seven theoretical frameworks outlined in table 1.

Generalization 1. The more emotional facilitative behaviors by parents associated with warmth, companionship, and acceptance, the greater the maturity in adolescent personality development. Support for this generalization can be found in data summarized in figure 1. The most mature (identity achieved) adolescents perceived their parents as emotionally supportive by providing them with companionship, physical affection, and interpersonal support. Further, mothers have been found to perceive themselves as highly affectionate toward their identity-achieved adolescents. In study 1 of our longitudinal investigations, we likewise found companionship to be a significant predictor of continual progressive growth in identity formation over three years of college. Similarly, foreclosed adolescents who made some identity gains perceived their mothers as affectionate and involved with them.

Generalization 2. The more cognitive facilitative behavior by parents that is associated with setting reasonable behavioral standards, independence training, acceptance of others' perspectives, disciplined compliance to behavioral expectations, and enabling behaviors that provide explanations and focus on relevant communication issues, the greater the maturity in adolescent personality development.

Once again, as summarized in figure 1, we find that low levels of control or regulation of behavior, high encouragement of independence, fairness in disciplinary practices, and the use of praise as an enabling behavior are correlated with the highest levels of maturity in identity. Further, in study 2 of our longitudinal research we have found that moderate levels of conflict, which we interpret to suggest acceptance of a moderate degree of difference in opinions, is predictive of progressive growth in maturity from the senior year of high school through the first year of college.

Generalization 3. The greater the encouragement of self-expression, the acceptance of unique viewpoints, and the degree of respect for, or acceptance of, others' perspectives, the greater the personality maturity of the adolescent.

The primary support we have for this generalization has been noted earlier. However, independence training that is associated with being identity achieved would suggest that parents who encourage autonomous and independent behavior are also encouraging greater maturity in their adolescents.

Generalization 4. The greater the hostility, restrictiveness, emotional distance, or perceived parental rejection, the less the psychological maturity of the adolescent. Clearly the lowest level of identity development is associated with rejection, control, and poor affectionate relationships. This conclusion is readily supported by findings summarized in figure 1. Further, in study 2 of our longitudinal research, controlling and over-organizing parental behavior has been observed to predict continual regressive development in identity formation, while study 1 demonstrated that rejection-control and withdrawal are predictive of regression in maturity during the college years.

Generalization 5. The greater the frequency of parental binding behaviors, systemic rigidity, or chaos in the family's ability to adjust to the child's growth toward maturity, the less the maturity of the adolescent's personality. We have not assessed the basic elements of this generalization; however, indirectly we find that over-controlling behaviors as binding behaviors are associated with lower identity status development and that withdrawal (as a form of withholding) is predictive of regressive growth patterns in identity.

Generalization 6. The greater the maturity of the parents' personalities, the greater the maturity of the personality of the adolescent. Social learning theory suggests that parents provide a role model that is likely to be emulated by the child. To assess this possibility within the context of identity formation, Adams (1985) assessed both parents' and adolescents' identity statuses and compared them to determine if greater parental maturity is predictive of greater maturity in adolescents. While lower level identity status parents had a mixture of lower and higher identity status youths, the more mature identity status parents (moratorium and achievement statuses) had an overwhelming majority of equally mature adolescents. Further, an analysis of the perceived interaction styles of the mature identity status parents revealed they used many of the positive behaviors that are facilitative of maturity in their adolescents as identified in generalizations 1, 2, and 3.

IMPLICATIONS FOR PARENTING

Our heuristic analysis of several data sets useful in examining the six generalizations suggests considerable theoretical promise for using them in parenting recommendations. While numerous implications from the findings partially supporting the generalizations can be made, we wish to focus on just four.

First, the importance of emotional facilitating behaviors must be underscored. It is important to treat one's child in a warm and accepting way and engage the youth with companionship that enhances communication. However, extreme patterns of affectional expression can discourage the youth from searching for self-evaluated and self-defined answers. It may lock the youth into an enmeshed environment that is too uncomfortable to leave. Autonomy striving and independence behavior may be seen by the adolescent, the parents, or both as disappointing or rejecting the expectations of loving parent(s). Therefore, as is true with most good things, a careful balance is needed. Lots of love coupled with independence training or encouragement of self-exploration may defeat the over-affectional patterns that are otherwise inhibitive.

Second, setting reasonable standards for behavior, using praise to encourage compliance and reinforce expected conduct, and enabling behaviors that allow reciprocity and enhance clarity in communication appear important to the facilitation of maturity by adolescents. Parents should discuss boundaries of acceptable behavior with their adolescents. But parents should listen to the perspective of their youth and give some degree of latitude for autonomous striving and independence experiences.

Third, hostility, rejection, withdrawal, control, and emotional distance are unproductive forms of parental behavior. Adolescents need to know they are loved even when they engage in unacceptable behaviors. A balance of loving attention and reasonable standards of behavior is needed to help facilitate an adolescent's growth toward maturity.

Finally, our evidence suggests a broad pattern of affection, encouragement of independence, fairness in discipline, and encouragement to express one's viewpoints are needed to maximally facilitate growth. Such findings suggest that a complex "array" of parenting skills is needed to be fully effective. This means that we as parents must grow, adapt, change, and listen to our adolescents as they themselves mature. The family system, to be effective, must also be adaptive to the changing needs and abilities of its children.

REFERENCES

Adams, G. R., Family correlates of female adolescents' ego identity development. *Journal of Adolescence*, 1985, *8*, 69-82.

Adams, G. R., & Gullotta, T. *Adolescent life experiences*. Monterey, CA: Brooks/Cole, 1983.

Adams, G. R., & Jones, R. M. Female adolescents' identity development: Age comparisons and perceived childrearing experiences. *Developmental Psychology*, 1983, *19*, 249-256.

Baumrind, D. Parental disciplinary patterns and social competence in children. *Youth and Society*, 1978, *9*, 239-276.

Becker, W. C. Consequences of different kinds of parental discipline. In M. L. Hoffman & L. W. Hoffman (Eds.), *Review of child development research*. New York: Russell Sage Foundation, 1964

Bell, D., & Bell, L. Family climate in the role of the female adolescent: Determinants of adolescent functioning. *Family Relations*, 1982, *31*, 519-527.

Bell, D., & Bell, L. Parental validation and support in the development of adolescent daughters. In H. D. Grotev & C. Cooper (Eds.), *Adolescent development in the family: New directions in child development*, 27-42. San Francisco: Jossey-Bass.

Campbell, E., Adams, G. R., & Dobson, W. R. Familial correlates of identity formation in late adolescence. *Journal of Youth and Adolescence*, 1984, *13*, 509-525.

Cooper, C., Grotevant, H., & Condon, S. Individuality and connectedness in the family as a context for adolescent identity formation. In H. D. Grotevant & C. Cooper (Eds.), *Adolescent development in the family: New directions in child development*. San Francisco: Jossey-Bass, 1983.

Erikson, E. H. *Identity: Youth and crisis*. New York: Norton, 1968.

Grotevant, H., & Cooper, C. Patterns of interaction in family relationships and the development of identity exploration in adolescence. *Child Development*, 1985, *56*, 415-428.

Hauser, S., Powers, S., Noam, G., Jacobson, A., Weiss, B., & Follansbee, D. Familial contexts of adolescent ego development. *Child Development*, 1984, *55*, 195-213.

LaVoie, J. C., & Looft, W. R. Parental antecedents of resistance-to-temptation behavior in adolescent males. *Merrill-Palmer Quarterly*, 1973, *19*, 107-116.

Leigh, G., & Peterson, G. *Adolescent in families*. Cincinnati, OH:
   South-Western Publishing Company, 1986.

Maccoby, E. E., & Masters, J. C. Attachment and dependency. In P. H. Mussen
   (Ed.), *Carmichael's manual of child psychology* (3rd ed.). New York:
   Wiley, 1970.

Marcia, J. Development and evaluation of ego identity status. *Journal of
   Personal and Social Psychology*, 1966, *3*, 551-558.

Montemayor, R., Adams, G. R., & Brown, B. B. *Contributions of the family to
   ego-identity development during middle and late adolescence*. Ohio State
   University, Department of Psychology, in press.

Olson, D. H., McCubbin, A., Barnes, H., Muxen, M., Larsen, A., & Wilson, M.
   Families: What makes them work. Beverly Hills, CA: Sage, 1983.

Olson, D. H., Russell, C. S., & Sprenkle, D. H. Circumplex model of marital and
   family systems: VI. Theoretical update. *Family Process*, 1983, *22*, 69-83.

Powers, S., Hauser, S., Schwartz, J., Noam, G., & Jacobsen, A. Adolescent ego
   development and family interaction: A structural-developmental
   perspective. In H. D. Grotevant and C. Cooper (Eds.), *Adolescent
   development in the family: New directions in child development*. San
   Francisco: Jossey-Bass, 1983.

Rollins, B. C., & Thomas, D. L. Parental support, power, and control techniques
   in the socialization of children. In W. R. Burr, R. Hill, F. I. Nye, & I. L.
   Reiss (Eds.), *Contemporary theories about the family* (Vol. 1). New York:
   Free Press, 1979.

Stierlin, H. *Separating parents and adolescents*. New York: Quadrangle, 1974.

Thomas, D. L., Gecas, V., Weigert, A., & Rooney, E. *Family socialization and
   the adolescent*. Lexington, MA: Heath, 1974.

Wynne, L., Jones, J., & Al-Khayyal, M. Healthy communication patterns:
   Observations in families at risk for psychopathology. In F. Walsh (Ed.),
   Normal family processes. New York: Guilford, 1982.

Of all the stages of life, adolescence is the most difficult to describe. Any generalization about teenagers immediately calls forth an opposite one. Teenagers are maddeningly self-centered, yet capable of impressive feats of altruism. Their attention wanders like a butterfly, yet they can spend hours concentrating on seemingly pointless involvements. They are often lazy and rude, yet, when you least expect it, they can be loving and helpful (Csikszentmihalyi and Larson, 1984:xiii).

2

Family Interiors of Adolescent Ego Development Trajectories

STUART T. HAUSER, SALLY I. POWERS, GIL NOAM, AND MARY KAY BOWLDS

This engaging comment highlights the shifting complexities of teenage life. For many years we have been studying one especially prominent setting of this life--the family. Our research program (Hauser et al., 1983, 1984) maintains a dual emphasis, following individual adolescent socioemotional development *within* the family. Developmental paths of early adolescent psychiatric patients and high school students are traced over several years; simultaneously, the relationships of these teenagers with their parents are observed. Basic underlying questions involve how these family relationships contribute to variations in adolescent development and how families may be changed by this development. This paper presents recent longitudinal findings based on annual developmental assessments, clinical interviews, and family discussions. We begin by introducing a new set of constructs, adolescent ego development trajectories. Then, using specific cases, individual and family aspects of these trajectories are illustrated.

Stuart T. Hauser, Sally I. Powers, Gil Noam, and Mary Kay Bowlds • Harvard Medical School, Cambridge, Massachusetts 02115.

The overall focus of ego development, measured by a specially designed 36-item sentence completion test (Loevinger and Wessler, 1970), is upon the framework of meaning that the individual imposes upon both inner experience and the perception and experience of other people and outside events. This perspective conceptualizes sequential stages of socioemotional development. In the earliest measurable stages, impulses are predominant forces in the individual's life. Control over these impulses is experienced as undependable. Conscious concerns involve satisfaction of physical needs, including sexual and aggressive. The view of the world is egocentric and concrete. In the self-protective stage, following the impulsive one, there is an understanding that rules exist, but it is only out of self-interest that they are obeyed. Interpersonal relations are primarily exploitative and manipulative. Conscious concerns are with control and domination. Later intermediate stages are the conformist stages. Rules are obeyed simply because they are rules. Morality is partly internalized. Some reciprocity begins to emerge, although relations with others are seen in terms of concrete events and actions, rather than feelings and motives (Loevinger, 1976).

The higher postconformist stages are marked by increasing self-awareness and realizations that the "right ways" of living are relative to situations. Moral standards are internalized. Interpersonal relations come to be seen in terms of feelings and motives, rather than actions. There is greater understanding of emotional interdependence, rather than simply independence (Loevinger, 1976).

ADOLESCENT EGO DEVELOPMENT TRAJECTORIES

Besides considering specific stages of ego development, a second way to conceptualize adolescent ego development is in terms of "trajectories," the form of development, the profile of stages, that the adolescent shows over a period of several years. A range of ego development trajectories can be found during adolescence. Some boys and girls begin their adolescent years in the early stages of ego development, continuing to be highly dependent on their parents, almost unaware of differences between themselves and others, and relating to peers and adults through largely exploitative styles. In addition, these adolescents use relatively simply cognitive constructions, responding to situations and questions with few options (either/or, "black and white" thinking). If they remain at these stages over two or more years, they represent *arrested* ego development.

A second group of adolescents are intensely involved with acceptance by friends and compliance with prevailing social rules. Their awareness of individual differences and complex views is, at best, limited. They hold and rarely question socially prized categories and slogans. In terms of ego development, these adolescents are at the conformist stages, frequently found during adolescent years. If they do not advance to higher stages, we classify them as *consistent conformists*, exemplified by one of the high school students, Lou.

A third trajectory includes adolescents who express higher, postconformist ego stages. They show adherence to norms based on inner standards, increased distance or autonomy from parental views, abiding interest in mutuality with others, and a strong interest in complexity of experience, in paradox or contradiction. If they remain at these high levels, they represent *precociously advanced* ego development, and contrast most strikingly with ego development arrests. Sarah, one of our psychiatric patients, illustrates this unusual trajectory.

Finally, a fourth trajectory is *progressive* ego development, where the adolescent shifts upward from earliest preconformist stages to conformist, or from conformist to postconformist, over a two- to three-year period. This trajectory is illustrated by a second high school student, Lois.

FAMILY RELATIONSHIPS

Families vary enormously in their tolerance for the differentiation and autonomy of their members, a matter especially salient during adolescence. At one extreme are those families that applaud new steps (physical and psychological) of adolescent and adult members. At the opposite extreme, and the one given most attention in clinical work, are families that are highly perturbed by ways an individual member changes as he or she prepares to, or actually does, depart from the family group. This departure may be physical or psychological, and may challenge a single family member or rock the entire family system by the ensuing change. Tightly held emotional bonds may be jeopardized, a rigid power structure may no longer be enforceable, or the family's unyielding moral beliefs may become more apparent and fragile when scrutinized by the shrewd, skeptical adolescent.

A clarifying perspective for thinking about how family relationships may contribute to adolescent ego development trajectories involves the overarching concept of *individuation*, a quality of dyadic relationships generated by family members and "seen in the interplay between the individuality and connectedness of the partners" (Grotevant and Cooper, 1986:87). Individuality is marked by *separateness* (descriptions of the self as distinct from others) and *self-assertion* (expressing one's own viewpoint, taking responsibility for expressing it clearly). In adolescence, where differentiation is so important yet so problematic, separateness and self-assertion are crucial properties of family relationships and can potentially enhance or deter adolescent ego development, since these properties support or undermine the holding of different opinions and feelings by family members.

The second component of individuation in family relationships that can enhance or impede adolescent ego development is *connectedness*. The sustaining of either gradual changes or sudden spurts in adolescent autonomy requires more than the family's acknowledgement of separateness and encouragement of self-assertion. Continuing bonds between adolescent and parent, although now transformed, provide a crucial backdrop for growth through adolescence and into adulthood (Coelho et al., 1963). Connectedness is expressed through *mutuality* (the individual's respect for the views and feelings of others) and *permeability* (the individual's openness and responsiveness to others) (Grotevant and Cooper, 1985, 1986).

These relational qualities appear in ongoing verbal and nonverbal discourse within the family. The family's stance toward such fundamental qualities is ordinarily "taken for granted," not questioned or made explicit until challenged by a new family member, by a major change in a member (such as adolescence), or by a therapist. With respect to ego development trajectories reflecting growth (progressive, precociously advanced), separateness is expressed through distinct perceptions and descriptions of how one family member differs from another. Lois and her family illustrate this pattern for progressive ego development. Self-assertion may appear through the clear account by a family member of how she has arrived at a particular point of view, as will be seen in the cases of both Sarah and Lois. Forms of connectedness that enhance adolescent ego development include respect for others' views and responsiveness to them. In some families, encouragement for others' views is conveyed through the offering of self-disclosures, as parents share with their adolescent touching details of their own early history and inner conflicts, thereby offering the adolescent permission to reciprocally disclose such difficult complexities.

Family relationships can also interfere with, or inhibit, adolescent ego development. With respect to separateness, there may be a failure to see the self, and others, as distinct or unique, responding as though members were "two peas in a pod." During adolescence, there are especially strong countervailing pressures against the adolescent's expanding and contracting movements toward new autonomy; an autonomy that appears unpredictably and often back-to-back with almost transparent yearnings to be closely held. Parents and adolescent may combat clear recognition of how they now increasingly differ from one another--in ideas, feelings, and actions. Yet the differences surface in many forms, through struggles over the car, dating practices, and curfews. This reluctance to acknowledge and appreciate new differences is especially clear in the family of Lou, one of the consistent conformists.

Besides resistance to separateness, another family aspect of arrested or sluggish adolescent ego development is restrained self-assertion. The adolescent, or one of his parents, is vague about his ideas, or quickly abandons them when challenged. In terms of connectedness, problematic features are painfully familiar, and can be even more dramatic. Instead of mutuality, there is self-centeredness and asynchrony, where parent and adolescent are on "different wavelengths," on tangents from one another as they talk about either completely different subjects or variations of the same one. Disengagement or nonparticipation by a teenager, and asymmetric participation or domination by a parent or adolescent, also reflect nonmutuality in relationships. Similarly, there are forms of diminished permeability that characterize families in which the adolescent's development has been slowed or arrested. Consider the pressure toward rapid solution of a family conflict resulting in premature resolution or closure, as mother imposes the "right" answer, in contrast to continued openness to unexpected solutions or new ideas from other family members. Impatience and anxiety over sharp differences can also fuel disrespect, ridicule, and abuse directed toward family members taking different paths. The result is a wall, a distinct barrier or opaqueness. New thoughts or perceptions are unwelcome in these closed systems. Further signs of opaqueness are the presence of relatively immutable coalitions or alliances within the family, ones that do not shift with the changing perceptions or development of members. The family system lacks elasticity, it does not move in response to individual members' changing awareness, needs, and learnings.

In summary, there are dimensions of family life that may "matter" for varying ego development trajectories--trajectories that reflect advances and derailings of adolescent ego development. We have focused on the likely importance of specific family *relationships*, the ongoing bonds between family members and how they may underlie different paths of adolescent ego development. Our assumption is that clarifying relationship contributions will provide one "window" into understanding the complex interplay between family context and adolescent ego development. Through several case studies, links between these family relationships, parent development, and adolescent ego development trajectories can be illustrated.

Such insights about the family context require a way to watch families in action. Our method is based on a "revealed differences" procedure (Strodtbeck, 1958) where family members discuss their different solutions to perplexing moral dilemmas constructed by Kohlberg (1969). One dilemma, for example, involves "Heinz," whose wife is dying of cancer. He cannot afford the steep price ($2,000) that the druggist is charging for the radium that can cure his wife. But the druggist will not sell it to him for the amount ($5) that he can afford, despite the fact that this was the druggist's cost. Heinz decides to break into the store to steal the drug in order to save his wife's life. After offering their individual solutions in separate interviews immediately preceding the family discussion, the family is instructed to discuss their specific differences about questions such as Heinz's decision to steal the drug and possible punishment. Besides arguing these differences, they are asked, if possible, to come to a *family* solution of these differences. Transcripts are made of the audiotapes of these discussions, which occur after the interviewer has left the room.

THREE ADOLESCENTS AND THEIR FAMILIES

The first of the ego development trajectories is one most familiar to clinicians. These are adolescents who have prematurely halted in their development. They have a limited repertoire of emotional responses to stresses or other events and restricted cognitive styles, relying heavily on stereotypes. Their interpersonal styles emphasize giving to or taking from other people, and dominance/submission relationships. They are impulsive. With respect to rules and impulse control, what is important is getting away with it, breaking or not breaking the law. Abstract principles and conflicts over ethics or values are simply not relevant.

Within families of arrested adolescents, there are few instances of connectedness between these teenagers and their parents. Instead, there are many moments of disengagement, turning away, or indifference between parent and child, as each seems to be speaking a different language. Rather than being permeable in their responses to one another, they express opaqueness, rejecting and devaluing ideas and feelings from one another. Both parents and adolescent participate in these problematic relationships, ones that usually have a long and tortured history. These family relationships are often traceable to repeated earlier wounds, unexpected mother-child separations, multiple marriages, and severe school difficulties. Within these families, most apparent are the severe ruptures or gulfs between parents and adolescents; the absence of support from both parents; the limited or total lack of self-assertion or separateness from the adolescent; and the striking imbalances in the family.[1]

Rather than continue to catalogue the difficulties so rampant in these strikingly impaired families, we now turn to three specific cases, ones that highlight *other ways* family relationships may link with adolescent trajectories. These cases represent adolescent paths that may be closely influenced by their current family contexts. In contrast to the early arrests, there are clear signs that the families are responding to current pressures from the adolescent toward differentiation and separation. An additional reason to

---

[1]Several boys and girls who show arrested ego development, from normal and psychiatric samples, are presented at length in the forthcoming book, *Family interiors of adolescent development* (Hauser et al., 1988).

focus on these other families is that they suggest aspects of the family that may be especially sensitive to adolescent-specific issues. With an increasing awareness of ripples or waves issuing from the adolescent, current family responses can be disentangled from the historical percipitate that is usually so painfully obvious in the more disturbed families. By being clear about which family patterns are more adolescent-specific, it may be possible to be more precise about *new* issues now activated in the more disturbed families of arrested adolescents.

Consistent Conformist: Lou

In contrast to the early arrests, adolescents who reach and remain at the conformist level are perhaps least problematic to adults as well as their peers. They participate in group activities, they have friends, they do not puzzle anyone, and, by and large, are "team players." Group norms, regulations, and rules do not generate problems. For the most part, they see the importance of cooperating and going along with standards set within the school, within their families, and within the larger social setting. Consistently conformist adolescents are aware of their feelings, but most often in general terms, or as cliches. Lou[2] was at the conformist level of development in the first and subsequent years of our annual observations.

In the early spring of his freshman year, Lou was amazed and conflicted over the "freedom" that he had in high school. In his grade school, tight rules and control were the order of the day.

I went to [North School] and I had Dr. Doe as a principal, and the school was run like a private, like an . . . almost like an institution. He was very, he was like an excellent principal, and very strict you know, it was things like, if you would do something wrong, they'd send you to The Bench. . . . You would have to stay after school, and it's like here I run around all the time, go up the wrong staircases.

Although Lou was somewhat critical of this "strictness," his overriding reaction was a welcoming one. It was a relief for him to have his time so well-structured by outside authorities. Lou felt uncomfortable with more independence; he felt greater confidence when watched over, when told what to do, and when clear actions

[2] All names of adolescents and parents are fictitious. Moreover, any specific identifying details (school, work, etc.) have been changed to preserve anonymity.

followed his violations of any of these rules. His family was run much like the North School. Lou was grounded the moment his grades slipped:

And, uh, my parents immediately took action. . . . No telephone calls, uh, I don't have any TV anyway. I'm sort of used to it. I'm not allowed to watch TV on school nights.

In Lou's eyes, this firm discipline led to his better school performance. Through the careful regulation of his time, Lou raised his grades, a significant accomplishment for both him and his parents. As his grades improved, Lou's parents decided that he should, nonetheless, continue adhering to all the restrictions, a position that he readily accepted. The establishing and enforcing of these rules serves as a powerful link between Lou and his parents. His vision: "If I do something [to violate the rules], I'll get creamed," reflects the significance of parental monitoring in the relationship between Lou and his parents, a relationship that certainly does not proclaim separateness and self-assertion.

A significant force behind Lou's preoccupation with rules is his fear of losing control. It is important to be "cool," not "emotional." Lou actively worries about the dangers of erupting when upset by others:

Most of the time I'm, most of the time I'm just cool. . . . I don't like to get annoyed. I don't like to get very emotional, cause I think you sort of make a fool of yourself when you're very emotional.

Through the descriptions Lou presents in his interview, and their own sentence completions, pictures of his parents emerge-- pictures that abound with rules, parental concerns, and "love" of parents. Mrs. Jackson is at a higher level of ego development than her husband or son, and expresses many complex perceptions and conflicts about herself and others. She is seen by Lou as the more receptive parent. Mr. Jackson appears to be conventional and rigid. Moreover, and perhaps most relevant, it is likely that Mr. Jackson is less empathic toward Lou, in light of his moodiness and brittle sensitivity to others' criticisms. The influence of the different developmental levels, preoccupations, and mood states of its members is apparent in the Jackson family relationships.

Differentiation of its members poses a special threat for the Jackson family. A basic feature of the family is the demand for a high degree of consensus, the need for its members to tightly adhere to the same beliefs and values. Family members occasionally venture from the group, experimenting with different views and "fantasies." But a confluence of powerful familial forces always leads each member to return to the family's established views, through either a blunting or rejection of their deviant ideas. Although this dynamic is most visible in Lou's negotiations with his parents, it is important to recognize that consensus and opposition to intrafamilial differentiation is a prominent characteristic of the Jackson *family*. In other words, we would be overlooking a basic dimension were we to see Lou's frequent conflicts with each parent as simply evidence of child-parent problems, or as a transient phase in the life of this family occurring while Lou is an oppositional teenager.

Early in their moral dilemma deliberations, the Jacksons lucidly express their discomfort with separateness. Mrs. Jackson thinks that Officer Brown should not report Heinz's stealing of the drug for his wife, while Mr. Jackson and Lou both think that the policeman should report him. The following sequence is triggered by the interviewer's announcement of this difference:

Mother: Can I please talk since the two of you agree? All right?
Lou: We'll get her Dad! (laughs) This is it, pal . . .
Mother: Be quiet.
Lou: Okay. Right, I won't say a word. You have the floor.
Mother: (interrupting) I have the floor . . . I have the floor.
Father: I've been alone before, so don't get too uptight about it.
Mother: All right . . . I'm not uptight!
Lou: Okay (laughs). She'll beat us both bloody (laughs). Okay? . . .

Mr. Jackson's comment about his wife's anxiety over her potential isolation from the other family members, and Lou's "joke" about her "beating us both bloody," point to the powerful forces set off as Mrs. Jackson deviates from both of them. Eventually, after hearing much from Mr. Jackson about the "logic" of a policeman fulfilling his duties, Mother shifts her position, announcing, "I agree . . . I give in. We give in."

In the individual interview, weeks before the family discussion, Lou described how his parents force him ("cream him") to conform. Lou sometimes provokes his parents' forceful actions, but more than this is involved. At stake is the importance of Lou's ideas being in line with those of the family. The Jacksons express mounting impatience toward Lou, as he insists that Heinz should not steal the drug for his wife if he doesn't love her.

Lou: Well, all right, let's say when they, they're on the grounds for divorce. Let's say they can, couldn't stand, let's say they, let's say they . . . they almost killed each other. Let's say that . . .

Father: (interrupting) You're mixing apples and oranges, Lou.

Lou: (interrupting): All right, but you don't know that. It could have been a . . .

Mother: (interrupting) It doesn't matter!

There follow intermittent interruptions and "acting" by Lou. Yet mixed with his irritating antics is his persistent position that he would not steal for a wife, or anyone, that he disliked.

Lou: You save a life! Anybody's? Even the kid that just punched me? . . . But why should I risk my neck for him? No way. I'm not morally obligated to him.

Mother: We're not talking about your kid in the hall. We're talking about a man and wife.

Mr. Jackson then tells Lou that he's not being very "logical" in his thinking, a comment clearly not to Lou's liking. Lou goes on to elaborate his own "logical assumptions," leading to yet another confrontation between him and his parents:

Lou: You're saying that I think all emotionally about it?

Father: Absolutely! If you hate her, you're not going to save her, if you don't hate her, and she's your wife, you're going to save her . . . I mean, it's crazy!

Lou: All right, let's think about this logically. Logically.

[After a brief exchange between Lou and his mother.]

Lou: (interrupting) Yeah, but you see, you two, because you're teamed up, have morally influenced me, like you do in a lot of cases.

Mother: We do our best.

Father: (laughing) That's my job, kid!

[Lots of laughter and confusion now ensue.]

Lou: Okay, we've settled that.

The family then tells the interviewer that they "agreed" and Mother makes a revealing joke:

Mother: We didn't even have to hit him [Lou] very hard . . . It didn't matter . . . we hit quietly.

It is in the final discussion of the evening that Lou most clearly identifies this most important family dynamic. Lou is once again pitted against both parents in his opposition to suspending the sentence for Heinz. The family's fervent feelings about members being too different from the group, and needing to "rejoin," rapidly surfaces after the interviewer announces this newest difference.

Mother: Well, I think he's [Lou] gonna change his mind.

Lou initially defends himself. Both parents become increasingly active in their participation, emphasizing the importance of a judge's "humanity" and the cruelty of "throwing Heinz in jail." Lou feels their combined pressure: "You're pushing me into a corner again" (laughs). "They always do this."

And they continue to hammer home their point, using such persuasive expressions as jail being for "hardened criminals," the "bread and water" of jail. They press hard by offering examples of how Lou might one day be in extenuating circumstances and have to steal, as further ways to try to persuade him of his incorrect position. Mrs. Jackson frequently reiterates her metaphor of "the balance of the scales of justice," and Mr. Jackson reminds Lou over and over of "logic." Faced with all of these arguments, persuasions, and pressures, Lou eventually capitulates, joining his parents' position.

Father: Now you have a chance to save him.

Lou: I'd like the judge to suspend the sentence.

Father: Okay. All right. Then we agree.

Lou: (to parents and interviewer) So I never win.

Mother: Right.

Lou: Put that down. I never win (in staccato voice). I never win. Me.

Mother: (laughs)

Father: Were you the only, the only one that's been the minority opinion tonight?

Lou: No!

Father: All right. That's better.

Lou: I've never on still. Not on my own.

The theme that emerges is one of the pressure to "conform," through ideas and actions. The pattern is at times difficult to discern, since Lou often presses his parents to "cream him," to force him to behave more in line with the rest of the family. But the

family, in more muted form, treats each of the members in similar
ways.

Precociously Advanced: Sarah

Our first contrast with these two ego development trajectories,
representing early and intermediate stages, is a precociously advanced adolescent girl. Unusually mature adolescents frequently
evoke delighted and, at times, perplexed reactions from adults, as
these adolescents express unexpectedly insightful perceptions
about themselves and their surroundings. Far earlier than most of
their peers (and many adults), they seem to understand complex
personal relationships and subtle aspects of their inner lives.
These children may be considered "gifted," but not in the ordinary
sense of academically gifted children. Rather, their strengths lie in
their abilities to see and convey "shades of gray," contradictory
ideas, paradoxes, and novel observations and understandings.
They are aware of many, often inconsistent, feelings. Differences
among friends are welcomed, not simply "tolerated" or rejected in
favor of more palatable stereotypes.

Sarah was 16 years old when she entered the study. In her
second year at the hospital, now living in a less structured setting,
she was clearer about her mood swings and the desperate feelings
that had led to overdoses and wrist slashings in the past three
years. Sarah is one of three psychiatric patients who began the
study with high ego development levels. Sarah then functioned at
a slightly lower stage (transition to postconformist) over the following two years before returning to her initially high postconformist stage in the final year, four years later. Her interview is
marked, from the first moments, by clear indications of her very
advanced development, as she describes her recent history and
feelings with much nuance and complexity. At the same time, she
conveys her intense but vacillating self-depreciation, telling the interviewer how she is the "screwed up one in my family."

Although it is now a less pervasive problem, Sarah still alludes
to her desitation in disclosing these feelings to others. Before her
hospital admission, Sarah used more dramatic actions--such as
suicide attempts--to convey desperate and unhappy feelings about
herself. While no longer suicidal, the mood swings remain with
her.

*When I'm in an up mood, I feel very hopeful (nervous laugh);
and when I'm in a down mood (nervous laugh), I feel very hope-
less . . . and little things can set me off . . . little things, I guess, can
put me in really good moods, too. They change very fast (nervous
laugh).*
Through her sentence completion responses, Sarah describes
some of the feelings that may underlie her "low moods."
When I feel angry "I often contain my anger or else direct it
toward myself."
My conscience bothers me "if I'm mean to somebody without in-
tending to be."
My main problem is "I'm too self-critical."
Sarah reminds us of her persistent "lows."
I am "still very far away from getting over being really
depressed."
And she also conveys her discomfort with peers.
What gets me into trouble is "dealing with kids my age."
Being with other people "my own age sometimes makes me
nervous and self-conscious."
Despite this unease, the people most important in Sarah's life
were friends, once connected with both her school and hospital settings. She spoke of the increasing importance of friends as she
tried to develop more independence from her family in recent
years. She refers to her conflict over separating from her parents
and being with close friends, "I'd rather spend time with my
friends than my family . . . but I still like to do things with my
family on weekends." Her friends are varied. With some she en-
joys relaxing or being drunk, not "partying that much." With
others, there are parties and more "aggressive" times. She tells of
both an interest in and tolerance of diverse friends:
*I usually can overlook [things that bother me in other people]
and they put up with an awful lot of bad things (nervous laugh)
about me too. I'm a very moody person (pause). I don't see how
people can stand me when I'm in one of my bad moods.*
Although here she again touches on her self-hatred, there are
other important features within this self-reflection. There is her
perceived similarity to others, her tolerance of others' foibles, and
her recognition of their acceptance of hers. She tells how important it was for a friend to be listening, "sympathetic and every-

thing." For example, Andrea, a close and supportive friend, listened during the summer before Sarah's hospitalization.

Sarah's parents are health service and teaching professionals. On first glance, her family appears to be cohesive; family members are involved with one another through skiing, tennis, apple picking, and going to restaurants together. Yet the tension between her isolation and her wishes to be more disclosing to them is almost palpable. There is a surface togetherness, belied by her sense that "we're just not all that close." She expands upon her perceived lack of closeness within her family as she describes how her parents tell each other their feelings, "but not really half as much." The theme of closeness threads through her descriptions of each parent.

Her mother, Mrs. Smith, is 40 years old, and functions at one of the higher ego development levels. Since being in the hospital, Sarah has become closer to her mother, as well as more aware of her wishes to separate from her.

I think I have become a little closer, especially to my mother (long pause). And that's funny, because at the same time that I say we're not that close, I'd like to be a little more close, I'm also feeling that I'm ready to, you know (laugh), to let . . . leave home.

The yearning for her mother and the idea that this yearning is not fulfilling is also expressed in one of her sentence completions: *If my mother* "and I had talked more about problems when I was younger, I might not have gotten as depressed as I am now."

Although she recognizes some regrets or concerns, these feelings are but minor ones in her awareness, as Mrs. Smith clearly gives precedence to her "positive attitude to life." Possibly Sarah's perceived lack of "closeness" with her mother has to do with Mrs. Smith's leanings toward devotion and tenacious holding on to optimistic visions. As a consequence of these emphases, Mrs. Smith may be reluctant to see Sarah's "darker," more disquieting feelings and degraded views of herself.

Mr. Smith is a 42-year-old health professional, functioning at an especially high level of ego development. Sarah expresses less conflict as well as less disappointment with him. She sees him as very "intellectual." He less openly expresses feelings, especially "upset" ones. "I've seen my dad before when he's very upset and tried to hide it by acting angry." When upset with her after an overdose, her father questioned her "sternly," "but I knew that he wasn't angry, he was really upset, he was just trying to hide it." In contrast to the several one-dimensional descriptions expressed by Mrs. Smith, Mr. Smith expresses multifaceted views of people and situations. He stresses difficulties, sadness, regrets, and coping. In describing *the thing I like about myself*, Mr. Smith says, "I seem to be able to survive and function completely, even in the face of adversity of major proportions." These themes appear in several other stems. For instance, *I feel sorry* "that I did not spot the symptoms of my daughter's depression much earlier, for I suspect treatment years before might well have saved her a lot of pain." And, *My main problem is* "that I do not seem to communicate well the warmth of my feelings to those whom it is most important to do so."

The "communication" regret touched on in this last response is reminiscent of Sarah's disappointment with the limited communication in her family. Besides father's awareness of his difficulties conveying "warm" feelings, the seemingly large gap between his own and his wife's perceptions may also contribute to Sarah's idea of the family's "communication problems." Her parents differ dramatically in their views of themselves, others, and the surrounding society. In contrast to Mrs. Smith's idea that a wife should "be a good companion and friend," Mr. Smith says she should "be supportive of her husband emotionally, and be sensitive to his moods and problems, but should be able to expect the same in return and should not subordinate her individuality to his." Mr. Smith's sensitivity to the consequences of his actions on others is yet another important theme, one not found for Mrs. Smith.

There are, then, unmistakable differences between Sarah's parents' perceptions and interpretations. Overall, her mother's level of ego development is *conscientious*, at the start of the postconformist stages. Her father is functioning at the transition between the conscientious and autonomous stages, solidly within the postconformist range of development. How do these varying inner worlds and views of both parents intersect with those of Sarah who is functioning at a developmental level most similar to her mother's?

In the family discussion there are many lively exchanges and challenges. In addition, we see numerous signs of members' receptiveness to each other's ideas. Through their self-assertive challenges, family members tell one another when they veer from the question at hand.

The Smiths engage in complex discussions about the rationale for their specific answers and their underlying logic, illustrated when Sarah and her father try to resolve their difference with Mrs. Smith over whether Heinz should steal the drug. Father and Sarah both believe that Heinz should steal the drug while Mrs. Smith thinks that he should not steal it.

Father: (to his wife) "Want to defend yourself?"

Mother: "Uh hum. I said that my answer, my feeling was that he should then, according to the story, explore other alternatives before he broke the rules of society. That it was important that he try to explore every single alternative, ah, because if we had people going around breaking rules, breaking society's rules, such as stealing, we'd have total anarchy, no matter how severe the reasons were and I . . ."

Sarah: (interrupting) "Well, I felt it was implied in the story that there wasn't any other choice, that this was, you know, the one thing that would save his wife, and in that, if that was the only thing, I think he should. I think the, um, druggist is in the wrong. Of course he's breaking the law, but he's, he has a, a very, very, strong motive to steal it."

Mother: "But it wasn't a proven, wasn't a proven cure."

Father: "Well, what they're dealing with is, you know, not a guarantee of cure, but, the right or wrong of the act."

Mother: "Right, and I think the act is wrong, and I also said that I thought that one of the things they hadn't tried was the very people that had loaned the ah, Heinz, the money could, perhaps, as peer pressure be brought to bear on the druggist, that that hadn't been tried, that they ought to get together and try--I just felt that every motive should still be explored and that the story hadn't explained."

[After brief continued discussion.]

Mother [to father]: "Why do you think that he should steal?"

Father: "Well, I didn't, and that's why I am so amused . . . because I started out saying, 'Now, he shouldn't steal,' and then I sort of weaseled my way around to the fact that if, indeed, this hypothetical was intended to ask you the question, 'which is a higher priority of value--the human life or, breaking the rule, the law,' then I've got to say that if that's the real question, then cer-

*tainly the human life is the higher value, and I changed my answer
(laughing) from no to yes, that he should steal it."*
[After an interchange between Sarah and Mother.]
*Sarah: "That's what I felt it came down to; is it okay to break
the law when it's for a human life? I felt also that, um, I made a
distinction between somebody who is family or close friend and a
stranger, but [the interviewer] said, 'Well, should he have done
that for a stranger?' And I said, 'No, because he doesn't have the
same kind of concern for a stranger's life.' You know, I'm sure he
feels, you'd feel very badly if the stranger died, but I don't think
that he would, Heinz would feel that it's his duty whereas you
know, his wife, somebody he loves and cares about, if indeed he
does love and care about (nervous laugh) her."*
*Father: "See, I think I'm probably more doctrinaire than you
are because I felt it's a question of human life versus the abstract
principle of theft, that any human life, even the stranger's, is worth
stealing for."*

In this long excerpt, all three members express much separateness and connectedness, as they pursue their own arguments *and*
are permeable to each other's perspectives. Mrs. Smith's level of
participation is high, as is her responsiveness. She eventually
modifies her position, reflecting the impact of the discussion:

*Well, okay, if it's a question of, if it's brought down to the moral
issue of human life versus stealing, I will agree with the two of you.*

But her involvement becomes more and more restrained as the
discussions unfold. What emerges is a strong pairing of father and
Sarah, excluding Mrs. Smith in subtle and direct ways. After a
few speeches, Mrs. Smith virtually "drops out" of the discussion,
leaving the active dialogue to Sarah and her father.

Mrs. Smith's participation is episodic. Her disagreements and
challenges are especially obvious in a charged argument about
whether relationships between fathers and sons differ from those
between mothers and daughters. Moreover, she consistently hears
Sarah proclaim that, "Daddy is right," following disagreements.
We see in these interactions much evidence of compatibility between Sarah and her father, coupled with their not allowing Mrs.
Smith access to the discussion or minimizing her contributions.

In this family of a precociously advanced adolescent there is
much evidence of individuated relationships, especially between
Sarah and her father. The special additional feature in this family

is the powerful coalition between Sarah and her father, repeatedly leaving mother behind. The presence of this imbalance in the system, reflecting both the strong alliance between daughter and father, as well as longstanding difficulties between the parents, reveals the important point that adolescent ego development is not necessarily impaired by familial disturbance--particularly if the adolescent remains connected with, not isolated from, at least one of the parents.

Progressive: Lois

We now come to the fourth trajectory--progressive ego development--those subjects who entered the study at either very low or intermediate stages, and within the next years began to function at clearly higher levels of development. Lois, one of the high school students, rose from an intermediate conformist stage to one of the more advanced postconformist ones.

Uppermost for Lois was "other people," their support and understanding--her connections with them were pervasive and constantly important. From the first minutes of the interview with this 15-year-old high school freshman, the heightened significance of friends and family members and the continuity of relationships with them was apparent. When asked about the new transition to high school, most students commented on "being lost" and "getting adjusted" to the new classes or to the new "freedom." For Lois, the fundamental issue had to do with friends.

It was a big change because I don't see all my friends as much as I used to. I used to hang around with a bunch of kids . . . we had all been pretty close . . . and I thought it was going to be . . . the end of the group, but apparently it was a strong nucleus, 'coz we managed to stay together and I see them almost every day. . . . And I also made a lot of new friends that all made my transition a lot easier.

Much of Lois' pleasure with others seems related to being accepted and acknowledged by them. She describes, in much detail, several friendships and group "antics" on weekend nights. The contact and consistent companionship are basic components of Lois' experiences with her friends. On the more negative side, Lois' delight with others leads to her intense sensitivity to being left alone or in the least way excluded. Being excluded in a somewhat less visible way set off considerably more disturbing waves for Lois. One of the most public displays of being neglected or left out was her not being invited to a party, certainly a major theme for many teenagers. What is especially noteworthy about Lois is that she brought up this disturbing moment early in the interview, detailing its intensity, together with her ways of surmounting the painful episode. At first Lois was stunned and dismayed:

> . . . *I was very depressed. A lot of crying. I did a lot of yelling at my mother, but she knew why. I told her . . . so I talked to her for awhile and I told her that I was going to be real crabby because I was really in a bad mood and she said she understood.*

Lois turned to her mother, older brother, and her father.

With more convincing clarity than many of the other adolescent subjects, Lois builds a strong case for her family's contribution to her generally high self-esteem, high optimistic visions of the future, her altruistic wishes, and resilience--her "bouncing" back from her dismay over feeling rejected by friends from the party, and from her no longer being "top dog" in the large high school. Lois provides narratives of each family member's contributions. She also tells us of an emotional brittleness that was particularly evident early in her development. As will be seen, these more problematic issues also have important meanings within her family.

Early in her first-year interview Lois introduced her mother. Mrs. Weller plays a dual role in Lois' life: mother and "best friend"--a description repeatedly presented by Lois in interview and sentence completions. Mrs. Weller is 48 years old, has completed a master's degree, and functions at an especially high stage of ego development. Her own sentence completions make it clear that relationships with family members are of the utmost importance.

Lois' father, Mr. Weller, is a 49-year-old executive of a large institution. He has completed his doctoral degree and functions at the transition between the two postconformist stages, similar to his wife. Lois portrays him as available to her at times that she is upset, such as when she was not invited to the recent party. She feels close to him, "but we're not close the way I am close with my mother. I can't confide in my father." Although her relationship with her father does not have the intensity and near total openness that she experiences with her mother, there are several distinctive qualities highlighted by Lois. He is appreciative of her observations and understandings.

He confides in me . . . he respects me in a different way than
most people do. He respects my opinions and he's willing to listen
to me a lot of the time.

The other highly visible members of Lois' family are her older
brothers. In contrast to any of the other adolescents, Lois goes on
at length about their importance, the special ways that they affected her and continue to influence her development. She recalls
how they regaled her about her overreactions as she was growing
up and her apparent brittleness. She clearly distinguishes between
her brothers. Most influential as a force toward change, and a fervent supporter of hers, is Ted, her older brother by five years.

The portrait of her family offered by Lois is noteworthy for
several reasons. It is consistent with her articulate and open dis-
closures, sharing her views of her inner experience and interpersonal world. Second, we are introduced to *siblings* as well as
parents, not at all a usual feature of the other interviews with the
adolescents. Although we might speculate about the input of siblings in the maturation or arrested growth of each of the adolescents, it is through Lois that we are afforded detailed perceptions
of these other family members. Third, Lois' elaborate description
of each family member and her relationships with them represent
how salient her family is in her life. Especially moving is her picture of how much protection and guidance she feels from this
group. This is a family that has much awareness of itself as a unit,
holding--for many years--formal "family council meetings," where
common questions or problems could be considered amidst
safeguards from intrusion or domination of other (older) family
members.

Alongside of the other adolescents, whether precociously advanced or arrested in development, Lois provides us with one of
the most complete pictures of a family in our study. We see
aspects of her family ranging from individual members (her
mother) to the special functions of the whole unit (family council
meetings). Outstanding strengths cited by Lois include the ap-
preciation/respect, and available intense trustworthy relationships
(her mother, sometimes her older brother, and her father). Given
these ingredients, plus strong motivation to "improve" and change,
it is not surprising that Lois' ego development progressed over the
years. However, important questions remain. To what extent are
these features of the family visible in their actual family interac-

tions? Are there yet other family relationships unarticulated by Lois, or her parents?

The Wellers discussed two different dilemmas, both where Lois opposed the conclusion of her parents. These circumstances provide an excellent vantage point for seeing how the Wellers promote and contend with Lois' differences and transient "separations" from them. There are also tracings of Lois' influences upon the experiences of her parents.

With great clarity and tenacity, Lois presents and reiterates her ideas, at times verging on highly opinionated positions. The many slight "okays" and "ums" in her parents' responses are indications of their mutuality, and permeability, toward her. Lois first concludes that Heinz should steal to save his wife's life. Both parents thought that Heinz should not steal.

Lois: "Oh, I'm going to have to be alone against both of you!"

Mother: "Okay, That's super! How come you said yes?"

Father: "Lois, why don't you tell us why you think he should steal it?"

Lois: "Well, I didn't really say 'yes' he should definitely steal it. I said that he should go and look for help and see if someone else can help her and he should go to other people . . . I didn't say definitely 'yes' . . ."

Mother: (interrupting) "Well, that's a very good idea."

Lois: (interrupting) "Then [the interviewer] said 'suppose he couldn't get any help . . .' Then . . . I think it is more important for him to steal it because it's a person's life and a human life is a human life so . . ."

Mother (interrupting) "That's true, but what about the quality of life?"

Lois: "What do you mean about the qual . . ."

Father: (interrupting) "Well, suppose everybody stole, what do you think the society would be like?"

Lois: "But it's not a question of everybody stealing. It's a question about one person stealing to save someone's life. I'm not saying that everybody should go around stealing . . . I mean he should steal because it's his wife that's dying. That's the big difference."

Lois amplifies her position following the challenging questions from her parents. It is not that she simply is more verbose after the questions and challenges, as a way to subtly overwhelm her parents or mask her resistance to their challenges. Rather, what she shows is a cumulative engagement with them and inclusion of their ideas in her ever more complex contributions to the unfolding discussion. Yet in the midst of what seems to be a series of challenges and responses, Lois' father suddenly orchestrates the group, now pressing his wife to describe her thoughts. Mrs. Weller clearly wishes to continue questioning Lois, countering her husband's pressures. In part, her father is not wanting to continue probing Lois' position. He goes on to protect her, warning his wife to avoid trying to persuade Lois to change her mind. Not only does her father intervene to shield Lois and orchestrate the situation, but Lois then protects and encourages her mother to express her position--as if to say, "let her continue with me; she's not going to push me to her position, let her speak."

The readiness of Mr. Weller to restrain his wife from pressing Lois allows Lois to maintain her special connection with her mother and elaborate her ideas. What is of further interest is Lois' seeming parallel response to her mother, as if shielding *her* from the father. In her interview, Lois dwelt at length upon the specialness of her relationship with her mother, perhaps leading to special sensitivities on her part, to her mother not being in any way "cut off" from this connection with Lois.

The family agrees the druggist should in some way make the drug available to save the wife's life. In another family this may have been a sign that an agreement had been reached, or that a partial consensus could be read as a total consensus and perhaps mask a deeper disagreement, a sidestepping of the original differences between members. Mr. Weller seems to recognize the possibility that they may slip away from facing their actual disagreement. He thereby directs the family to confront their differences yet again.

Mother: "Well, I agree, and far as that's (the druggist making the drug available) concerned, that's that . . ."

Father: (interrupting) "But that's not the issue that's confronting us. We have to deal with the dilemma they have laid out for us--can you see?"

Mother (interrupting) "In other words you have to . . ."

Father: (interrupting) "Can you see, I mean, if we're supposed to come to some consensus, can you see the point we're trying to make?"

Lois: "Oh, I understand what you're trying to . . . is it a question of one person's life and of society's rules?"
Father: "That's right."
Lois: "But I don't see that society's rules are as important as life."
Father: "I see."
Lois: "I mean, you know, it's important to have rules because otherwise everything would fall apart and . . . it's a human life. I just can't see setting rules against a human life."
Father: "So you're saying that . . . it's not possible then for us to come to a consensus as a family?"
Lois: "Well, I don't think we're gonna get very far because I think life is more important and you guys think that society's rules are more important."
Father: "Mmmmm."
Mother: "It isn't a question. Well, I guess it is really a question of that."

The consequences of father's self-assertions are dramatic: Lois most clearly perceives and expresses her father's point and he is then able to recognize the depth of their differences.

Several features of individuated relationships are visible in the Weller's discussions. There is the continuing acceptance and recognition of Lois' points; the unflinching, yet thoughtful recognition of differences; the "protective cycles"; and the summarizing that does not "close off" the flow. In fact, following one summary by both parents, Lois goes on to recommend how the judge should respond, that he should deal with the wife. Both parents applaud Lois for recognizing the wife's predicament, since they had not attended to her in their deliberations.

There are examples throughout the discussion that demonstrate how the Wellers' very high levels of ego development clearly shape and form these discussions and give clear instances of the "multiperspective" to Lois. Elsewhere in the discussion, Mr. Weller noted the two points of view (Lois' and theirs) and that both were acceptable ("two different points--I think there's obvious validity for both points"). This was followed by Mrs. Weller's description of how differing experience in the world (Lois' and theirs) might contribute to the "generation difference" that Lois pointed to, since through "living longer" the parents' responses have been colored by many situations they have seen where laws were broken. The idea that their responses are "colored" by other beliefs and perceptions recurs a number of times and obviously conveys complexity yet again to Lois. This student and her parents offer magnificent examples of a spectrum of individuated relationships occurring between a progressive adolescent and her parents.

DISCUSSION

In this paper we have taken a new look at our observations of individual development and family processes. There are several ways that this contribution differs from our previous reports, thereby leading to new directions for analysis. Conceptually, we present and apply new constructs to our adolescent and family data. Rather than considering the individual adolescents along the lines of specific ego stages and whether they increase (or decrease) over successive years, we have argued for constructing new, theoretically derived categories based on how ego development in early adolescence changed or did not change over subsequent years. This strategy for arraying individual ego development profiles generates a number of clinically meaningful "trajectories," or developmental paths, through adolescence. Individual and family features associated with four of these profiles-- arrest, consistent conformist, precociously advanced, and progressive--were discussed at length within this paper. There are two other theoretical and clinical possibilities, regression and moratorium (successive advances and regressions over the years). Although not discussed or illustrated here, these additional but less frequent types are included in the array of adolescent ego development trajectories (Hauser et al., 1987c, 1988).

The six ego development trajectories represent individual differences within adolescence. During the era between puberty and late teenage years, many powerful forces impinge on the adolescent and can lead to subtle and dramatic changes, often manifest as conflicts or crises. While the forces may be similar for individuals within these years, the ways that each individual copes with the diverse biological and social forces vary. One expression of these variations is through the ego development trajectories. Since this is a new conceptualization, we do not yet know its theoretical and empirical linkage with other classifications of adolescents, such as identity statuses (Marcia, 1980) or coping patterns (Haan, 1977). In addition, while of clinical interest, concurrent and predictive relationships between the trajectories and adolescent psychopathology are also unknown. We do know, from recent applications of these new distinctions to diabetic adolescents, that ego development trajectories strongly predict adjustment to diabetes (Hauser et al., 1987c). A second new direction within these analyses is a probing of *parents'* ego development, and how it may inform their relationships with the adolescent. While we have some understanding of links between parent ego and family interactions (Hauser et al., 1987a), explorations of how this development may shape *relationships* is a new contribution.

A third way that this contribution differs from our previous work is through its inclusion of relationship constructs referring to individuation--new tools for exploring links between family context and adolescent ego development. These clarifying distinctions have been previously used to study family components of identity formation and role taking in normative adolescents (Grotevant and Cooper, 1985, 1986). We have expanded the categories to allow for their relevance to non-normative (psychiatrically hospitalized, developmentally arrested) adolescents. Thus, within the individuality domain we conceive of inhibition of self-assertion and impaired separateness. With respect to connectedness, of importance is opaqueness, rather than permeability--and nonreciprocity or asymmetry, rather than mutuality. By widening the scope of these constructs, we extend their applicability to the complete set of trajectories. An important aim of our intensive case studies was to illustrate the pertinence of these constructs in understanding how the family may influence adolescent ego development trajectories. More systematic work operationalizing these newly extended relationship categories is currently in progress in our laboratory (Allen and Hauser, 1987). The family discussions will soon be systematically analyzed with the coding scheme generated by these efforts.

Investigating family relationship levels is a clear departure from our prior analyses (Hauser et al., 1984), in which we examined separate family member speeches and discrete interactions. The rationale for this new direction is our recognition that theoretically significant family bonds were not being assessed by microanalyses of specific moment-to-moment, molecular interactions such as problem solving, explaining, accepting, and distracting. Important questions concern the connections between family relationship and family interaction variables. Are relationships organized sets, or "threads" of specific interactions? Can interactions be considered as "markers" of relationships, not fully representing them, yet providing traces of their presence, and perhaps clues to mediating mechanisms between relationships and adolescent development? Or are there no linkages, are these *different* sets of dimensions, based on distinct levels of observation and conceptualization?

Besides these specific questions about how family relationships ultimately shape individual development, there is a more fundamental theoretical issue regarding direction of effect. Most simply, are family relationships *reactive* to adolescent ego development, or do they actively contribute to these trajectories? Putting the question in such stark either/or terms does not allow for the more complex possibility of reciprocal effects. The likely model is one of such reciprocal influences. For instance, a given adolescent, such as Lois, may elicit--through her very strengths--more mutuality and permeability from her family, and these contributions in turn promote her continued growth. In contrast to such "benign cycles," there may be "vicious cycles," where especially abusive and indifferent adolescents evoke and sustain detached, opaque, and inhibited relationships from their parents. Our position, similar to that recently presented by Bell and Chapman (1986), is that we must first identify the parent and adolescent components as precisely as possible. Then, through our longitudinal studies of adolescent and family change, and sequential family processes (Hauser et al., 1987a, 1987b), we can construct and test models of the directional significance of family and individual factors and their reciprocal effects. Through our new offering in this paper, introducing a new set of individual and family constructs together with qualitative analyses documenting their applicability, we set the stage for continued longitudinal analyses, incorporating repeated measures of both the individual and his or her family surroundings. Next steps point to systematic family relationship analyses and more extensive exploration of the empirical and theoretical meaning of adolescent ego developmental trajectories.

REFERENCES

Allen, J. R., & Hauser, S. T. *The autonomy and relatedness coding system.* Unpublished coding manual. Harvard Medical School, 1987.

Bell, R. Q., & Chapman, M. Child effects in studies using experimental or brief longitudinal approaches to socialization. *Developmental Psychology*, 1986, *22*, 595-603.

Bronfenbrenner, U. Ecology of the family as a context for human development: Research perspectives. *Developmental Psychology*, 1986, *22*, 723-742.

Coelho, G., Hamburg, D., & Murphey, E. Coping strategies in a new learning environment. *Archives of General Psychiatry*, 1963, *9*, 433-443.

Csikszentmihalyi, M., & Larson, R. *Being adolescent: Conflict and growth in the teenage years.* New York: Basic Books, Inc, 1984.

Grotevant, H. D., & Cooper, C. R. Patterns of interaction in family relationships and the development of identity exploration in adolescence. *Child Development*, 1985, *56*, 415-428.

Grotevant, H.D., & Cooper, C. R. Individuation in family relationships. *Human Development*, 1986, *29*, 82-100.

Haan, N. *Coping and defending.* New York: Academic Press, 1977.

Hauser, S. T., Jacobson, A. M., Noam, G., & Powers, S. Ego development and self-image complexity in early adolescence. *Archives of General Psychiatry*, 1983, *40*, 325-332.

Hauser, S. T., Powers, S. I., Noam, G. G., & Jacobson, A. M. Familial contexts of adolescent ego development. *Child Development*, 1984, *55*, 195-213.

Hauser, S. T., Houlihan, J., Powers, S. I., Jacobson, A. M., Noam, G., Weiss-Perry, B., & Follansbee, D. Interaction sequences in families of psychiatrically hospitalized and non-patient adolescents. *Psychiatry*, 1987.

Hauser, S. T., Houlihan, J., Powers, S. I., Jacobson, A. M., Noam, G. G., Weiss-Perry, B., Follansbee, D., & Book, B. B. Adolescent ego development within the family: family styles and family sequences. *International Journal of Behavioral Development*, in press.

Hauser, S. T., Jacobson, A. M., Milley, J., Wolfsdorf, J., & Herskowitz, R. Developmental trajectories and family context: Adolescents with acute and chronic illness, presented at Penn State Invitational Conference, "Emotion and Cognition in Child and Adolescent Health and Development: A Two-Way Street," October 9, 1987.

Hauser, S. T., Powers, S. I., Weiss-Perry, B., Follansbee, D., Rajapark, D. C., & Greene, W. Constraining and Enabling Family Coding System, revised version. Unpublished. Harvard Medical School, 1987.

Hauser, S. T., Powers, S. I., Jacobson, A., & Noam, G. *Family interiors of adolescent development.* New York: Free Press, under contract.

Kohlberg, L. Stage and sequence: The cognitive developmental approach to socialization. In D. A. Goslin (Ed.), *Handbook of socialization theory and research.* New York: Rand-McNally, 1969.

Loevinger, J. *Ego development: Conceptions and theories.* San Francisco: Jossey-Bass, 1976.

Loevinger, J. Construct validity of the sentence completion test of ego development. *Applied Psychological Measurement,* 1979, *3,* 281-311.

Loevinger, J., & Wessler, R. *Measuring ego development* (Vol. 1). San Francisco: Jossey-Bass, 1970.

Loevinger, J., Wessler, R., & Redmore, C. *Measuring ego development* (Vol. 2). San Francisco: Jossey-Bass, 1970.

Marcia, J. E. Identity in adolescence. In J. Adelson (Ed.), *Handbook of adolescent psychology.* New York: John Wiley and Sons, Inc., 1980.

Shapiro, R. L. Action and family interaction in adolescence. In J. Marmor (Ed.), *Modern psychoanalysis.* New York: Basic Books, Inc, 1968.

Stierlin, H. *Separating parents and adolescents.* New York: Quadrangle, 1974.

Strodtbeck, F. L. Husband-wife interaction and revealed differences. *American Sociological Review,* 1958, *16,* 468-473.

Swenson, C. Ego development and a general model for counseling and psychotherapy. *Personnel and Guidance Journal,* 1980, *6,* 382-388.

Structural equation analysis was used to test models of marital and parental relationships as predictors of adolescent self-esteem in a sample of 103 intact families. The findings support the independence of three dimensions of self-esteem and the utility of including multiple measures when investigating their relationship to family factors. Marital quality was directly related to one dimension of self-esteem, and indirectly to the other two dimensions by way of parental supportive behavior. Results also highlighted the role of gender. Substantially more variance in fathers' supportive behavior was accounted for by marital quality than in mothers' support. Further, fathers' support contrasted to mothers' support was more strongly related to adolescents' self-esteem. Relationships were stronger for boys than for girls.

3

Marital Quality, Parental Behaviors, and Adolescent Self-Esteem

BRIAN K. BARBER

INTRODUCTION

Consistent with a reemergence of theoretical interest in the self within the social sciences (Gecas, 1982), there has been an increase in recent decades in empirical attempts to understand the development of self-esteem. In the present decade a particular emphasis has been placed on the family as a primary context of influence for adolescent self-esteem. Studies have yielded rather consistent findings, particularly with regard to the role of the parent-child relationship. Specifically, parental supportive behavior has consistently been found to be positively related to adolescent self-esteem, and various dimensions of parental control have been found to be negatively related to adolescent self-esteem (Barber and Thomas, 1986a;

Brian K. Barber • Department of Child and Family Studies, University of Tennessee, Knoxville, Tennessee 37996-1900.

49

Demo et al., 1987; Gecas and Schwalbe, 1986; Hoelter and Harper, 1987; Openshaw, Thomas, and Rollins, 1984; Rollins and Thomas, 1979).

The present study attempts to contribute to this literature in two fundamental ways. First, with a few recent exceptions, the bulk of the research on family and adolescent self-esteem has focused on the parent-child dyad. This emphasis is typical of much social science research, particularly that which investigates socialization processes (Lewis, 1984). Recently, however, we have come to acknowledge the complexity of the family system and that measurement of a broader range of family contexts is necessary in order to better understand the socialization process (Belsky, 1981; Lamb, 1978; Rollins and Galligan, 1978). The role of the marital relationship, for example, is beginning to receive a fair amount of attention in socialization studies. These studies have varied in design and sophistication of analysis, but have not yet provided a clear picture of the role of the marital relationship in the socialization process. Some studies, for example, focus primarily on measuring the impact of marital quality on parenting patterns. Other studies attempt to relate marital quality directly to self-esteem in children or adolescents, with some suggesting that the parental relationship may be an important intervening variable. Thus the possibility of both direct and indirect effects of marital quality on child characteristics has been raised. As Belsky (1981) concluded, however, studies that have incorporated measures of the child, the parental relationship, and the marital relationship simultaneously in causal models are not available. The absence of such analyses prevents a clearer determination of the role of the marital relationship in the socialization process. Accordingly, a major purpose of this study is to test models of adolescent self-esteem that simultaneously include the parental and marital relationship.

The second way in which this study contributes to the literature is by employing multiple measures of adolescent self-esteem. There has been considerable variation in the measurement of self-esteem in past research. This inconsistency reflects in part a long-standing theoretical controversy about whether self-esteem is best conceptualized as a unidimensional or multidimensional construct. For example, some researchers (Coopersmith, 1967; Rosenberg, 1965, 1979) have emphasized global, unidimensional measures of self-esteem. Others have preferred to characterize self-esteem as multidimensional, differentiating either on the basis of the context in which self-evaluations occur, e.g., school, family, peers (Coopersmith, 1967; Gecas, 1972), or on different aspects of self-evaluation such as competence, worth, power, control, moral integrity, etc. (Coopersmith, 1967; Epstein, 1973; Gecas, 1971; Harter, 1983). Still others have suggested that both global self-esteem and more specific dimensions exist in some hierarchical order (see Harter, 1983). One result of this controversy is that a proliferation of self-esteem measures exist, and unfortunately few researchers have attempted to compare different measures in any given study. One exception to this is the work done by Openshaw et al. (1981, 1984). Building on their work, the present study employs two measures of self-esteem that are frequently used in studies of adolescent self-esteem and tests to see if they can be differentiated by measures of family processes.

ADOLESCENT SELF-ESTEEM

Two of the most frequently used measures of self-esteem in family research on adolescent self-evaluation are the Rosenberg Self-Esteem Inventory (Rosenberg, 1965, 1979) and various versions of the Osgood Semantic Differential (Osgood, 1962, 1964). The Rosenberg Scale is a 10-item scale initially designed for adolescents and adults, and it has traditionally been considered a unidimensional measure of global self-esteem (Harter, 1983). The Osgood Semantic Differential consists of a series of bipolar adjective pairs used to describe various personal attributes or qualities. Using this scale, both Gecas (1971, 1972) and Franks and Marolla (1976) identified two variables they conceptualized as dimensions of self-esteem. Since their work, other studies have replicated this pattern (Barber and Thomas, 1986b; Openshaw et al., 1981). Gecas (1971:463) originally labeled these variables Self-Esteem Power and Self-Esteem Worth and described them as "the person's feelings of competence, effectiveness, and personal influence, and his feelings of personal virtue and moral worth, respectively." Subsequent research has indicated that the items that load together consistently on the Worth factor are more social in nature than moral or virtuous, and hence the factor has been reconceptualized as Social Worth (Barber and Thomas, 1986b).

In an effort to determine whether or not these measures of self-esteem truly represent independent dimensions, Openshaw et al. (1981) combined the items from the Rosenberg Scale with those from the Osgood Semantic Differential. Varimax rotated factor analysis revealed four dimensions: Self-Esteem Power and Worth (Social Worth) and two dimensions made up of the Rosenberg items. These two Rosenberg factors were the same as those found by Kaplan and Pokorny (1969) and provided further evidence that the Rosenberg Scale may indeed represent two qualitatively different dimensions of self-esteem. These dimensions have been conceptualized as Positive Self-Esteem, referring to a positive evaluation in a person based on his/her personal qualities (Openshaw et al., 1981), and Self-Derogation, "a relatively negative effect evoked in a person by his . . . consideration of his personal qualities, achievements, and behavior" (Kaplan and Pokorny, 1971:330). This distinction between one's evaluation of his/her qualities, achievements, or behavior and the effect associated with the evaluation is consistent with other research (Harter, 1983).

With regard to this issue of the dimensional structure of the Rosenberg Scale, other researchers have raised the possibility that the dimensions derived may simply be methodological artifacts (Zeller and Carmines, 1976, 1980). Miller, Rollins, and Thomas (1982) note that this problem of distinguishing methodological artifacts from meaningful variation in theoretical constructs is common in family research and suggest that one way to help clarify the issue is to demonstrate that the individual dimensions relate differently to antecedent or consequent variables (Barber and Thomas, 1986a). Addressing this, Openshaw et al. (1984) tested the relationship of a number of parent-child measures to the four dimensions of self-esteem. Their findings supported the independence of the dimensions by showing that various parental behaviors (e.g., support and induction) differentially predicted individual dimensions of self-esteem.

The present study extends this work by providing another test of the dimensional structure of self-esteem. All items from the Rosenberg Scale will be used in combination with those from the reconceptualized Social Worth Scale. Self-Esteem Power is not used because some recent studies have shown that it is not predicted as well by family variables, particularly parental support (Barber and Thomas, 1986b; Openshaw et al., 1984). Items for each scale will be combined and factor analyzed, and resulting dimensions will then be tested in the models of family processes. This study improves upon past self-esteem research in two ways. First, dimensions of self-esteem will be tested simultaneously in models of family processes that extend beyond the parent-child dyad to include the marital relationship. Thus, in addition to parental behaviors, marital quality can be used to differentiate between dimensions of self-esteem. Second, the structural equation analysis used in this study significantly improves upon the analyses used in other studies, particularly with regard to the measurement of self-esteem. Although measures of self-esteem and many variables used to predict them typically comprise multiple items, past researchers have resorted to creating some form of scale score for each dimension in order to analyze the relationships between them. Structural equation analysis, however, employs each raw item as an indicator of a latent construct, estimates the error term for each indicator, and allows for the estimation of error term correlation. This procedure results in a much cleaner measurement of the constructs and should provide a more precise and accurate understanding of the relationship between the various dimensions of self-esteem and family variables.

THE FAMILY AND ADOLESCENT SELF-ESTEEM

Two classes of parental behaviors, parental support and control, have been identified repeatedly in parent-adolescent research as being critical in accounting for the development of adolescent self-esteem (Openshaw and Thomas, 1986). The relationship between parental supportive behavior (warmth, nurturance, affection, etc.) and positive child outcome is one of the most consistent in the social science literature (Barber and Thomas, 1986a; Rollins and Thomas, 1979). In reviewing seventeen studies that measured parental support and tested its relationship with adolescent self-esteem, Openshaw and Thomas (1986) found that 21 out of 23 analyses revealed a positive relationship. Since their review, other studies have offered further confirmation of this relationship (Barber and Thomas, 1986a; Hoelter and Harper, 1987).

The research relating parental control to child characteristics has been less consistent (Baumrind, 1978; Peterson and Rollins, 1987; Rollins and Thomas, 1979). In their review of eight studies

using undifferentiated forms of control, Openshaw and Thomas
(1986) found a positive relationship between control and adolescent self-esteem in four studies, a negative relationship in one, and
no relationship in the other three studies. This inconsistency appears largely to be a result of the complexity of this aspect of
parental behavior. Parents can exercise control over their children
in many different ways, and apparently different types of control
have contrasting influence on child characteristics. For example,
some dimensions of control have been shown to have positive
relationships with child outcomes, e.g., induction (Hoffman, 1980;
Rollins and Thomas, 1979), autonomy granting, and maturity
demands (Baumrind, 1966). Other types of control attempts have
evidenced a negative relationship, e.g., coercion (Hoffman, 1980;
Rollins and Thomas, 1979; Steinmetz, 1979;), punitiveness, and
love withdrawal (Baumrind, 1966), and inconsistent control attempts (Patterson and Stouthamer-Loeber, 1984; Thornburg,
1986). In order to contrast with the positive parental behaviors
(support) already introduced, this study focuses on parental control
attempts that are expected to be negatively related to adolescent
self-esteem by including measures of coercion and inconsistent
control attempts.

For both parental support and parental control, symbolic interaction theory (Cooley, 1902; James, 1890; Mead, 1934) is useful in
explaining the relationship to self-esteem. In this theory, the self
is seen to develop through interaction with the social environment.
Cooley's notion of "looking-glass self" (1902) implies an
individual's cognitive capacity for role taking, where the individual is able to see himself as he imagines others see him. The
behavioral patterns of others, particularly significant others, become important symbols to the child and communicate meaning
about the self. Thus, parental supportive behavior communicates
acceptance on the part of the parent who attributes value and
worth to the child (Rollins and Thomas, 1979). Parental support is
therefore expected to be related positively to healthy levels of self-
esteem. Similarly, parental coercion can be interpreted by the
child as a direct attack on her worth and value as a person, or as an
implicit distrust for her ability to function effectively without
parental intrusion. Inconsistent control attempts do not supply a
stable flow of information to the child and can communicate that
parents do not care enough to be consistent in their treatment of

the child. Accordingly, both forms of control are expected to be negatively related to self-esteem.

Marital Quality

There appear to be at least three distinct bodies of literature that have investigated the relationship between marital functioning and child characteristics: the family process literature, the divorce literature, and the child development literature. Each of these focuses in its own way on marital quality.

The family process literature. This literature is primarily concerned with family interaction patterns that describe two basic types of processes: (a) establishment of boundaries, or the family's self-regulation of interaction with information, persons, or groups outside the family; and (b) the establishment of appropriate forms of connectedness and separateness among family members (Broderick and Pulliam-Krager, 1979). The impact of the marital relationship on the child is seen in the interaction patterns that occur between one or both parents and the child subsequent to problems in the marriage. Families can establish what Haley (1971) has called a perverse triangle, where counternormative coalitions develop between parents and children. Minuchin (1974) sees one such coalition occurring when one parent (usually the mother) establishes a relationship of inappropriate intensity with a child to compensate for the insufficient satisfaction occasioned by the disengagement of the spouse (usually the father) from the marital relationship. This relationship with the child is not seen as supportive, but establishes a "paradoxical bond" that is confusing to the child and could complicate the process of establishing his or her own identity.

Similarly, another paradoxical relationship can develop through the process Vogel and Bell (1960) have called "scapegoating." Here parents focus criticism on a child as a means of diverting attention from their own marital conflict. The child then becomes the apparent source of the conflict.

It is not difficult to see how children exposed to either inordinate emotional demands or to unwarranted criticism resulting from these paradoxical relationships would have difficulty establishing a healthy sense of self. There is some support in the family process literature that the presence of such coalitions between parents and children are related to a variety of personality disorders (Broderick and Pulliam-Krager, 1979; Minuchin, 1974). *The divorce literature.* Much of the literature on the effects of divorce on children has concluded that it is parental discord or conflict rather than the divorce itself that exercises a negative impact on children (see Emery, 1982). A more recent review provides support for this conclusion in summarizing findings where marital quality (conflict, hostility, or harmony) has been found to be related to children's maladjustment, social and work behavior, self-concept, psychosocial adjustment, self-esteem, delinquency, and antisocial behavior (Amato, 1986). Of these studies focusing particularly on self-concept or self-esteem, mixed results have been found. Raschke and Raschke (1979) and Holman and Woodroffe-Patrick (1986) have found marital conflict to be negatively associated with self-concept in subjects ranging from third graders to early adolescents in the U.S. and Tobago. Amato (1986), on the other hand, found inconsistent relationships between parental conflict and self-esteem in Australian children. Conflict was negatively associated with self-esteem in primary school girls but not in boys, whereas for adolescents, weak negative associations were found for males and females.

One issue that remains unclear in this research is the precise role that marital quality plays in a child's self-esteem. Is marital quality directly related to self-esteem as some studies seem to imply? If so, how is this relationship to be explained theoretically? Or is the effect of marital quality indirect through key intervening variables such as parenting practices? Some of the divorce literature would support this latter position as several studies have documented that in homes burdened by high levels of marital conflict the parent-child relationship deteriorates (Hess and Camara, 1979; Hetherington et al., 1979; Wallerstein and Kelly, 1980).

The child development literature. The child development literature has focused primarily on the impact of marital quality on the parental relationship. Marital quality has been found to be related to various aspects of early parenting: adjustment to mothering (Grossman et al., 1980; Shereshefsky and Yarrow, 1973); adjustment to fathering (Russell, 1974; Wente and Crockenberg, 1976); extent of negative affect displayed toward the infant (Pedersen, 1975); the extent of active parenting (Belsky, 1979); parent-child teaching interactions (Brody et al., 1986); and parental attitudes, behavior, and perceptions (Goldberg and Easterbrooks, 1984). In general, the findings suggest that the higher the marital quality, the more positive the parenting patterns.

In sum, the research from the three bodies of literature are consistent in suggesting either theoretically or empirically that marital quality impacts the well-being of children. The family process literature provides some clinical evidence and theoretical rationale for an impact of marital quality primarily through the parental relationship. Similarly, the child development literature offers support for the impact of marital quality on parenting behavior, albeit with samples of very young children. The divorce literature suggests both direct and indirect effects. However, as Belsky (1981) notes, no study has incorporated a design that permits the estimation of both effects.[1]

METHODOLOGY

Sample and Data Collection

The data used for this study come from a random sample of families from the state of Utah. The data were collected in 1985 and represent the first phase of an ongoing international family research project.

A random sample of 500 households from each of three Utah counties was drawn from the relevant telephone directories. A packet containing a cover letter explaining the study, two-parent questionnaires, a teenage questionnaire, and three self-addressed business reply envelopes was sent to each household via first-class mail. Both parents and the oldest teenager, if the household contained any, were requested to fill out the appropriate questionnaire. Following established mail survey techniques (Dillman, 1978), a series of three follow-up mailings was made to those who had not responded to the first mailing. The first follow-up was sent approximately two weeks after the first mailing and consisted of a

---

[1]Hoelter and Harper (1987) included measures of both the marital and parental relationship in a structural equation model of adolescent self-conception. However, they focused on the direct effect of each of these on self-conception, and appear not to have estimated a relationship between the marital and parental measures. Hence, no information about indirect effects of marital quality on self-conception was available.

postcard reminder. Two to three weeks later a second complete packet with a new cover letter was sent to each household that had not yet responded. Finally, three weeks after the second packet, a third packet with a different cover letter was sent.

Response Rates

Of the total sample of 1525 names from the telephone directories, 156 were returned as undeliverable. At least one completed questionnaire was received from each of 674 households. Because the survey was intended for two-parent families, many households (e.g., singles, widows, widowers, and divorced persons) were ineligible for the study and selected themselves out of the sample. In order to account for this, 1980 census data was used to estimate the number of two-parent families in the original sample. Using this figure as a base, the estimated response rate for the study was 64%. Of the 420 couples who responded, 106 had at least one adolescent between ages 14 and 19. For 103 of these families, complete data is available for the variables used in this study.

Sample Characteristics

The mean age of respondents was: 44 for fathers, 42 for mothers, and 16 for adolescents. Ninety-three percent of the fathers were employed full-time; 33% of the mothers worked full-time, and 24% were employed part-time. Fathers' median income was between $25,000 and $35,000. The sample was predominately white (97%) and Mormon (83%).

MEASURES

Self-esteem. As discussed earlier, two measures of self-esteem were used; data for each was collected from the adolescents' perspective. The Social Worth Scale (Barber and Thomas, 1986b) consists of four bipolar adjective pairs (good-bad, happy-sad, friendly-unfriendly, sociable-unsociable). Respondents were asked to rate themselves on a 5-point continuum between the adjective pairs. A low score represents the negative end of the continuum. The full 10-item Rosenberg Scale (Rosenberg, 1965, 1979) was used with a 5-point response scale (strongly disagree to strongly agree). Two sample items are: "I am able to do things as well as most people," and "I certainly feel useless at times." A high score represents strong agreement with the statements.

Parental support. A 3-item measure of General Support was used. These three items have been found in previous research to be the key items from a larger measure of general support (Barber and Thomas, 1986a; Ellis et al., 1976). Using a 5-point scale from "never" to "very often," the items measure the extent to which the adolescent over the past several years has felt a sense of security in his/her relationship with parents, the extent to which the adolescent has felt parents were there when needed, and whether the adolescent has been able to talk with parents about problems. Adolescents responded to each question for both mothers and fathers. In addition, both mothers and fathers were asked to report on the extent to which their adolescent felt secure and needed in his/her relationship with the parent.

Parental control. Four items were used to measure parental control, two coercion items and two inconsistent control items. Data for each item were collected from both the parents' and adolescent's perspective. The items measured the extent to which parents found fault with and complained about the adolescent, and the extent to which rules and punishment patterns changed. A 3-item response scale was used that reflected the extent to which a statement's description was "not like," "somewhat like," or "very much like" the parent.

Marital quality. Each parent responded to five questions about their relationship, which included measures of their happiness and satisfaction (very unhappy/unsatisfied to very happy/satisfied), the extent to which they can depend on their spouse for support (rarely to very often), whether or not they would marry the same person again (certainly not to certainly), and how often the thought of divorce has crossed their mind (often to never). The adolescent responded to one question comparing the happiness of his/her parent's marriage with that of friends' parents' marriages (very unhappy to very happy). All items had a 5-point response scale.

ANALYSIS

The first step in the analysis was to identify the number of dimensions of adolescent self-esteem represented by the items used. Varimax rotated factor analysis was performed on the combined list of items (14) from both the Social Worth Scale and the Rosenberg Scale. By combining the items we were able not only to test the factor structure of the Rosenberg Scale, but also to see to what extent the Social Worth items were related to the Rosenberg items. Next, structural equation analysis (LISREL, [Joreskog and Sorbom, 1984]) was used to test models of family variables and self-esteem. This procedure is especially appropriate for this data since each of the variables used in this study have multiple indicators. Raw items are used as indicators of latent constructs, and LISREL performs a confirmatory factor analysis on the items indicating each latent construct as well as testing the structural relationship between the particular constructs that the researcher expects to be related.

FINDINGS

Dimensions of Self-Esteem

The factor analysis of the 14 self-esteem items revealed a three-factor solution. The first two factors comprised Rosenberg items. Four of these items split-loaded on all three factors. Two of these ("feel I'm a failure" and "don't have much to be proud of") were the same items that split-loaded in the Openshaw et al. (1981) study. The other two were "satisfied with self" and "positive attitude toward self."

The third factor in the present analysis comprised the four Social Worth items. One of these (good-bad) split-loaded on both the Rosenberg factors. The problematic nature of this item has been demonstrated elsewhere (Barber and Thomas, 1986b).

Once having removed the items that did not discriminate well between factors, the analysis was redone and resulted in three clear factors. These results are presented in table 1.

This analysis provides confirming evidence both for the multi-dimensional nature of the Rosenberg Scale as well as the inde-

pendent nature of the Social Worth dimension. The three items for
each dimension of self-esteem were then used to indicate their
respective latent construct in the structural equation analysis.

Table 1

Varimax Rotated Factor Matrix of Rosenberg and Social Worth Items

	FACTOR 1 Self-Derogation	FACTOR 2 Social Worth	FACTOR 3 Positive Self-Esteem
Self-Derogation			
Feel Useless	.83	−.17	−.09
Think I'm no good	.83	−.06	−.22
Want more self-respect	.78	−.18	.08
Social Worth			
Sociable	−.19	.86	−.02
Friendly	.01	.82	.07
Happy	−.27	.80	.14
Positive Self-Esteem			
Have good qualities	−.17	−.01	.89
Equal with others	−.26	.10	.83
Do things well	.17	.09	.75
Eigenvalues	3.20	1.86	1.44
Cumulative % variance	35.6	56.3	72.3
Alpha reliability	.777	.805	.784

MARITAL QUALITY, PARENT BEHAVIOR, AND SELF-ESTEEM

Theoretical Model

One of the advantages of structural equation analysis is that the
researcher is forced to devise a hypothesized model before testing
empirical relationships. Once tested, the model can then be
revised using theoretical and empirical criteria, and retested until
the model fits the data acceptably. Based on the literature
reviewed for this study, a theoretical model of the impact of family
variables on self-esteem was designed. Given the number of variables involved, this model was too complex to be represented
clearly in figure form. It included positive relationships between
parental support and dimensions of self-esteem (negative to Self-
Derogation), negative relationships between parental control and
dimensions of self-esteem (positive to Self-Derogation), a positive

relationship between marital quality and parental support, and a negative relationship between marital quality and parental control. The literature regarding a direct relationship between marital quality and self-esteem is not clear or substantial enough to warrant specific hypotheses. Therefore, all paths from marital quality were estimated.

The first model tested used data strictly from the adolescent's perspective. Criteria used to revise the model were the Modification Index computed by LISREL and the statistical significance of individual parameters. In either case, no changes were made that violated the underlying theory.

Structural Model

The major revision in the structural model was the removal of the parental control variables. Neither father nor mother control showed a significant relationship to any dimension of self-esteem, nor were they meaningfully predicted by marital quality. There were some moderately strong bivariate correlations between the control items and the self-esteem and marital quality items, but once combined in the full model, the presence of the control construct did not contribute to the overall fit.

Other revisions of the structural model included the fixing of various structural parameters between the family variables and self-esteem. Those parameters close to zero were no longer estimated.

Measurement Model

No revision was necessary for the observed indicators of endogenous or exogenous latent constructs. That is, all of the individual items used to measure constructs proved to be statistically significant. This provides important confirmatory evidence of the dimensional structure of self-esteem, as well as indicating that the items used to measure the family variables (parental support and marital quality) were significantly predicted by their respective latent construct.

The fact that there was only a single item measuring the adolescents' perception of marital quality forces the assumption that this item is a perfect measure of marital quality. Although such an assumption is common among other statistical procedures (e.g., multiple regression), it does not take good advantage of the properties of structural equation analysis. In order to address this, the parent item most closely related in content to the adolescent item (how happy the parents' marriage is) was included. This new latent construct of marital quality was thus indicated by father, mother, and adolescent reports. This device was supported empirically by high bivariate correlations between the adolescent report of marital quality and that of father (.54) and mother (.63). (It should be noted here that bivariate correlations between parent and adolescent report of support and control items were not strong enough to warrant using each person's perception simultaneously.)

Two further revisions in the measurement model were suggested by the Modification Index. Both regarded the estimation of correlated error terms. Accordingly, error terms between the adolescents' perception of mother and father support (all three items) and between two items from the Social Worth variable were allowed to be correlated. The freeing of these parameters substantially improved the fit of the model.

Finally, in order to determine any effect of social class, a latent variable indicated by husband's education, occupation, and income was added to the model. Social class was not related to marital quality or to parental support. Its only significant relationship was with Self-Derogation, indicating that adolescents from higher socioeconomic status are more likely to derogate themselves. This is an interesting finding and should be investigated more thoroughly in future work. Despite this one relationship, the inclusion of the social class variable did not improve the fit of the model, suggesting that for this sample social class was not a critical variable in the relationships under study, and it was therefore deleted from the final model. Figure 1 depicts the final model.

The chi-square for the model was 153.94 ($df = 120$, $p = .020$), and the goodness of fit index was .865. This fit is somewhat lower than the arbitrary cutoff of .90 typically used with LISREL for an acceptable fit. What this suggests is that there may be other relationships among variables in the model that, if estimated, would improve the fit. It is not unlikely that some of these could be the interrelationships among the dimensions of self-esteem, and/or between the two measures of support. As the model stands, the error terms (PSI) for these constructs were estimated. Also, as noted earlier, error terms for the individual indicators of parental

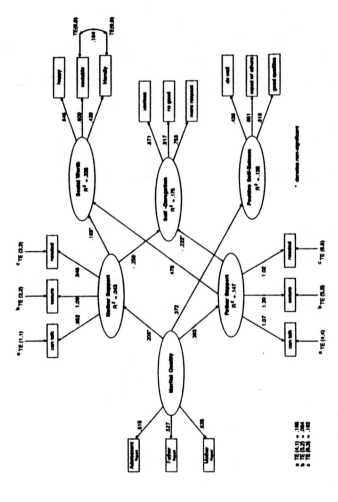

Figure 1. Final LISREL Model of Marital Quality (Parent and Adolescent Report) and Adolescent Report of Self-Esteem and Parental Support.

support (THETA EPSILON) were correlated across parent. However, direct paths between mother and father support, or between the dimensions of self-esteem, were not freed for estimation. This is because with LISREL, since they are part of the endogenous end of the model, direction of effect would have to be delineated. Since there is no theoretical basis for identifying direction of effect between subdimensions of self-esteem or between mother and father support, direct relationships between these constructs were not estimated. This is acceptable for our purposes because the primary function of the model was to identify the structural relationships between family variables and self-esteem.

Parent Report Model

The same model was tested substituting parent reports of support and control and only using parental reports of marital quality. Except for the relationship between marital quality and parental support, there were no significant relationships in the model. This is not surprising given the relatively low correlations between adolescent and parent reports of parental behavior. It is clear in this data, as it has been in a number of other socialization studies, that it is the child's report of parental behavior that has the predictive power for self-reported child outcome (Ausubel et al., 1954; Heilbrun, 1973; Schaefer, 1965), and in particular adolescent self-esteem (Demo et al., 1987; Gecas and Schwalbe, 1986).

DISCUSSION

Adolescent Self-Esteem

The results of this study provide strong evidence for the multidimensional nature of adolescent self-esteem. This is seen first in the preliminary factor analysis that identified three separate factors--Social Worth, Positive Self-Esteem, and Self-Derogation-- and then verified in the confirmatory factor analysis conducted by LISREL. In each case the items loaded cleanly on their respective factors. Further evidence for the independence of these dimensions is seen in the patterns of relationships to other variables in the model. Both Social Worth and Self-Derogation are predicted by parental support, yet the strength of the relationships and the amount of variance accounted for differ substantially. Eighteen percent of the variance in Self-Derogation is accounted for relatively equally by mother and father support. On the other hand, while mother support has a weak (.16) relationship with Social Worth, father support has a much more substantial relationship (.48), and the two together explain 34% of the variance. Finally, Positive Self-Esteem is not related to parental behaviors but is predicted by marital quality (.37), explaining 14% of the variance. These different patterns offer compelling evidence for the utility of conceptualizing adolescent self-esteem as consisting of qualitatively distinct dimensions.

These findings highlight the role of family processes in the development of self and underscore the complexity of development and family. At least in this sample, it appears that family processes have different types of influence on distinct aspects of adolescent self-evaluation. Why is it that Positive Self-Esteem is unrelated to the parental relationship but related to the marital relationship? Or what is it about Social Worth and parental support that results in differential patterns of prediction based on the gender of the parent? Clearly, theoretical work needs to be done to better understand these constructs and their interrelationships. Empirically, an initial picture of how the self-esteem dimensions differ can be gained by looking at the bivariate correlations between the individual indicators of each dimension and the family variables. These correlations revealed that for each dimension of self-esteem one of the three indicators had a measurably stronger relationship to either parental support or marital quality. The critical item for Social Worth was the "happy" item; for Self-Derogation, the "think I'm no good" item; and for Positive Self-Esteem, the "think I'm on a equal plane with others" item. As work continues, efforts should be focused on better understanding these aspects of self-evaluation, how they differ theoretically, and why they are related differently to family processes.

Finally, with regard to the Rosenberg Scale, these findings obviously argue strongly that the scale is at least two dimensional and that use of it as a unidimensional scale may compromise our understanding of adolescent self-evaluation and its predictors. Studies that aggregate responses to all ten items may be losing valuable information.

FAMILY AND ADOLESCENT SELF-ESTEEM

Parental Behaviors

The findings regarding the general relationship of parental behaviors to self-esteem are not surprising. The failure of parental control in the model is consistent with other studies (most recently, Barnes et al., 1987, in this issue) and is further evidence for the problematic nature of the parental control construct.

Parental support was related as predicted to the dimensions of self-esteem, but what surfaces as very intriguing is the role of parent's gender. Largely due to methodological constraints, past socialization research has not done well at differentiating between parents. Some studies may report bivariate correlations using both parents; other procedures like multiple regression encounter problems typically with multicollinearity. The resulting instability in coefficients often forces the researcher to either aggregate mother and father scores into a global parent score, or simply report data from one parent. In the present case, every effort was made to determine if there was a problem with multicollinearity. First, the structural parameters between mother and father support and dimensions of self-esteem did not evidence any instability, either in the strength or direction of the relationships. Second, separate models were run using only one parent's support. The pattern of coefficient strength remained the same, that is, father support stronger to Social Worth and mother support stronger to Self-Derogation. These patterns are also apparent in the bivariate correlations.

Having dealt with the issue of multicollinearity, what remains striking is the predominant role of the father in this sample. While not significant, the relationship between father support and Self-Derogation is not substantially lower than for mother support. The relationship between father support and Social Worth, on the other hand, is dramatically stronger than the non-significant relationship between mother support and Social Worth. This is an intriguing finding. Given the legacy of literature that documents a meaningful relationship between maternal support and child outcome, it would be hasty to conclude from these findings that maternal support is not related to adolescent self-esteem. Alternatively, what may be happening is that, presuming a relatively constant level of maternal support, it is the presence of a highly supportive father that becomes the more powerful predictor of this dimension of adolescent self-evaluation.

Marital Quality

An important contribution of this study is the simultaneous analysis of the marital and parental relationships in predicting adolescent self-esteem. This has not been done previously, and by so doing, a more precise view of the role of marital quality in the socialization process can be realized. Marital quality was found to be a significant predictor of both mother and father support, explaining 4% and 15% of the variance, respectively. Interestingly, these findings also illustrate the prominent role of the father. Marital quality accounted for more than three times the variance in father support than in mother support.

For two of the dimensions of self-esteem (Social Worth and Self-Derogation), the impact of marital quality appears to be indirect through parental support. This supports past research from the family process, child development, and divorce literatures in suggesting that what happens in the marital relationship is related to the type of parenting that occurs in families. On the other hand, marital quality was related directly to Positive Self-Esteem. If this proves to be a reliable finding in future studies, then important theoretical work will need to be done to help explain why this particular dimension of adolescent self-evaluation is directly related to marital functioning.

Gender of Adolescent

Because of the relatively small sample size when split by gender of adolescent (males, $N = 42$; females, $N = 61$), and the complexity of the tested model, LISREL analyses were not conducted on individual genders for fear of instability in parameters. Bivariate correlations between the key variables in the model did however provide preliminary evidence for important gender differences. This evidence was consistent in suggesting that the model better represented the relationship of family to self-esteem for boys than for girls. Indeed, every relationship tested showed a higher correlation for boys; in some cases the differences were substantial. This finding is consistent with recent studies of adolescent self-esteem that have found boys' self-esteem to be more strongly related to family factors than girls' (Demo et al., 1987; Gecas and Schwalbe, 1986). While some cursory attempts to explain this finding by the studies' authors have been offered, no serious theoretical or empirical work appears to have been done. This signals another important direction for future family research.

LIMITATIONS AND FUTURE RESEARCH

The findings and contributions of this study must be considered, naturally, in light of the limitations of the data. As with all cross-sectional studies, it must be recognized that the direction of relationships in the model are imposed by the researcher and not derived from the data itself. Without longitudinal data, it is, of course, not possible to confirm the temporal sequencing of variables. Thus it cannot be concluded, for example, that marital quality causes parental support, or that parental support is responsible for higher levels of adolescent self-esteem. In each case, the reverse direction is also plausible (Barber and Thomas, 1986a). In the absence of longitudinal data, however, we have relied upon established theory to guide our decisions about relationship direction.

A further limitation of the study regards the sample. Although random, it does nevertheless only represent intact families in one geographical location in the U.S. The foremost consequence of this is the resulting religious bias. Future research will clearly want to test the model on other samples to test the degree to which the present results are influenced by the religious affiliation or practice of the respondents.

Given these parameters, the present study offers a number of interesting and compelling findings that both help clarify some past research as well as point a direction for future research. A primary contribution of the study is the evidence for independent dimensions of adolescent self-esteem. The confirming evidence for the two dimensions derived from the Rosenberg Scale and the independence of the Social Worth Scale permits a greater sensitivity in understanding, measuring, and predicting adolescent self-evaluation.

A further contribution is the confirming empirical evidence that family processes outside the parent-child dyad play a role in socialization. The simultaneous analysis of marital and parental variables in relation to adolescent self-evaluation has helped to provide some needed clarity to the role of marital functioning in the socialization process. Future research should test similar models with other measures of the marital relationship as well as include measures of other aspects of the family that may impact on adolescent development. Examples would be sibling relationships, the interface between peer and family relationships, as well as communication patterns within the family (Demo et al., 1987).

Finally, the role of gender in socialization processes is very clearly highlighted in this study. For both parents and adolescents gender appears to be a critical factor in understanding the relationship between family processes and adolescent self-evaluation. Future work needs to focus more intently on testing and explaining these differences both theoretically and empirically.

REFERENCES

Amato, P. R. Marital conflict, the parent-child relationship and child self-esteem. *Family Relations*, 1986, *35*, 403-410.

Ausubel, D. E., Balthazar, E., Rosenthal, I., Blackman, L. S., Schpoont, S. H., & Welkowitz, J. Perceived parent attitudes as determinants of children's ego structure. *Child Development*, 1954, *25*, 173-183.

Barber, B. K., & Thomas, D. L. 1986 Dimensions of fathers' and mothers' supportive behavior: The case for physical affection. *Journal of Marriage and the Family*, 1986, *48*, 783-794.

Barber, B. K., & Thomas, D. L. Dimensions of adolescent self-esteem and religious self-evaluation. *Family Perspective*, 1986, *20*, 137-149.

Barnes, G. M., Farrell, M. P., & Windle, M. Parent-adolescent interactions in the development of alcohol abuse and other deviant behaviors. *Family Perspective*, 1987, *21*(4), 321-335.

Baumrind, D. Effects of authoritative control on child behavior. *Child Development* 1966, *37*, 887-907.

Baumrind, D. Parental disciplinary patterns and social competence in children. *Youth and Society*, 1978, *9*, 239-276.

Belsky, J. The interrelation of parental and spousal behavior during infancy in traditional nuclear families: An exploratory analysis. *Journal of Marriage and the Family*, 1979, *41*, 749-755.

Belsky, J. Early human experience: A family perspective. *Developmental Psychology*, 1981, *17*, 3-23.

Broderick, C. B., & Pulliam-Krager, H. Family process and child outcomes. In W. R. Burr, R. Hill, F. I. Nye, & I. L. Reiss (Eds.), *Contemporary theories about the family*. New York: The Free Press, 1979.

Brody, G. H., Pillegrini, A. D., & Sigel, I. E. Marital quality and mother-child and father-child interactions with school-aged children. *Developmental Psychology*, 1986, *22*, 291-296.

Cooley, C. H. *Human nature and the social order*. New York: Scribner's Sons, 1902.

Coopersmith, S. A. *The antecedents of self-esteem*. San Francisco: Freeman, 1967.

Demo, D. H., Small, S. A., & Savin-Williams, R. C. Family relations and the self-esteem of adolescents and their parents. *Journal of Marriage and the Family*, 1987, (November), 705-716.

Dillman, D. A. *Mail and telephone surveys*. New York: John Wiley and Sons, 1978.

Ellis, G. J., Thomas, D. L., & Rollins, B. C. Measuring parental support: the interrelationship of three measures. *Journal of Marriage and the Family*, 1976, *38*, 713-722.

Emery, R. E. Interparental conflict and the children of discord and divorce. *Psychological Bulletin*, 1982, *92*, 310-330.

Epstein, S. The self-concept revisited or a theory of a theory. *American Psychologist*, 1973, *28*, 405-416.

Franks, D. D. and Marolla, J. Efficacious action and social approval as interacting dimensions of self-esteem: A tentative formulation through construct validation. *Sociometry*, 1976, *39*, 324-341.

Gecas, V. Parental behavior and dimensions of adolescent self-evaluation. *Sociometry*, 1971, *34*, 466-482.

Gecas, V. Parental behavior and contextual variations in adolescent self-esteem. *Sociometry*, 1972, *35*, 332-345.

Gecas, V. The self-concept. *Annual Review of Sociology*, 1982, *8*, 1-33.

Gecas, V., & Schwalbe, M. L. Parental behavior and adolescent self-esteem. *Journal of Marriage and the Family*, 1986, *48*, 37-46.

Goldberg, W. A., & Easterbrooks, M. A. Role of marital quality in toddler development. *Development Psychology*, 1984, *20*, 504-514.

Grossman, F. K., Eichler, L. S., & Winickoff, S. A. *Pregnancy, birth and parenthood*. San Francisco: Jossey-Bass, 1980.

Haley, J. Toward a theory of pathological systems. In G. Zuk & I. Boszormenyi-Nagy (Eds.), *Family theory and disturbed families*. Palo Alto, CA: Science and Behavior Books, 1971.

Harter, S. Developmental perspectives on the self-system. In P. H. Mussen (Ed.), *Handbook of Child Psychology*, Vol. 4 (4th ed.). New York: John Wiley and Sons, 1983.

Heilbrun, A. B., Jr. *Aversive maternal control: A theory of schizophrenic development*. New York: John Wiley, 1973.

Hess, R. D., & Camara, K. A. 1979 Post-divorce family relationships as mediating factors in the consequences of divorce for children. *Journal of Social Issues*, 1979, *35*, 79-95.

Hetherington, E. M., Cox, M., & Cox, R. Play and social interaction in children following divorce. *Journal of Social Issues*, 1979, *35*, 26-47.

Hoelter, J., & Harper, L. Structural and interpersonal family influences on adolescent self-conception. *Journal of Marriage and the Family*, 1987, *49*, 129-139.

Hoffman, M. L. Moral development in adolescence. In J. Adelson (Ed.), *Handbook of adolescent psychology*. New York: Wiley, 1980.

Holman, T. B., & Woodroffe-Patrick, M. *Family structure, conflict, and children's self-concept: A cross-cultural replication and extension.* Unpublished manuscript. Brigham Young University, 1986.

James, W. *Principles of psychology*. New York: Holt, 1890.

Joreskog, K. G., & Sorbom, D. *LISREL VI*. Mooresville, IN: Scientific Software, 1984.

Kaplan, H. B., & Pokorny, A. D. Self-derogation and adjustment. *Journal of Nervous and Mental Disease*, 1969, *5*, 421-434.

Kaplan, H. B., & Pokorny, A. D. Social class and self-derogation: A conditional relationship. *Sociometry*, 1971, *34*, 41-64.

Lamb, M. Influence of the child on marital quality and family interaction during the prenatal, perinatal, and infancy periods. In R. Lerner & G. B. Spanier (Eds.), *Child influences on marital and family interaction: A life-span perspective*. New York: Academic Press, 1978.

Lewis, M., (Ed.). *Beyond the dyad*. New York: Plenum Press, 1984.

Mead, G. H. *Mind, self, and society*. Chicago: University of Chicago Press, 1934.

Miller, B. C., Rollins, B. C., & Thomas, D. L. On methods of studying marriages and families. *Journal of Marriage and the Family*, 1982, *44*, 851-873.

Minuchin, S. *Families and family therapy*. Cambridge, MA: Harvard University Press, 1974.

Openshaw, D. K., & Thomas, D. L. The adolescent self and the family. In G. K. Leigh & G. W. Peterson (Eds.), *Adolescents in families*. Cincinnati: South-Western Publishing Co, 1986.

Openshaw, D. K., Thomas, D. L., & Rollins, B. C. Adolescent self-esteem: A multidimensional perspective. *Journal of Early Adolescence*, 1981, *1*, 273-282.

Openshaw, D. K., Thomas, D. L., & Rollins, B. C. Parental influences of adolescent self-esteem. *Journal of Early Adolescence*, 1984, *4*, 259-274.

Osgood, C. E. Studies of the generality of affective meaning systems. *American Psychologist*, 1962, *17*, 10-28.

Osgood, C. E. Semantic differential technique in the comparative study of cultures. *American Anthropologist*, 1964, *66*, 171-200.

Patterson, G. R., & Stouthamer-Loeber, M. The correlation of family management practices and delinquency. *Child Development*, 1984, *55*, 1299-1307.

Pedersen, F. A. *Relationships between paternal behavior and mother-infant interaction.* Paper presented at the annual meeting of the American Psychological Association, Chicago, 1975.

Peterson, G. W., & Rollins, B. C. Parent-child socialization: A review and application of symbolic interaction concepts. In M. B. Sussman & S. K. Steinmetz (Eds.), *Handbook of marriage and the family.* New York: Plenum, 1987.

Raschke, H. J., & Raschke, V. J. Family conflict and children's self-concepts: a comparison of intact and single-parent families. *Journal of Marriage and the Family,* 1979, *41,* 367-374.

Rollins, B. C. and Galligan, R. The developing child and marital satisfaction. In R. Lerner & G. B. Spanier (Eds.), *Child influences on marital and family interaction: A life-span perspective.* New York: Academic Press, 1978.

Rollins, B. C., & Thomas, D. L. Parental support, power, and control techniques in the socialization of children. In W. R. Burr, R. H., F. I. Nye & I. L. Reiss (Eds.), *Contemporary theories about the family* (Vol. 1). New York: Free Press, 1979.

Rosenberg, M. *Society and the adolescent self-image.* Princeton: Princeton University Press, 1965.

Rosenberg, M. *Conceiving the self.* New York: Basic, 1979.

Russell, C. Transition to parenthood: problems and gratification. *Journal of Marriage and the Family,* 1974, *36,* 294-301.

Schaefer, E. S. Children's report of parental behavior: An inventory. *Child Development,* 1965, *36,* 413-424.

Shereshefsky, P. M., & Yarrow, L. J. *Psychological aspects of a first pregnancy and early postnatal adaptation.* New York: Raven Press, 1973.

Steinmetz, S. Disciplinary techniques and their relationship to aggressiveness, dependency, and conscience. In W. R. Burr, F. I. Nye & I. L. Reiss (Eds.), *Contemporary theories about the family (Vol. 1).* New York: Free Press, 1979.

Thornburg, H. Adolescent delinquency and families. In G. K. Leigh & G. W. Peterson (Eds.), *Adolescents in families.* Cincinnati: South-Western Publishing, 1986.

Vogel, E. F., & Bell, N. W. The emotionally disturbed child as a family scapegoat. In N. W. Bell & E. F. Vogel (Eds.), *A modern introduction to the family.* New York: Free Press, 1960.

Wallerstein, J. S., & Kelly, J. B. *Surviving the breakup: How children and parents cope with divorce.* London: Grant McIntyre, 1980.

Wente, A. S., & Crockenberg, S. B. Transition to fatherhood: Lamaze preparation, adjustment difficulty and the husband-wife relationship. *Family Coordinator,* 1976, *25,* 351-357.

Zeller, R. A., & Carmines, E. G. Factor scaling, external consistency, and the measurement of theoretical constructs. *Political Methodology,* 1976, 215-252.

Zeller, R. A., & Carmines, E. G. *Measurement in social sciences: The link between theory and data.* New York: Cambridge University Press, 1980.

This study explored the association between effort in school and grade performance among a sample of over 7,000 high school students of various ethnic backgrounds in California. The major finding was that the expected relationship between effort and performance did not hold for black males, but only those coming from authoritarian, single parent families. Relationships between effort and performance held for other black males as well as all other gender-ethnic groups. Possible explanations for this unusual finding are discussed and suggestions for future research to clarify this issue are offered.

4

When Effort in School Does Not Produce Better Grades: A Family Environment Affects a School Process

SANFORD M. DORNBUSCH AND PHILIP L. RITTER

INTRODUCTION

Several years ago we published a volume summarizing our research on the factors affecting student effort in high school (Natriello and Dornbusch, 1984). Students who cut or don't do their homework are often portrayed as deviants, as if great effort by high school students is the norm. Just as factory and office workers tend to loaf as much as they tend to work, so students can be viewed as organizational actors whose efforts must be motivated. If students don't try, they don't learn. Effort is important.

Bronfenbrenner (1979) has long stressed the interpenetration of diverse systems in determining the nature and impact of social processes. In this paper we shall demonstrate the importance of

Sanford M. Dornbusch • Center for the Study of Families, Children, and Youth, Stanford University, Stanford, California 94305 that approach. In particular, we will show how the study of family structure and family processes can help us understand processes occurring within the school context.

We will examine here the failure among black males of greater effort in school to be associated with higher grades. Of all gender-ethnic groups, black males showed the least evidence that effort pays off. How can we explain this strange result? When we have orally reported this finding to groups of parents and teachers, they have often misinterpreted what we have said. We are not saying that black males do not expend effort; rather, we are trying to determine those conditions in which black males who expend more effort in school typically do not get higher grades than those who put out less effort.

One of the key tasks of parents and educators is the motivation of students, inculcating within them the desire to learn in school and to perform well according to the school's academic standards. Such motivation is assumed to produce greater effort, and the effort produces performances that are both better and more highly evaluated by teachers. The failure of effort to produce higher grades is discouraging to all those who want to raise the level of performance.   It is our task here to examine the circumstances that lead to this anomalous and disheartening condition, for we believe that knowledge of where things go wrong is the first step to improvement.

SOURCES OF DATA

The major source of data for this study is a questionnaire completed by 7,836 adolescents enrolled in six high schools in the San Francisco Bay Area, approximately 88% of the total enrollment of those schools, in the spring of 1985. The questionnaire contained numerous items. Those used in this paper include student background characteristics, self-reported grades, perceptions of parental attitudes and behaviors, and family communication patterns. From this questionnaire we used perceptions of family processes to construct indices of parenting style, background variables to serve as controls, and self-reported grades as the dependent variable.

Some questionnaire items were not answered by all students. Variations in sample size across tables reflects this fact. We chose to present all the available data rather than include only those cases where the data were complete.

For one school in our sample we had current grade point averages for nearly every student. Those data enabled us to assess the validity of the self-reported grades that we used as a dependent variable.

MEASURES

Measures of Student Performance

Self-reported grades. The measure of student performance used throughout this paper is the response by the student to a question that asks for the selection of a category that represents the usual grade the student receives. The categories were: Mostly A's, About Half A's and Half B's, Mostly B's, About Half B's and Half C's, Mostly C's, About Half C's and Half D's, Mostly D's, and Mostly Below D. A numerical scale of self-reported grades was then related to these responses, with 4.0 representing the top category.

We have consulted with educators about the use of grades as a measure of school performance. Their consensus was that grades, unlike scores on intelligence tests and measures based on standardized achievement tests, provide the most appropriate measure of current school performance. Grades have their difficulties as a measure of intellectual performance, for they often represent relatively arbitrary assessments by a teacher. But the typical grade, usual grade, or mean grade is the summation of many judgments about the extent to which a student is responding to the school curriculum.

Grade point averages. We found that grade point averages were available in most of our schools only for seniors approaching graduation. One school had up-to-date grade point averages for almost all its students. We therefore compared the questionnaire response, the self-reported grade, to the grade point average for each student in that school.

The correlation between grade point averages and self-reported grades was .76 ($N = 1,146$). We were concerned that there might be a systematic inflation of self-reported grades for students whose academic performance was low. Accordingly, we examined the responses of students at each grade level. There was a slight tendency to overstate grades only when one reached grades near the bottom of the distribution, mean grades of C and below.

Accordingly, throughout this paper we will use a single measure of school performance that was available for almost all students in the sample. Self-reported grades give a close approximation to the distribution of grades on the transcript and will be used as the measure of school performance in all analyses.

Measures of Student Effort

The use of questionnaire responses to determine the level of effort for each student in this large sample is obviously an approximation to direct observation or the collection of student diaries. Yet, because effort is a key variable in this paper, we must necessarily strive for the most accurate and detailed measures possible. Accordingly, for most of this paper, we will report on seven different and overlapping measures of effort. When our results are consistent across so many measures, we can have more confidence in our findings.

The seven measures we will describe here consist of two estimates, given at widely separated points in the questionnaire, of total time spent on homework; a measure of effort-engagement behaviors that incorporates four separate measures; and the four measures that form the effort-engagement scale for four subjects. The seven measures are as follows:

1. Estimate of total time spent on schoolwork after school on weekdays. This estimate comes from one of the responses to a set of questions inquiring about the way the student spends time after school from Monday through Friday. These questions allowed six possible categorical responses ranging from zero to 80 hours or more of homework.

2. Estimate of total time spent on homework each week. In another part of the questionnaire, students were asked the total amount of time spent on homework each week. There were eight possible categorical responses, ranging from no homework to more than 15 hours a week. Because the highest category for this question was lower than for the previous question, the estimates of the total hours of homework averaged less than for the first measure.

3. A Guttman scale measuring student reports on effort-engagement behaviors in math, science, English, and social studies classes. This Guttman scale was created for earlier studies of student effort (Natriello and Dornbusch, 1984) and continues to have high reproducibility. The scale is based on time spent on homework in each class, on a combination of mind wandering and really paying attention in each class, and on frequency of cutting each class.

Because of our interest in examining the relation of each detailed measure of effort to grades, we will also present data for each of the successive components of the effort-engagement measure. The following four measures are thus part of the measure of effort-engagement behaviors.

4. Frequency of mind wandering in those four classes.

5. Frequency of really paying attention in those four classes.

6. Frequency of cutting classes in those four classes.

7. Mean time on homework in those four classes.

All measures of effort have been coded so that a positive correlation is recorded whenever the relationship is in the expected direction (higher levels of effort are associated with better grades).

Measures of Parenting Style

We derived indirect measures of the style of parenting from the student responses to our questionnaire. In assigning scores on the three parenting styles, we relied on the face validity of questions and response categories. The reliability of our three measures and the consistency of our findings increase our confidence in the utility of this approach.

Three parenting style indices were developed to roughly conform with Baumrind's (1971, 1978) three styles of parenting (authoritarian, permissive, and authoritative). Twenty-five items or sets of items were identified in the student questionnaire as closely reflecting one of the three styles, and each index was constructed by taking the means of the appropriate items. No question was allowed to contribute to more than one of the indices, so that the three scores are not forced to be correlated with each other.

The authoritarian index was based on the mean response to the following eight questions concerning the frequency of certain family behaviors: in their family communication, the parents tell the youth not to argue with adults, that he or she will know better when grown up, and that the parents are correct and should not be questioned; as a response to poor grades, the parents get upset, reduce the youth's allowance, or "ground" the youth; as a response to good grades, parents tell the youth to do even better, and note that other grades should be as good.

The permissive index was the mean of eight responses: hard work in school is not important to the parents (the mean for four academic subjects), the parents don't care if the student gets bad grades, they don't care if the student gets good grades, there are no rules concerning watching television, and (using the highest involvement of the possible parent figures) the parents are not involved in education, they do not attend school programs for parents, they do not help with homework, and they do not check the child's homework.

The authoritative index was calculated from the mean frequency of nine responses concerning family behavior: in their family communication, parents tell the youth to look at both sides of issues, they admit that the youth sometimes knows more, they talk about politics within the family, and they emphasize that everyone should help with decisions in the family; as a response to good grades, parents praise the student and give more freedom to make decisions; as a response to poor grades, they take away freedom, encourage the student to try harder, and offer to help.

The reliability of these three quantitative indices of parenting style was assessed using Cronbach's alpha. The alpha coefficients were .70 for the eight items of the authoritarian index, .60 for the eight items of the permissive index, and .66 for the nine items of the authoritative index. The alphas for the authoritarian and authoritative indices were moderately high and satisfactory, and the alpha for the permissive index was only slightly lower.

DEMOGRAPHIC VARIABLES

Ethnicity. Each high school student was asked to select one of nine categories for ethnic identification: Asian, Black, Filipino, Pacific Islander, American Indian, Latino or Hispanic, White, and Other. Vietnamese respondents were combined with the Asian subgroup. Sample sizes provide sufficient cases for the analysis in this paper of responses from four groups: Asian, Black, Hispanic, and (non-Hispanic) White.

Family structure. Our measure of family structure came from student reports of who is present in the household. In our previous analyses (Dornbusch et al., 1987), family structure consisted of five categories: two natural parents; single mother; mother and stepfather; single father; and father and stepmother. In this paper, since we concentrate on black males and females, the small sample forces us to dichotomize the gender-ethnic groups into two-natural-parent households and not-two-natural-parent households.

RESULTS

Effort and Grades

Table 1 shows consistent moderate correlations for the two sexes between each measure of effort and self-reported grades for the total sample. One might wonder why the correlations are not even higher. Reflection will suggest that some of the best students need not pay attention to repetitive classroom material and need not take as long to do their homework. Moderate correlations are all that we should expect.

Table 1

Correlations Between Self-reported Grades and Diverse Measures of Effort, by Sex

	MALE	FEMALE	TOTAL
After-School Homework	.28*** (3346)	.33*** (3253)	.31*** (6599)
Weekly Homework	.46*** (3745)	.48*** (3557)	.47*** (7302)
Effort-Engagement Behaviors	.37*** (3623)	.43*** (3488)	.40*** (7111)
Mind Wandering	.21*** (3761)	.23*** (3566)	.22*** (7327)
Paying Attention	.27*** (3777)	.25*** (3577)	.26*** (7354)
Cutting Class	.36*** (3732)	.40*** (3537)	.38*** (7269)
Homework in Four Subjects	.34*** (3791)	.40*** (3582)	.37*** (7373)

Using a two-tailed test of significance, ^ indicates statistical significance at the .10 level, * indicates statistical significance at the .05 level, ** indicates statistical significance at the .01 level, and *** indicates statistical significance at the .001 level.

Table 2 presents, for each gender-ethnic group, both the mean on each measure of effort and the correlation of each measure of effort with grades. What is striking in table 2 is that among black males, the correlation of each measure of effort with grades tends to be markedly lower than in the other gender-ethnic groups. Among black males, the highest correlation is only .18, and one measure is statistically significant in the wrong direction. No other group, including black females, approaches the low level of relation between effort and grades found among black males.

Table 2

Means on Diverse Measures of Effort and Correlations of Each Measure
with Self-reported Grades, by Sex and Ethnicity

		MALE				FEMALE		
	Asian	Blk.	Hisp.	Anglo	Asian	Blk.	Hisp.	Anglo
After-School Homework								
Mean	11.6	6.6	7.7	8.0	12.3	9.2	6.4	8.6
	362	173	428	2047	324	173	422	2074
Corr.	.30***	−.15*	.32***	.28***	.30***	.23**	.21***	.34***
	(348)	(165)	(411)	(1966)	(314)	(158)	(396)	(2006)
Weekly Homework								
Mean	9.2	4.7	4.6	6.1	10.0	5.8	4.7	6.9
	(417)	(214)	(514)	(2224)	(374)	(194)	(506)	(2201)
Corr.	.47***	.17*	.34***	.44***	.40***	.40***	.40***	.47***
	(401)	(205)	(489)	(2140)	(363)	(177)	(473)	(2125)
Effort-Engagement Behaviors								
Mean	2.46	2.22	2.19	2.24	2.55	2.22	2.17	2.34
	(398)	(201)	(483)	(2178)	(367)	(186)	(487)	(2164)
Corr.	.30***	.18*	.38***	.37***	.40***	.35***	.38***	.41***
	(385)	(193)	(458)	(2095)	(356)	(170)	(457)	(2096)
Mind Wandering								
Mean	3.3	3.4	3.2	3.2	3.4	3.3	3.2	3.2
	(412)	(214)	(512)	(2250)	(376)	(193)	(507)	(2206)
Corr.	.24***	.06	.19***	.23***	.19***	.21**	.22***	.26***
	(398)	(204)	(486)	(2162)	(363)	(176)	(473)	(2134)
Paying Attention								
Mean	4.1	4.0	3.9	3.8	4.1	4.0	3.9	3.9
	(416)	(214)	(517)	(2254)	(380)	(193)	(510)	(2209)
Corr.	.21***	.12 ^	.28***	.28***	.25***	.32***	.25***	.24***
	(400)	(204)	(491)	(2166)	(367)	(176)	(476)	(2138)
Cutting								
Mean	4.7	4.5	4.3	4.4	4.7	4.4	4.3	4.5
	(410)	(213)	(510)	(2227)	(372)	(190)	(500)	(2196)
Corr.	.37***	.07	.26***	.38***	.42***	.33***	.32***	.39***
	(395)	(204)	(483)	(2141)	(360)	(174)	(467)	(2123)
Homework in Four Subjects								
Mean	3.9	3.3	3.2	3.4	4.0	3.4	3.2	3.6
	(416)	(218)	(519)	(2257)	(380)	(196)	(510)	(2211)
Corr.	.33***	.09	.36***	.33***	.36***	.28***	.32***	.39***
	(401)	(209)	(492)	(2170)	(368)	(179)	(476)	(2138)

Achievement Test Scores

Two possible explanations for the failure of effort among black males to be associated with grades required testing. One explanation was that this result was a product of poor academic preparation for high school level work. In a previous study (Natriello and Dornbusch, 1984) we noted that the reading level of 62% of all black males in San Francisco high schools was four years or more behind grade level. With such a low level of academic preparation, simply reading and trying to understand an assignment may take a great deal of effort. This explanation would suggest that our findings would apply only to students with a very low level of academic preparation.

A second, more racist, explanation of our results argues that many black males do not have the intellectual capacity to do work at the high school level. This explanation would predict that students with lower levels of intellectual ability would be the only group who usually fail to get higher grades with greater effort.

In table 3 we separate black males and females into two groups: those in the bottom quartile on nationally normed language achievement tests and those in the top three quartiles. Both explanations, in terms of academic preparation and in terms of intellectual capacity, would predict that the correlations between each of the three measures of effort and grades would be lower for students in the bottom quartile.

Table 3

Correlations Between Three Measures of Effort and Self-reported Grades, by Sex, Among Blacks Who Are Above or Below the 25th Percentile on a Language Achievement Test

		AFTER-SCHOOL HOMEWORK		HOMEWORK IN FOUR SUBJECTS		EFFORT-ENGAGEMENT BEHAVIORS	
Males	high on language test	.01	(41)	.11	(52)	−.02	(48)
	low on language test	−.25	(38)	.12	(48)	.40**	(43)
Females	high on language test	.27 ∧	(51)	.33*	(58)	.17	(58)
	low on language test	.22	(33)	.26	(36)	.41*	(30)

Neither explanation gets any support from table 3. The correlations between effort and grades for black males in the bottom quartile on test scores were not lower than the correlations for black males in the higher achievement quartiles. Effort is not paying off for black male students who are capable of performing the academic tasks of high school. Indeed, counter to both explanations, the only significant positive correlation between effort and grades is found for those black males who are in the lowest quartile on the achievement tests.

If we instead split at the 50th (national) percentile for language achievement tests (instead of the 25th), there are fewer cases in the high group, and the comparisons are less clear. We do not present the data here, but the conclusions are obvious. Looking at those males who scored above the 50th percentile in language achievement, the relationship between each of the effort scores and grades was lower for black males than for males in any other ethnic group. None of the relationships for black males with high test scores was statistically significant. Deficiencies in level of achievement upon entrance to high school cannot be the explanation of the low relation between effort and grades for black males.

Authoritarian Parenting

We reported our findings to various groups of school administrators, teachers, and parents, asking for alternative explanations. A suggestion by Dr. Mary Bacon, a black school administrator in Palo Alto, provided another testable hypothesis. She felt that blacks who come from authoritarian families are likely to perceive themselves as operating under an authoritarian regime in school. They try to conform, but they are not internally motivated to do the work; they see themselves as merely complying to external pressure when they fulfill academic assignments.

We began the exploration of this explanation in table 4, where the mean on each parenting index for each ethnic-sex group is compared to the appropriate mean for whites. Differences among ethnic groups are seen in that analysis. Of particular interest to us is that black families were significantly higher than non-Hispanic whites on authoritarian parenting. Indeed, black males and females reported a higher level of authoritarian parenting than did any other ethnic group, and a somewhat lower level of authoritative and permissive parenting. It thus seems appropriate to examine the impact of authoritarian parenting on the relation between effort and grades among black high school students.

Table 4

Mean on Each Parenting Style Index, by Sex and Ethnicity

	MALE Authoritarian Mean on Index	Permissive Mean on Index	Authoritative Mean on Index	N	FEMALE Authoritarian Mean on Index	Permissive Mean on Index	Authoritative Mean on Index	N
White	3.33 (.61)	2.95 (.57)	3.58 (.58)	2,314	3.25 (.59)	2.94 (.53)	3.61 (.52)	2,239
Asian	3.52*** (.63)	3.02* (.63)	3.45*** (.63)	418	3.45*** (.58)	2.97 (.58)	3.51*** (.53)	382
Black	3.65*** (.70)	2.70*** (.70)	3.62 (.68)	230	3.54*** (.59)	2.84* (.59)	3.51* (.64)	196
Hispanic	3.55*** (.65)	3.02* (.71)	3.49** (.63)	549	3.47*** (.63)	3.08*** (.63)	3.46*** (.60)	525

Note: Numbers in parentheses are standard deviations.
Tests of significance for means compare the mean on each index for a sex within an ethnic group with the mean on the same index for the same sex among whites, the largest group.

We begin with the relation of authoritarian parenting to grades. In general, table 5 shows that authoritarian parenting among non-Hispanic whites, blacks, Asians, and Hispanics is associated with lower grades among high school students (Dornbusch et al., 1987). Among blacks, the negative correlations of authoritarian parenting and grades are somewhat weaker but in the expected direction. These findings are consonant with the research and conceptualization of Baumrind (1971, 1978), although the measures of authoritarian parenting that we use are markedly different from those that she employed. New measures are necessary because we have extended Baumrind's typology of family parenting styles to a very large and diverse sample of high school students.

Table 5

Correlations Between Authoritarian Parenting and Grades, by Sex and Ethnicity

ETHNICITY	MALE		FEMALE	
White	−.21***	(2,214)	−.27***	(2,162)
Asian	−.18***	(403)	−.11*	(368)
Black	−.11	(218)	−.14∧	(179)
Hispanic	−.01	(517)	−.32***	(487)

Given the impact of authoritarian parenting on grades, we then tested Dr. Bacon's suggestion. In table 6 we split each gender-ethnic group into those families in the highest third in level of authoritarian parenting and those in the lower two-thirds in level of authoritarian parenting. The result is startling: for black males in the high authoritarian families, the relation between each measure of effort and grades tends to be negative or close to zero. Among black males who are not in high authoritarian families, we find the expected positive relations between effort measures and grades. The correlations between effort and grades among black females who come from high authoritarian families are lower than for black females in low authoritarian families, although the cor-

Table 6

Correlations Between Self-reported Grades and Diverse Measures
of Effort by Level of Authoritarian Parenting Style,
by Sex and Ethnicity

GROUP (RANGE OF N)	AFTER-SCHOOL HOMEWORK	WEEKLY HOMEWORK	EFFORT-ENGAGE-MENT BEHAVIORS	MIND WANDER-ING	PAYING ATTEN-TION	CUTTING CLASS	HOMEWORK IN FOUR SUBJECTS
Total Male							
Lo Auth. (2063+)	.32***	.48***	.38***	.22***	.26***	.38***	.36***
Hi Auth. (1252+)	.22***	.42***	.34***	.17***	.20***	.33***	.31***
Total Female							
Lo Auth. (2177+)	.35***	.51***	.43***	.23***	.23***	.40***	.40***
Hi Auth. (1071+)	.31***	.47***	.42***	.20***	.29***	.38***	.39***
Black Male							
Lo Auth. (81–87)	.14	.31**	.35**	.10	.23*	.25*	.22*
Hi Auth. (83–108)	−.37***	−.10	−.02	−.05	−.03	.00	−.05
Black Female							
Lo Auth. (89–95)	.27**	.44***	.44***	.30**	.33***	.35***	.34***
Hi Auth. (66–77)	.18	.30**	.16	.00	.30**	.29*	.17
Asian Male							
Lo Auth. (190–210)	.33***	.45***	.35***	.12 ^	.18**	.34***	.38***
Hi Auth. (156–184)	.27***	.49***	.27***	.34***	.27***	.42***	.30***
Asian Female							
Lo Auth. (185–209)	.29***	.47***	.43***	.18**	.30***	.31***	.42***
Hi Auth. (129–150)	.31***	.32***	.34***	.14 ^	.26***	.48***	.32***
Hispanic Male							
Lo Auth. (206–227)	.32***	.39***	.43***	.24***	.30***	.39***	.38***
Hi Auth. (196–237)	.29***	.34***	.38***	.16*	.33***	.17*	.38***
Hispanic Female							
Lo Auth. (229–268)	.23***	.43***	.34***	.16**	.15*	.30***	.32***
Hi Auth. (166–198)	.15 ^	.33***	.39***	.24***	.34***	.31***	.28***
Non-Hispanic White Male							
Lo Auth. (1325+)	.31***	.45***	.37***	.23***	.29***	.39***	.34***
Hi Auth. (624+)	.21***	.38***	.33***	.18***	.26***	.35***	.28***
Non-Hispanic White Female							
Lo Auth. (1459+)	.36***	.48***	.42***	.27***	.26***	.40***	.39***
Hi Auth. (546+)	.29***	.43***	.36***	.20***	.18***	.35***	.37***

relations remain positive. Authoritarian parenting in black families seems to have an impact, especially on males, that reduces the expected relation between effort and grade point average.

Family Structure

We have found so far that, for black males, authoritarian parenting is associated with a low level of payoff for effort. Lawrence Steinberg of the University of Wisconsin, noting that black families have by far the lowest proportion of two-natural-parents families, suggested that we also examine the impact of family structure. He speculated that authoritarian parenting may have a more negative impact on the payoff for effort in families without two natural parents. Thus, we might find that non-two-natural-parents households that are high in authoritarian parenting depress the relation between effort and grades in every ethnic group. The reason that we observed the impact for blacks might be the higher proportion of broken homes among blacks.

In order to test this idea, we divided each gender-ethnic group into two-natural-parents households and non-two-natural-parents households, and then we looked at the impact of authoritarian parenting upon the relation between effort and grades. Table 7 shows the results among black and non-black males and females. It is only among black males in households without both biological parents that high authoritarian parenting is associated with a lack of relation between effort and grades. Six of the seven measures of effort are negatively correlated with grades among black males in families that are both high authoritarian and do not contain two natural parents. That pattern is not found among black females nor in any other gender-ethnic group. There is no evidence of a pervasive influence of family structure on the payoff for effort; the impact of family structure on the relation between effort and grades appears to be limited to black males.

DISCUSSION

The empirical results of this study can be briefly summarized. It is among black males that a higher level of effort in school is not correlated with higher grades, and not among other gender-ethnic groups. It is among black males in families high on our measure

Table 7

Correlations Between Diverse Measures of Effort and Self-reported Grades,
Within Two-Natural-Parent Households and Non-Two-Natural-Parent
Households, by Level of Authoritarianism, Sex, and Black or Nonblack Ethnicity

	MALES				FEMALES			
	Two-Nat.-Parent Household		Non-Two-Nat.-Parent Household		Two-Nat.-Parent Household		Non-Two-Nat.-Parent Household	
	High Auth.	Low Auth.	High Auth.	Low Auth.	High Auth.	Low Auth.	High Auth.	Low Auth.
After-School Homework								
Blacks	−.20	.12	−.50***	.21	.07	.04	.25	.39**
	(35)	(31)	(43)	(40)	(19)	(30)	(44)	(55)
Nonblacks	.26***	.31***	.20***	.34***	.31***	.37***	.31***	.30***
	(754)	(1278)	(369)	(638)	(612)	(1318)	(365)	(724)
Weekly Homework								
Blacks	.20	.42*	−.28*	.27 ^	.10	.49**	.40**	.45***
	(42)	(32)	(58)	(45)	(22)	(33)	(50)	(56)
Nonblacks	.46***	.47***	.40***	.45***	.48***	.49***	.43***	.47***
	(809)	(1366)	(433)	(700)	(659)	(1403)	(402)	(787)
Effort-Engagement Behaviors								
Blacks	.34*	.33 ^	−.19	.47**	.14	.40*	.19	.47***
	(40)	(31)	(58)	(43)	(21)	(32)	(47)	(57)
Nonblacks	.36***	.38***	.35***	.39***	.42***	.43***	.39***	.41***
	(809)	(1355)	(428)	(690)	(653)	(1392)	(401)	(776)
Mind Wandering								
Blacks	.17	.13	−.17	.06	.20	.25	−.05	.32*
	(41)	(32)	(60)	(45)	(22)	(32)	(49)	(57)
Nonblacks	.21***	.23***	.22***	.24***	.20***	.21***	.24***	.24***
	(830)	(1376)	(434)	(708)	(664)	(1407)	(402)	(787)
Paying Attention								
Blacks	.25	.25	−.19	.12	.32	.12	.28 ^	.54***
	(41)	(32)	(59)	(44)	(22)	(33)	(49)	(57)
Nonblacks	.32***	.28***	.34***	.24***	.27***	.23***	.29***	.19***
	(829)	(1380)	(438)	(707)	(668)	(1408)	(403)	(789)
Cutting Class								
Blacks	−.25	.26	.13	.28 ^	.43*	.24	.21	.40**
	(44)	(31)	(59)	(46)	(22)	(33)	(49)	(57)
Nonblacks	.40***	.38***	.28***	.41***	.36***	.38***	.40***	.43***
	(833)	(1376)	(437)	(712)	(665)	(1402)	(404)	(787)
Homework in Four Subjects								
Blacks	.24	.19	−.17	.29 ^	.21	.38*	.14	.34*
	(44)	(32)	(60)	(45)	(22)	(33)	(51)	(57)
Nonblacks	.34***	.36***	.29***	.37***	.41***	.41***	.37***	.36***
	(838)	(1383)	(440)	(709)	(666)	(1409)	(408)	(791)

of authoritarianism that we find the lack of relation between effort
and grades, and not among black males who are not in highly
authoritarian families. It is among black males who are in families
that do not contain both biological parents and that also are highly
authoritarian, that greater effort does not typically produce higher
grades. The lack of payoff for effort is not found among any other

gender-ethnic groups, nor is it present among black males who live with both natural parents.

Two measurement issues have been suggested as possible causes of these findings. One suggestion is that this subgroup of black males in single-parent authoritarian homes show less variability in their scores on both effort and grades, thereby making it difficult to demonstrate a relationship between those two variables. We have checked and found that this group of black males has higher standard deviations on each of these measures than do other groups of black males.

A second possibility is a tendency of this group of black adolescent males to inflate their level of effort as a resistant response to adult domination. We cannot check the validity of this explanation, but, even if true, it is puzzling that such inflation does not take place among other groups of students in single-parent authoritarian households.

To repeat, authoritarian parenting within a home that does not contain both natural parents is associated with a lack of payoff for effort, but only among black male students. The result is clear, but it is unexpected. Behavioral scientists search for universal generalizations that apply within given scope conditions. To say that a phenomenon is limited to black males is to evade the issue. What processes could be producing this result? We don't know, but we can speculate in an attempt to assist future research.

Obviously, we need continuing intensive studies of the relation of family structure and processes to school processes and outcomes (Clark, 1983). We will present here some ideas for investigation.

1. Is authoritarian parenting different for black males, and especially for black males who are not living with both their natural parents? For example, the level of physical punishment may differ from one gender-ethnic group or family type to another. We capture only some aspects of parenting in our analyses of family parenting styles.

2. A large proportion of the black families without two natural parents have a single mother as the head of the household. Since our lack of payoff for effort is primarily found among sons in these families, comparative analyses of mother-son interaction are needed. These analyses should be done within black families, as well as in other ethnic groups.

3. We believe that we are dealing here with issues of attribution, the actor's perception of the causes of his or her behavior. As we have noted, the domain of the family and the domain of the school are not impermeable. Our findings show that family structures and processes can influence school behaviors. One of the mechanisms by which this interpenetration takes place may be the pattern of causal attributions made by the student in school.

We know that an individual's perception that external pressure is the main cause of his or her behavior makes it less likely that the individual will be motivated internally to perform that behavior in the future (Lepper, 1983). Since pressure from outside is perceived as having forced the behavior, the actor does not view the behavior as internally caused.

Children from roughly 6 to 16 must physically be in school. The fact that schooling is compulsory should not lead to the view that students perceive all their school tasks as externally motivated. That view overlooks the extent to which, when students are given an assignment, they can personally commit themselves to it or just go through the motions. There is a voluntary component to student effort that increases the importance of a tendency toward external attribution (Folger et al., 1978). Students who emphasize their own internal motives for performing school tasks are likely to invest more of themselves and to do better.

Authoritarian parenting in black families without both natural parents may be reducing the internal motivation of young males with respect to school behaviors. These black males may be carrying over to the school arena their vision of regimes that prescribe behavior and allow little latitude for personal choice and efficacy. We need to study the mechanisms that lead to such results in some types of families and not in others.

4. Finally, we propose investigation of the complex interaction between the worlds of peers, family, and school. In this study we have examined only the overlap between family and school. Black males from broken homes may, on the average, have markedly different experiences in their relations with peers when compared with any other group of adolescents. In our next round of research, we will add the study of peers to our previous emphasis on family and schools.

REFERENCES

Baumrind, D. Current patterns of parental authority. *Developmental Psychology Monographs*, 1971, *4*, 1-103.

Baumrind, D. The development of instrumental competence through socialization. In A. D. Pick (Ed.), *Minnesota symposium on child psychology (Vol. 7)*. Minneapolis: University of Minnesota Press, 1978.

Bronfenbrenner, U. *The ecology of human development: Experiments by nature and design*. Cambridge, MA.: Harvard University Press, 1979.

Clark, R. M. *Family life and school achievement: Why poor black children succeed or fail*. Chicago: University of Chicago Press, 1983.

Dornbusch, S. M., Ritter, P. L., Leiderman, P. H., Roberts, D. F., & Fraleigh, M. J. The relation of parenting style to adolescent school performance. *Child Development*, 1987, *58*.

Folger, R., Rosenfield, D., & Hays, R. P. Equity and intrinsic motivations: The role of choice. *Journal of Personality and Social Psychology*, 1978, *36*, 557-564.

Lepper, M. R. Extrinsic reward and intrinsic motivation: Implications for the classroom. In J. M. Levine & M. C. Wang (Eds.), *Teacher and student perceptions: Implications for learning*. Hillsdale, NJ: Erlbaum, 1983.

Natriello, G., & Dornbusch, S. M. *Teacher evaluative standards and student effort*. New York: Longmans, 1984.

This study explored the mediating role of adolescent self-esteem in the relationship between parental behaviors and adolescent academic achievement. The sample consisted of families with both parents and at least two adolescents present in the home. Controlling for socioeconomic status, IQ, and older sibling academic achievement, structural equation analyses revealed that the expected relationships between parental supportive and coercive behaviors and academic achievement was significantly mediated by levels of adolescent self-esteem. Implications of these findings for theory, research, and practice are discussed.

5

ADOLESCENT SELF-ESTEEM AS AN INTERVENING VARIABLE IN THE PARENTAL BEHAVIOR AND ACADEMIC ACHIEVEMENT RELATIONSHIP

CRAIG K. MANSCILL AND BOYD C. ROLLINS

Achievement in the academic setting is highly prized by contemporary American society. An individual's academic achievement can have important consequences for his school and later life. Within the school setting academic achievement often determines whether or not the student is allowed to participate in extra-curricular activities, and it is also used as a criterion for scholarships and/or admittance to college. In an individual's career path, academic performance often determines career choice as well as job opportunities.

Craig K. Manscill • LDS Church Educational System, Poughkeepsie, New York, 12601. Boyd C. Rollins • Department of Sociology, Brigham Young University, Provo, Utah 84602.

The impact of academic achievement on the larger society is perhaps most clearly seen in the association between poor achievement and school dropouts. Bachman et al. (1971) report that dropouts are more likely to have lower self-esteem than adolescents who continue their education. In addition they appear to be more subject to negative affective states, such as depression, and are often associated with delinquent behavior.

Most dropouts do not return to school and thus fail to receive a diploma. The lack of a diploma bars many young people from opportunities that might otherwise be open to them, and often results in the school dropout becoming a burden upon society as he joins the ranks of unemployment and/or government support.

Lavin (1965), in reviewing over 300 studies published during the period between 1953 and 1961, identified 29 types of variables which have been used as predictors of school achievement. In these studies, two variables appear to surface consistently as being meaningful predictors of achievement: 1) the student's self-concept and 2) the student's family experience.

The purpose of this chapter is to formulate and empirically test a theoretical model of parental socialization factors as antecedents of academic achievement in adolescent youth, with the adolescent's self-concept as an intervening variable. The major hypothesis of the model is that an adolescent's perceptions of his or her parents' supportive and coercive behaviors *indirectly* influence the adolescent's academic achievement through the impact of the parental behaviors on the adolescent's self-esteem worth. The self-esteem worth then directly influences academic achievement.

SELF-CONCEPT

There has been a considerable amount research on the relationship between self-concept or self-esteem and academic achievement (Brookover, 1964; Coppersmith, 1959, 1967; Faunce, 1984; Lavin, 1965; Nelson, 1970; Nicholls, 1967; Rubin et al., 1977; Scheirer and Kraut, 1979; Watkins and Astilla, 1980; Williams, 1973; Wylie, 1979; Youngblood, 1976). Purkey (1970:14) suggested that "if the child perceives himself to be able, confident, adequate and a person of worth, worthy of respect rather than condemnation, he has more energy available to spend on academic achievement. On the other hand, if he perceives himself as worthless, incapable to cope with life's problems, he may not find it convenient or possible to identify with academic achievement and may fail in spite of being intellectually capable of achieving more."

Brookover (1967) concluded from his extensive research on self-image and achievement, that the assumption that human ability is the most important factor in achievement is questionable, and that the student's attitudes limit the level of his achievement in school.

In his review of self-image (self-acceptance, self-image, self-esteem, and self-confidence) Lavin (1965:39) concluded that, "although research findings below the college level are spotty, the studies suggested a positive self-image is associated with higher performance." Wylie (1979) reviewed numerous studies in which self-concept has been related to achievement test scores in children. Across these studies she finds that the correlations tend to range from .10 to .50 and more typically fall within the .30s and low .40s. The empirical research clearly demonstrates a positive relationship between self-esteem and academic achievement.

PARENTAL BEHAVIORS

Of the many different persons children are exposed to, parents likely exercise the major influence on their achievements (Haller and Portes, 1973; Otto, 1979; Sewell and Hauser, 1975). In particular, two dimensions of parental behavior, support and control attempts, have been identified repeatedly in parent-child research as important in accounting for the parents' socialization influence on children (Goshen-Gottstein, 1975; Thomas, Gecas, Weigert, and Rooney, 1974; Rollins and Thomas, 1975, 1979).

Parental Support. One of the most reliable and consistent relationships found in socialization research is that of the positive relationship between parental supportive behavior and positive child outcomes. In reviewing 235 empirical studies focusing on parental support and numerous child outcome behaviors, Rollins and Thomas (1979) noted a remarkable consistency of results across time, developmental stages, cultural contexts, methodological variations, and sex-of-parent-sex-of-child variations. In general, this literature suggests that children reared in supportive environments tend to develop socially valued characteristics. With

particular regard to academic achievement there is a large amount
of research which indicates that parental supportive behavior such
as praise, approval, encouragement, help, cooperation, expression
of terms of endearment, and physical affection is positively related
to academic achievement in children (Baumrind, 1971; Baumrind
and Black, 1967; Dornbusch, Ritter, Leiderman, Roberts, and
Fraleigh, 1987; Hoffman, 1960; Kagan and Moss, 1962; Kohn,
1977; Kohn and Schooler, 1983; Maccoby, 1961; Rollins and
Thomas, 1979; Walters and Stinnet, 1971).

   Parental Control Attempts. There are a variety of ways in
which parents exercise control attempts in relating with their
children. Some theorists have made general distinctions between
these such as Rollins and Thomas' (1979) "coercion, "induction",
and "love withdrawal". The empirical relationships between parental control attempts and child outcome have not been consistent.
This inconsistency has to do in part, no doubt, with the different
operational definitions of control attempts. Some dimensions of
control attempts appear to be positively related to a child's characteristics while others demonstrate a negative relationship.

   This study concerns itself with that domain of parental control
attempts which impact negatively on child outcomes. Particular
emphasis is placed on coercive parental behavior. Coercion is
defined as behavior of the parent in a contest of wills, which
results in considerable external pressure on the child to behave according to the parents' desires (Rollins and Thomas, 1979). In
reviewing the research on discipline techniques, these same researchers found that parental coercive behavior tended to be related to lower levels of social competence, self-esteem, and moral
development in children. With particular reference to achievement, other researchers have found that coercive parents, those
who are punitive in their discipline, deprive their children of
material objects or privileges, apply direct application of force, or
the threat of any of these impede achievement in their children
(Aaronson, 1966; Barton et al., 1974; Becker, 1970; Berg, 1963;
Biglin, 1964; Dornbusch, et al., 1987; Hoffman, 1960).

PARENTAL BEHAVIORS, SELF-CONCEPT, AND
ACADEMIC ACHIEVEMENT

   The literatures relating parental support and coercive control attempts to academic achievement in children are fairly clear in iden-

tifying a positive relationship with support and a negative relationship with coercion. What these literatures have not done, however, is to consider the role of self-concept in the relationship between parental behaviors and academic achievement. There is a well established literature relating self-concept to academic achievement. But in addition to this there is also a very well established literature relating parental behaviors to dimensions of the self-concept (Comstock, 1973; Coopersmith, 1967; Gecas, 1971, 1972, 1979; Laitman, 1975; Miller, 1976; Mote, 1966; Openshaw, Thomas and Rollins, 1983; Openshaw, Rollins, and Thomas, 1984; Ragland, 1978; Rosenthal, Peng, and McMillan, 1980; Saavdra, 1978; Streitmatter and Jones, 1974; Thomas et al., 1974; Toto, 1972; Turnberg, 1966). In many cases the very same two parental socialization variables, support and coercive control attempts, are identified as predicting levels of both academic achievement and self evaluation. Given this, it seems only logical then that when considering the impact of parental behaviors on academic achievement, the self-concept of the student ought to be considered. Since it has been shown that self-concept is related to academic achievement and that parental behaviors which have been shown to predict academic achievement are also strong predictors of self-concept it may well be that self-concept serves as an intervening variable in the parent behavior and academic achievement relationship. It is this notion which is the major thrust of this study. We therefore hypothesize a positive relationship between parental support and self-esteem worth, and a negative relationship between parental coercion and self-esteem worth but that the previously documented relationships between these parental behaviors and academic achievement will not be present when self-esteem worth is simultaneously included in the model as an intervening variable.

Such relationships between parental supportive and coercive behaviors, childrens' self-esteem worth, and childrens' academic achievement can be understood in terms of symbolic interaction theory (Cooley, 1902). Basic to symbolic interaction is the notion that humans live in a symbolic environment as well as a physical environment, and that through this interaction they acquire a complex set of symbols. Parental behaviors such as support and coercive control attempts as perceived by the child are symbols which can be interpreted as indications of how the parents views the

child's worth. Thus supportive behaviors on the part of parents
are interpreted as validations or confirmations of worth, while
coercive behaviors communicate disregard for the child's worth.
Subsequently, the self definition of worth enables or disables the
child in pursuit of instrumental goals such as academic performance. A conceptual model for these theoretical ideas is depicted
in Figure 1.

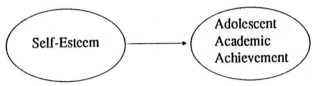

Figure 1. Hypothesized relationship between adolescent self-esteem and
adolescent academic achievement.

CONTROL VARIABLES

In her review of studies relating self-concept to academic
achievement, Wylie (1979) suggests the need to control for certain
factors which left uncontrolled may be contributing to some of the
difficulty in interpreting past findings. In particular she recom-
mends controlling for the socioeconomic level of parents and the
child's intellectual ability. Other researchers also suggest the importance of sibling performance when considering a child's
achievement level.

Socioeconomic Status. Several researchers have attempted to
identify the relationship between socioeconomic status and
academic achievement. Their work has resulted in findings which
document a positive relationship between socioeconomic status
and child academic achievement (Baker, Shutz, & Hinze, 1961;
Bayley and Schaefer, 1960; Dunnell, 1971; Gecas, 1979; Lambert,
1970; Thomas, 1962). To control for this relationship, we simultaneously included father's occupational status, father's and
mother's educational attainment, and father's income as independent variables in the empirical model while testing the theoretical relationships.

Intellectual Ability. In the case of high school adolescents, intellectual ability has been found to be highly correlated (up to .60)
with academic achievement, accounting for as much as 20 to 36%

of the variance (Brookover, Thomas, and Paterson, 1962; Lavin, 1965). To control for this strong correlation, we simultaneously included a measure of the subjects' intellectual ability (IQ) as an independent variable in the empirical model while testing the theoretical relationships.

Sibling Academic Achievement. Social learning theory suggests that learning can take place vicariously by a child observing significant others in the child's life (Bandura, 1969, 1977; Bandura and Kupers, 1964). Specifically, in two child families younger siblings have been found to copy or model the behavior of their older siblings more so than older children model the behavior of their younger siblings. To control for an older sibling's academic achievement we also included an older siblings cumulative grade point average (GPA) in the empirical model while testing the theoretical relationships.

The structural model of this study including control variables simultaneously with the variables in the theoretical model is depicted in Figure 2.

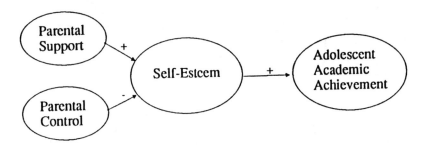

Figure 2. Hypothesized relationships between adolescent self-esteem, parental support, and parental control with adolescent academic achievement.

SAMPLE

The present study used data from a larger research project on parent-adolescent relationships collected in 1974. The population for the study consisted of the households of 13,100 junior and senior high school students enrolled in the metropolitan Salt Lake City School District in 1973. From that population a random sample of 348 households with two adult resident parents and two

or more adolescent children ages 14 to 18 enrolled in junior and
senior high schools were selected. An honorarium of $20 was of-
fered to each family for their participation.

MEASUREMENT

Selected data from the questionnaire responses of the youngest
of two adolescents and from both parents along with school
records on both adolescents were used to operationalize the variables in this study. The questionnaire responses were obtained
from family members at their home residence. A research assis-
tant monitored the filling out of the questionnaire responses to
provide an atmosphere of confidentiality for each respondent.

Academic Achievement. Cumulative grade point averages
(GPA) for adolescents were used as an indicator of their academic
achievement. The grade point averages of the two adolescents in
each household were obtained from the school district records.
The grading scale used in the schools provided a term grade point
average of 0.0 (E) to 4.0 (A). For the older siblings in the sample
the mean of academic achievement was 3.0 with a standard deviation of .78 while the mean and standard deviation for the younger
siblings was 3.0 and .73 respectively

Self-Esteem. The measure of self-esteem worth for the youngest
of the referent siblings in each household was based on a number
of items from a modified version of Osgood's (1964) semantic differential scale similar to that used by Gecas (1971, 1972) and
Thomas et. al. (1974). Such a method employs bipolar adjective
pairs, each set on a five point Likert-type scale. The items in this
instrument asked adolescents to describe how they saw themselves
in their families. From a principle components factor analysis of
the responses a three factors solution emerged, one of which was
identified as self-esteem worth. The adjective pairs with factor
loadings of 0.40 or more on self-esteem worth were in order of
magnitude:

1. Happy - Sad
2. Sociable - Unsociable
3. Friendly - Unfriendly
4. Confident - Unsure
5. Good - Bad
6. Dependable - Undependable

7. Honest - Dishonest

The value for the internal consistency reliability coefficient on this factor was 0.84. Standardized factor weighted scores with a mean of zero and a standard deviation 1.0 were used for this variable in the data analysis.

Parental Behaviors of Support and Coercive Control Attempts. For the present study, only scores of the youngest adolescents perception's of their parents behavior were used. The parental behaviors of support and coercive control attempts were operationalized from 2 dominant factors in a 16 factor solution to responses on a 70 item parent behavior inventory. Fifty-one of the items came from a revision of Schaefer's (1965) Parent Behavior Inventory. The procedure used was a factor analysis employing varimax rotation. From pilot studies, the original 192 item inventory was reduced by this principle components factor analysis procedure to 51 items. These items were combined with a 9 item scale constructed from a factor analytic study comparing the Heilbrun and Cornell measures of parental support (Ellis, et. al., 1976). An additional 16 items were developed through a series of pilot studies on an initial set of 64 items designed to measure parental inductive control attempts. Questionnaire items which had factor loadings of .40 or greater were examined for the purpose of assigning meaning and naming the factors. From the 16 factors, 2 were identified as parental support and parental coercive control attempts. The individual items making up each parental dimension by order of magnitude are as follows:

Support

Over the past several years.....

1. I experienced a feeling of security in my relationship with this parent.

2. This parent made me feel he/she was there if I needed him/her.

3. This parent felt affection for me and I was certain of it.

4. This parent seemed to trust me in my role as a family member.

5. Whenever I had any kind of problem, I could count on this parent to help me out.

6. This parent has shown positive interest in and support of me in my daily affairs as part of the family.

7. This parent seemed to have approved of the things I did.

8. This parent taught me things I wanted to learn.
9. This parent said nice things about me.
Parental Coercive Control Attempts
This parent.....
1. is always getting after me.
2. is always finding fault with me.
3. is not very patient with me.
4. often complains about what I do.
5. gets cross and angry about little things I do.
6. always tries to change me.
7. seems to see my faults more than my good points.
8. does not give me any peace until I do what he/she says.

The internal consistency reliability coefficient values for the variables of parental support and parental coercive control attempts were .85 and .76 respectively.

Socioeconomic Status and IQ. Parents responses to the questionnaire were used to index socioeconomic status. Each parent specified the amount of their education and fathers indicated their annual income and the type of occupation if employed. The occupations were rated according to a rating scale developed by Siegal (1971) which ranges from 0 to 100. The mean for father's occupational status was 52.57 with a standard deviation of 16.49. The mean years of educational attainment for mothers and fathers were 13. 23 and 14.79 respectively while the standard deviations were 2.54 and 3.51. The modal yearly income for fathers was in the category of $16,000 - $18,500.

School records were used to obtain information on IQ for the youngest adolescent. The mean score was 109.20 with a standard deviation of 13.54.

CORRELATIONS AMONG THE VARIABLES

Before presenting the results of the test of the theoretical model the simple bivariate correlations between the independent variables (SES, parental behaviors, and IQ) and the dependent variable (academic achievement) and the intervening variables (self-esteem worth) are presented (See Table 1). Socio-economic status of the household is indexed by father's occupational status, father's income, father's education and mother's education. Parental behaviors are operationalized by the referent child's report of his/her

Table 1. Correlates of Adolescent Self-Esteem Worth and Academic Achievement

	GPA	SE-W	FA DSE-W	MO DSE-W
Father Occupation Status	.18**	-.03	.02	-.03
Father Education	.17**	-.03	.04	.01
Father Income	.17**	-.09	-.02	.02
Mother Education	.23**	.00	.06	.04
IQ	.35**	-.08	-.11	-.13*
Father Support	.04	.33**	.37**	.23**
Mother Support	.14*	.38**	.34**	.34**
Father Coercion	-.16*	-.25**	-.44**	-.26**
Mother Coercion	-.04	-.29**	-.30**	-.40**

* p<.05
** p<.01

father's supportive behaviors, mother's supportive behaviors, father's coercive behaviors, and mother's coercive behaviors. The referent child's intelligence is operationalized by a standardized test intelligence quotient (IQ). Academic achievement is operationalized by (GPA), and the referent child's self-esteem is operationalized by a self report of self-esteem worth (SE-W), the child's perception of the father's definition of the child's self-worth (FA DSE-W) and the child's perception of the mother's definition of the child's self-worth (MO DSE-W).

The simple bivariate correlations data clearly indicate that the socio-economic status and IQ variables have a positive relationship with academic achievement but have minimal or no relationships with self-esteem worth. The parental support variables demonstrate a fairly strong positive correlation with self-esteem worth but a minimal positive or no relationship with academic achievement. The parental coercion variables demonstrate a fairly strong negative correlation with self-esteem worth but a minimal negative or no relationship with academic achievement.

RESULTS

A structural equations (EQS) procedure similar to LISREL (Bentler, 1985) was used to evaluate the goodness of fit between a carefully specified theoretical model (including structural and measurement components) and values in a covariance matrix of relevant variables. EQS implements a general mathematical and statistical approach to the analysis of linear structural equation systems. The mathematical model of EQS (Bentler & Weeks, 1979, 1980, 1982) subsumes a variety of covariance structure models including multiple regression, path analysis, simultaneous equations, first and second higher-order confirmatory factor analysis, as well as regression and structural relations among latent variables. The statistical theory allows for the estimation of parameters and testing of models using traditional multivariate normal theory, based on a maximum likelihood least squares and minimum chi-square approach. EQS is best suited to confirmatory analyses. In the confirmatory approach, both a measurement model and a structural model must be clearly specified and identified. The measurement model provides for the specification of correlated errors among the independent variables as well as relationships between unobserved (latent) variables and measured indicators. The structural model specifies theoretical relationships between antecedent and dependent variables. Both models are specified as one complete model and tested simultaneously. In this way EQS tests the *measurement model* by performing a confirmatory factor analysis on the measurements indicating each latent variable. Simultaneously, EQS tests the *structural model* by estimating coefficients between the independent and dependent variables. Thus the researcher, must first identify a complete model (both the measurement and structural aspects) to test. When the model is tested estimates of the measurement and structural parameters are made and a chi-square test performed to evaluate whether the model fits the data well. This is a goodness of fit test. The goodness of fit index is a measure of the relative amount of covariation in a set of data accounted for by a model. It has an upper limit of 1.00, the closer to 1.00, the better the fit of the model. The average absolute standardized residual is an average of the covariation remaining in the data after the covariation accounted for by the model is removed. The closer to 0.0 this score is the better the fit of the model.

   Measurement Model. In this study, the measurement model consisted of four unobserved (latent) variables, namely, adolescent self-esteem, parental support, parental coercive control attempts,

and socioeconomic status. The indicators in the measurement
model are three indicators for self-esteem (SE-W, FA DSE-W and
MO DSE-W), two indicators for support (FA SUP and MO SUP),
two indicators for coercive control attempts (FA COERC and MO
COERC), and four indicators for socio-economical status (FA
EDUC, MO EDUC, FA OCCUP STAT and FA INCOME). Each
of the indicators of these variables, except those constrained to be
1.00 were significant at the .05 level of confidence. The amount
of variance accounted for ranged from .348 for mothers education
to .984 for mother support (see Table 2). Compared to factor loadings in exploratory factor analysis the coefficients in the measurement model are relatively high.

Table 2. Statistical Values for Measurement Model

Measurement Relationships	Standardized Coefficients	R^2	Unstandardized Coefficients	Standard Errors
SES:				
Father Occupation Status	.923	.852	1.000	----
Father Education	.845	.714	.194	.015
Father Income	.701	.491	.119	.011
Mother Education	.581	.348	.098	.016
Parental Support:				
Father Support	.742	.551	1.000	----
Mother Support	.992	.984	1.126	.155
Parental Coercion:				
Father Coercion	.797	.635	1.000	----
Mother Coercion	.751	.564	.952	.166
Self-Esteem Worth:				
Fahtier DSE-W	.913	.834	1.000	----
MO DSE-W	.837	.701	.923	.057
SE-W	.928	.861	.902	.046

Structural Model. The results of the test of the complete EQS
model are depicted in Figure 3, including both measurement and
structural values. The initial test of the model suggested a change
in the specification of the control variables with SES directly relating to IQ as well as GPA. With this revision, the test of the final
model supports all of our hypotheses. The strongest relationships
in the model were among the parental behaviors and self-esteem;
parental support predicted self-esteem worth (.470) and parental
coercive control attempts also predicted self-esteem worth (-.472)
and in the expected directions. But most important and central to

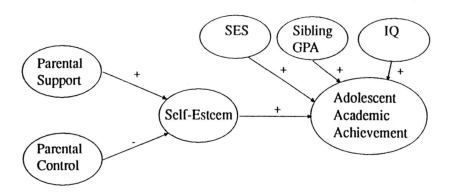

Figure 3. Complete hypothesized relationship of the independent variables of
parental support and control, and Self-esteem, the control variables of SES, I.Q.,
and sibling G.P.A. and the dependent variable adolescent academic achievement.

this study, self-esteem was found to serve best as a intervening
variable between the two parental behaviors variables (support and
coercive control attempts) and adolescent academic achievement.
Though the coefficient is moderate (.235) between self-esteem
worth and GPA, it is still significant at the .05 level and accounts
for .055 of the variance in academic achievement after controlling
for the effects of the other variables. The control variables of IQ,
SES and sibling GPA were related to academic achievement as
predicted.

The goodness of fit measures indicate that this model fits the
data well. This is seen in the chi-square of 62.07, not particularly
a low value but with a reasonable probability value of .580 and a
high goodness of fit index of .953. The standardized residual of
.034 suggests that the specified model accounts well for the
covariance among the variables in the covariance matrix.

The squared multiple correlations for the structural equations
(the amount of variance accounted for in each theoretically
specified dependent variable) are 44% for self-esteem and 35% for
academic achievement.

Table 3 shows the relevant statistical values for the structural
model. These causal coefficients are standardized path analysis
type coefficients; that is, all variables have been rescaled to have
unit variance. Standardization is done for all variables in the system, including errors and disturbances. Consequently, all coeffi-

cients in the equations have a similar interpretation, and the magnitude of these standardized coefficients may be easier to interpret than the magnitudes of the coefficients obtained from the covariance or raw data metric. Each of the structural paths in the final model are statistically significant at the .05 level or above. The variance (R^2) along the structural paths range from 4% for the relationship between socioeconomic status and academic achievement to 22% for the relationship between parental support and self-esteem worth.

Table 3. Statistical Values for Structural Model

Structural Relationship	Standardized Coefficient	R^2	Unstandardized Coefficient	Standard Error	Z-Value
Self-Esteem Worth					
to GPA	.235	.055	.162	.044	3.664
IQ to GPA	.384	.147	2.184	.351	6.225
Sib GPA to GPA	.257	.066	.240	.055	4.355
SES to GPA	.201	.040	.092	.030	3.082
Parental Support					
to Self-Esteem	.470	.221	.531	.075	7.115
Parental Coercion					
to Self-Esteem	-.472	.223	-.568	.100	5.688
SES to IQ	.276	.076	.022	.066	3.654

Coefficient of Determination:
GPA   = .352
Self-Esteem Worth = .443

As control variables, socioeconomic status predicted academic achievement (.201) and IQ (.276) and sibling academic achievement predicted adolescent achievement (.257). As expected IQ accounted for the greatest amount of variance in academic achievement with a coefficient of .384. A Z-value above 1.0 is statistically significant at the .05 level of confidence. All tests reached the .05 level or better.

EQS has the utility within it to suggest other paths that would provide a better fit of a model to the data. This utility was employed as a check to assess whether the data suggested a direct relationship between the parental behaviors and academic achievement. No such relationship was suggested.

As a further check of this finding, a regression analysis was performed. When self-esteem was not included in the analysis, a significant direct effect was found between the parental behaviors and academic achievement. When self-esteem was included in the regression model, the direct effect of the parental behaviors of support and coercive control attempts was not found, but an indirect effect was found for the parental behaviors of support and coercive control attempts and academic achievement through self-esteem. These procedures gave us confidence that the finding of self-esteem as an intervening variable is reliable.

DISCUSSION OF THE FINDINGS

Socioeconomic Status. As reported in the findings, the positive relationship found between socioeconomic status and intellectually ability (IQ) was not initially hypothesized. A search of the literature, supports this overlooked finding, suggesting a positive relationship between various socioeconomic variables and intellectual ability (Williams, 1976; Dickson, et al., 1979; Hess and McDevill, 1984). Consistent with numerous previous studies, socioeconomic status of the family was also positively related to the adolescents' academic achievement. Fathers' occupation was the strongest indicator of family background while mothers' education was the weakest indicator of socioeconomic status. This finding suggests that families with high socioeconomic background (probably the upper middle class) are more apt to have children with high intellectual ability and high academic achievement. This might be due to the fact that more resources are accessible in the adolescents' environment because of greater income. Also, those parents who have achieved higher education place a greater value on academic success.

Intellectual Ability. As expected, IQ was the strongest predictor of academic achievement in adolescents. Adolescents with higher IQ's obtained higher academic achievement compared to those adolescents with lower IQ's.

Sibling Academic Achievement. The academic achievement of the older sibling was found to be positively related to the younger sibling's academic achievement, as expected. This finding gives support to that of Brimm (1958) and the modeling theoretical notion proposed by Bandura (1969, 1977) and Thomas and Calonico (1972). The older sibling, seen as having more power and responsibility in the family, is being imitated by the younger sibling. If the older sibling obtains high academic achievement, the specific behaviors that resulted in such achievement, e.g. making frequent visits to the library, completing daily homework assignments, spending time reading and writing, asking questions of parents and teachers, studying long hours of examinations, etc., are more apt to be imitated by the younger sibling.

Self-Esteem. Self-esteem was positively related, albeit moderately, to adolescent academic achievement. A adolescent who believes in himself will achieve academically, whereas if the prevailing attitude is a belittled sense of self-worth, the lower self-esteem will help contribute to lower academic achievement. This notion is consistent with many previous investigations (Brookover, 1964; Coopersmith, 1967).

Parental Support and Coercion. Parental supportive behavior had a positive relationship with and strongly predicted adolescent self-esteem, while a negative correlation was found in similar magnitude between parental coercion and self-esteem. In this study, if adolescents perceived their parent's behavior as warm, nurturing, and highly interactive they reported positive feelings of self-esteem. In contrast, if the adolescents perceived their parents behaviors as coercive and punitive they reported feelings of inferiority, inadequacy, and lower self-esteem. Such findings are consistent with those of Freedman, Carlsmith and Sears (1970) and are clearly understood when one considers the fact that the reflected appraisal the adolescent receives from the parent indicates to the adolescent his/her ability or ineptness in controlling behavior in social settings.

The findings of this study lead to the conclusion that the effect of parental behaviors upon adolescents' academic achievement is indirect. Parental support and coercion influence self-esteem which, in turn, influences academic achievement. This suggests if parents choose to modify academic achievement in their adolescent children, they should interact with them in a warm, nurturing manner. Further, parents should avoid harsh, punitive forms of discipline. Following such advice, parental behaviors should increase adolescent childrens' self-esteem, (feelings of adequacy and self-confidence) which should result in greater academic achievement.

IMPLICATIONS OF THE FINDINGS

In a very broad sense, we view academic achievement as suscep-
tible to socialization processes. That is, it is shaped indirectly by
the interaction between the developing cognitive processes of the
child and the influence of socializing agents. In many ways, the
family and/or school cannot control cognitive activities; children
remember, perceive, form categories, make associations, derive
generalizations, and develop strategies for dealing with stimuli in
ways that are linked to biological characteristics of our species. In
many other ways, however, socializing agents affect the outcome
of these basic mental operations. To some degree they control the
content, the raw material of experience, that children use in
developing their mental worlds by restricting, enlarging, or select-
ing the material that is to be learned. They also give cultural and
personal meaning to knowledge the child acquires, making some
knowledge salient and valued and other information irrelevant.
Socializing agents can assist the child in developing specific cognitive strategies and thus can affect performance on measures of
ability. However, we see that role as facilitating normal developmental processes rather than affecting them directly.

If parents and other agents help control the acquisition of
knowledge and cognitive strategies, they also affect social processes that govern ways the child will use these resources in academic
settings. A central social process identified in this study which is
affected by the socializing authorities in the adolescent's life is
self-esteem. The outcome of this process depends to a great degree on two features of the social world in which the child lives:
positive parental supportive behavior and negative parental coercive control attempts.

The findings regarding the role of self-esteem as an intervening
variable between parental behaviors and academic achievement
has important theoretical and practical implications. We have
been able to demonstrate that the interactional processes within the
family impact on academic achievement. Theoretically this is important because it forces us to reexamine the dyadic processes in
parent-child relationship, with self-esteem of the child at center
stage. By so doing we can incorporate a broader range of theoreti-

cal notions in our work and hopefully produce a more adequate understanding of the complexities of human experience.

Practically, the value of these findings is partly one of providing some empirical support for important notions already highly valued in particular areas of family study and education. For the family life educator, the school counselor and parents alike the intervening role of self-esteem in the parental behavior and academic achievement relationship merits incorporation into their counseling and curricula for improving academic achievement. Self-esteem building and maintaining processes are clearly called for.

LIMITATIONS OF THE FINDINGS

There are two major limitations in the present study. The first, has to do with structural model assumptions that are forced upon the data in specifying the model during analysis. As great as the analytic utility as EQS is, it can not determine the direction of cause and effect among relationships. Yet the researcher must posit structural paths based on previous research or theoretical notions and test those paths in order to further understand human phenomena. However, a great deal of caution is needed before one assumes cause and effect. We have for example the case with self-esteem and academic achievement. Caution is advised in assuming that self-esteem determines academic achievement. It is possible the relationship is reversed, that is, academic achievement determines self-esteem. Though, evidence from this study supports the former hypothesis there is some empirical evidence from other studies suggesting that later relationship. Similarly, it would also be conceivable to reverse the interpretation of the parental behavior-self-esteem relationship. It is possible that parents employ levels of support and control based in part on existing levels of self-esteem in their children. These matters of direction are important issues that deserve further empirical and theoretical attention.

The second limitation is concerned with the sample. The sample contained a disproportionate number of subjects from one religious group, the Latter-day Saints (Mormons). Thus the generalizability of the findings to broader populations is compromised. The data represents a relatively small group of families in one urban area and the reader is cautioned not to generalize inappropriately. It is suggested that the model in this study be tested on different samples to add validity to our findings.

This material is a revision of the doctoral dissertation of Craig K. Manscill, "Adolescent Self-Esteem as an Intervening Variable in the Parental Support and Academic Achievement Relationship. The original data were collected in a study partially supported by N.I.M.H. grant 24754-02SP.

REFERENCES

Aaronson, A. J. *Relationship between maternal attitudes toward child rearing and the success of boys in beginning reading.* Unpublished Ph. D. Dissertation, New York University, 1966.

Bachman, J. G., Green, S., & Wirtanam, I. D. Youth in Transition. Vol. 3: Dropping Out--Problem or Symptom. Ann Arbor: Institute for Social Research, University of Michigan, 1971.

Baker, R.E. Shutz, & R.H. Hinze Influence of mental ability on achievement when socioeconomic status is controlled. *Journal of Personality and Social Psychology*, 1961, *35*, 365-380.

Bandura, A. Principles of Behavior Modification. New York: Holt, Rinehart and Winston, 1969.

Bandura, A. *Social learning theory.* New Jersey: Prentice Hall, 1977.

Bandura, A. & Kupers, C. J. The transition of patterns of self-reinforcement through modeling. *Journal of Abnormal and Social Psychology*, 1964, *69*, 1-9.

Barton, K., Dielman, T. E., & Cattell, R. B. Child rearing practices and achievement in school. *Journal of Genetic Psychology*, 1974, 124-155-65.

Baumrind, D. Current patterns of parental authority. *Developmental Psychology Monographs*, 1971, *4*(1), 1-102.

Baumrind, D., & Black, A. E. Socialization practices associated with dimensions of social competence in preschool Boys and Girls. *Child Development*, 1967, *38*, 2911-327.

Bayley, N., & Schaefer, E. S. Relationships between socioeconomic variables and the behavior of mothers toward young children. *Journal of Genetic Psychology* 1960, *96*, 61-77.

Becker, A. J. *Reading achievement of boys as influenced by the child rearing attitudes of their fathers.* Unpublished Ph.D. Dissertation, Case Western Reserve University, 1970.

Bentler, P. M. *Theory and implementation of EQS: A structural equations program.: Manual for Program Version 2.0.*, BMDP Statistical Software, Inc. Los Angeles, California, 1985.

Bentler, P. M. & Weeks, D. G. Interrelations among models for the analysis of moment structures. *Multivariate Behavioral Research*, 1979, *14*, 169-185.

Bentler, P. M. & Weeks, D. G. Linear structural equations with latent variables. *Psychometrika*, 1980, *45*, 289-308.

Bentler, P. M. & Weeks, D. G. Multivariate analysis with latent variables. In P. R. Krishnaiah & L. Kanal (Eds.), *Handbook of Statistics*, Vol. 2. Amsterdam: North-Holland, 1982.

Berg, R. H. *Mothers' attitudes on child rearing and family life compared for achieving and underachieving elementary school children.* Unpublished Ph.D. Dissertation, University of Southern California, 1963.

Biglin. *The relationship of parental attitudes and children's academic and social performance.* Unpublished Ph.D. Dissertation, University of Nebraska, Teachers College, 1964.

Brimm, O. G. Family structure and sex role learning by children: A further analysis of Helen Kock's data. *Sociometry* 1958, *21*, 1-16.

Brookover, N. *The sociology of education.* New York: American Book, 1964.

Brookover, W. B., LePere, J. M., Hamacheck, D. E., Thomas, S., & Erickson, E. L. *Self concept of ability and school achievement II.* East Lansing: Bureau of Educational Research Services, College of Education, Michigan State University, 1967.

Brookover, W. B., Thomas, T., & Paterson, A. *Self-concept of ability and school achievement.* Paper presented at the annual meeting of the Ohio Valley Sociological Society, East Lansing, Michigan, May 1962.

Comstock, M.L.C. *Effects of perceived parental behavior on self-esteem and adjustment.* Unpublished Ph.D. Dissertation, University of North Carolina at Chapel Hill, 1973.

Cooley, C. H. *Human nature and the social order.* New York: Charles Scribner's Sons, 1902.

Coopersmith, S. *The antecedents of self-esteem.* San Francisco: W.H Freeman, 1967.

Coopersmith, S. A method for determining types of self-esteem. *Journal of Abnormal and Social Psychology* 1959, *59*, 87-94.

Dickson, W. P, Hess, R. D., Miyake, N. & Azuma, H. Referential communication accuracy between mother and child as a predictor of cognitive development in the United States and Japan. *Child Development*, 1979, *50*, 53-59.

Dornbusch, Ritter, Leiderman, Roberts, & Fraleigh The relation of parenting style to adolescent academic performance. *Child Development*, *58*, 1244-1257.

Dunnel, J. P. *Input and output analysis of suburban elementary school districts.* Paper presented at the American Educational Research Association, New York, 1971.

Ellis, G. J., Thomas, D. L., & Rollins, B. C. Measuring parental support: The interrelationship of three measures. *Journal of Marriage and the Family*, 1976, *38*, 713-722.

Faunce, W. A. School achievement, social status, and self-esteem. *Social Psychology Quarterly*, 1984, *38*, 713-722.

Freedman, J. C, Carlsmith, J. M., & Sears, D. O. *Social psychology*. New York: Prentice Hall, 1970.

Gecas, V. Parental behavior and adolescent self-evaluation. *Sociometry*, 1971, *34*, 466-482.

Gecas, V. Parental behavior and contextual variations in adolescent self-esteem. *Sociometry*, 1972, *35*, 332-345.

Gecas, V. The influence of social class on socialization. In W. R. Burr, R. Hill, F. J. Nye, & A. L. Reiss (Eds.), *Contemporary theories about the family*. New York: Free Press, 1979.

Goshen-Gottstein, E. R. Potentially harmful childrearing practices. *Israel Annals of Psychiatry and Related Disciplines*, 1975, *13*(2), 85-104.

Haller, A. O. & Portes, A. Status attainment process. *Sociology of Education*, 1973, *46*, 51-91.

Hess, R. D. & McDevitt, T. M. Some cognitive consequences of maternal intervention techniques: A longitudinal study. *Child Development*, 1984, *55*, 2017-2030.

Hoffman, L. W., Rosen, S. & Lippitt, R. Parental coerciveness, child autonomy, and child's role at school. *Sociometry*, 1960, *23*, 15-22.

Kagan, J. & Moss, H. A. *Birth to maturity*. New York: Wiley, 1962.

Kohn, M. L. *Class and conformity: A study in values*. 2nd Ed. Chicago: University of Chicago Presses, 1977.

Kohn, M. L., & Schooler. *Work and personality: An inquiry into the impact of social stratification*. Norwood, J.J.: Ablex, 1983.

Laitman, R. J. Family relations as an intervening variable in the relationship of birth order and self-esteem. *Dissertation Abstracts International*, 1975, *36*(6-B), 3051.

Lambert, N. M. Paired associate learning, social status and tests of logical concrete behavior as univariate and multivariate predictions of first grade reading achievement. *American Educational Research Journal*, 1970, *1*, 511-528.

Lavin, D. E. *The prediction of academic performance*. New York: Russell Sage Foundation, 1965.

Maccoby, E. R. The choice of variables in the study of socialization. *Sociometry*, 1961, *24*, 257-371.

Miller, T. W. The effects of core facilitative conditions in mother on adolescent self-esteem. *Journal of Social Psychology*, 1976, *100*(1), 147-148.

Mote, F. B. *The relationship between child self-concept in school and parental attitudes and behaviors in child rearing*. Unpublished Ph.S. Dissertation, Stanford University, 1966.

Nelson, G. L. *An investigation of selected correlates of self-concept in children*. Unpublished Ph.D. Dissertation, University of Minnesota, 1970.

Nicholls, J. G. Anxiety, defensiveness, self-esteem, and responsibility for intellectual achievement: Their relations to intelligence and reading achievement test scores. *New Zealand Journal of Educational Studies*, 1967, *2*, 125-135.

Osgood, C. E. Semantic differential technique in the comparative study of cultures. *American Anthropologist*, 1964, *66*, 171-200.

Openshaw, D. K., Rollins, B. C., & Thomas, D. L. Parental influences on adolescent self-esteem. *Journal of Early Adolescence*, 1984, *4*(2), 259-74.

Openshaw, D. K., Thomas, D. L., & Rollins, B. C. Socialization and adolescent self-esteem: Symbolic interaction and social-learning explanations. *Adolescence*, 1983, *18*(70), 317-29.

Otto, L. B. Antecedents and consequences of marital timing. In W.R. R. Burr, F. I. Hill, Nye, & I. L. Reiss (Eds.), *Contemporary theories about the family.* Vol. 1. New York: Free Press, 1979.

Purkey, W. W. *Self-concept and school achievement.* Englewood Cliffs, N.J.: Prentice-Hall, 1970.

Ragland, E. K. Social and sexual self-esteem in women and perceived father-daughter relationships during early adolescence. *Dissertation Abstracts International*, 1978, *38*(9-A), 5365.

Rollins, B. C., & Thomas, D. L. Theory of parental power and child compliance. In R. E. Cromwell & D. H. Olson (Eds.), *Power in families.* New York: Halstead Press, 1975.

Rollins, B. C. & Thomas, D. L. Parental support, power, and control techniques in the socialization of children. In W. R. Burr, R. Hill, R. E. Nye, & I. L. Reiss (Eds.), *Contemporary theories about the family.* Vol. 1. New York: Free Press, 1979.

Rosenthal, D. M., Peng, J. D., & McMill, J. M. Relationship of adolescent self-concept to perceptions of parents in single- and two-parent families. *International Journal of Behavioral Development*, 1980, *3*(4), 441-53.

Rubin, R. A., Forle, J. & Sandridge, E. Self-esteem and school performance. *Psychology in the Schools*, 1977, *14*, 503-07.

Saavedra, J. M. The interaction between adolescents' perceptions of parental warmth and control and the association of these dimensions of parenting with self-esteem and self-adequacy among Puerto Rican males. *Dissertation Abstracts International*, 1978, *38*(7-B), 3372.

Schaefer, E. S. Children's reports of parental behavior. *Child Development*, 1965, *36*, 552-57.

Scheirer, M. A. & Kraut, R. E. Increasing educational achievement via self concept change. *Review of Educational Research*, 1979, *49*(1), 131-150.

Sewell, W. H. & Hauser, R. M. *Education, occupation, and earnings.* New York: Academic Press, 1975.

Siegal, P. M. *Prestige in the American occupational structure.* Unpublished Ph.D. Dissertation, University of Chicago, 1971.

118   Craig K. Manscill and Boyd C. Rollins

Streitmatter, J., & Jones. Perceived parent and teacher socialization styles on
    self-esteem in early adolescence. *Journal of Marriage and the Family*,
    1974, *36*, 13-29.

Thomas, D. L. & Calonico, J. M. Birth order and family sociology: A
    reassessment. *Social Science*, 1972, *47*, 48-50.

Thomas, D. L., Gecas, V., Weigert, A. & Rooney, E. *Socialization and the
    adolescent*. Lexington, Mass.: D.C. Heath, 1974.

Thomas, J. A. Efficiency in education: An empirical study. *Administrator's
    Notebook*, 1962, *11*, 1-4.

Toto, S. E. *Altering parental attitudes toward child-rearing practices and its
    effect on adolescent self-esteem*. Unpublished Ph.D. Dissertation, Boston
    University, 1973.

Turnberg, J. *An investigation of the association of maternal attitudes and
    childhood obesity and the self-concept of the obese child*. Unpublished
    Ph.D. Dissertation, New York University, 1966.

Walters, J., & Stinnett, N. Parent-child relationships: A decade review of
    research. In C. B. Broderick (Ed.), *A decade of family research and action*.
    Minneapolis: National Council on Family Relations, 1971.

Williams, J. H. The relationship of self-concept and reading achievement in first
    grade children. *Journal of Educational Research*, 1973, *66*, 378-380.

Williams, T. R. Abilities and environments. In W. Sewell, et al., (Eds.),
    Schooling and achievement in american society. New York: Academic
    Press, 1976.

Wylie, R. *The self-concept Vol. 2*. Lincoln, Nebraska: University of Nebraska
    Press, 1979.

Youngblood, R. L. Self-esteem and academic achievement in Filipino high
    school students. *Educational Research Quarterly*, 1976, *1*(2), 27-36.

The present study uses a general population sample of families with adolescents to assess the effects of parent-child relations on alcohol abuse and other related deviance among adolescents. Structural equation modeling procedures are used to specify and test hypothesized relationships between parental support, parental inductive and coercive control attempts, peer orientation and adolescent substance abuse and other deviant behaviors. The findings show that parental support has a significant inverse relationship to adolescent problem behaviors, both by a direct effect and by an indirect effect by way of peer reference group influences. Parental control factors are not statistically related to adolescent outcome variables after statistically controlling for parental support. The findings are discussed in the context of symbolic interaction and socialization theory.

6

Parent-Adolescent Interactions in the Development of Alcohol Abuse and Other Deviant Behaviors

GRACE M. BARNES, MICHAEL P. FARRELL, AND MICHAEL WINDLE

It is commonly accepted that alcohol problems occur more often in some families than in others. Some explanations for this phenomenon involve growing support for the notion that there is a genetic component in the development of alcoholism (Goodwin, 1984; Schuckit, 1987). However, biological vulnerability for alcoholism at best explains the occurrence of some types of *severe* alcoholism; furthermore, biologically predisposing factors have only been shown for *sons* of *male* alcoholics. Biological vulnerability does not include an explanation of decisions to initiate the use of alcohol in adolescence and the variety of adolescent drinking patterns, including alcohol-related social problems and their relationships to drug abuse and delinquency among both males and females.

Grace M. Barnes, Michael P. Farrell, and Michael Windle • New York State Research Institute on Alcoholism, Buffalo, New York 14260.

In contrast to the biological vulnerability theory, there is a large body of empirical research showing the importance of parent-child interactions for the development of a wide range of childhood behaviors, including cognitive development, achievement, aggression, and social competence (for a review, see Rollins and Thomas, 1979). In general, the research shows that supportive and controlling behaviors on the part of parents are related to personality and social behavior outcomes in children. Recently, aspects of parental support and control have been linked to the development of drinking behaviors in adolescents (Barnes et al., 1986; Barnes and Windle, 1987; Kandel and Andrews, 1987).

There is a range of theoretical explanations for the empirical findings of the relation between measures of parental support and control and measures of child outcomes. Research leading to these findings has been guided by theories ranging from social learning to functional systems theory. One characteristic the theories have in common is the assumption that the parents mold the behavior of the child. Although this assumption has been criticized by those who examine the effect of children on parents (e.g., Maccoby and Martin, 1983), it seems reasonable to argue that parent-child relationships typically are asymmetrical in terms of power and that the intentional socialization behavior of the parents has a more profound impact on children than the less sophisticated behavior of children has on parents (Baumrind, 1980), especially when the outcome variables are social competence or social deviance.

Recently, Peterson and Rollins (1987) have suggested that the parental support and control findings may be interpreted using symbolic interaction theory. Parents and children have the ability to create and share common meanings and to take the roles of one another. Supportive behaviors such as praise, physical affection, and encouragement are gestures that convey that the child's "self" and actions are valued by the parents. As children take the roles of the parental others who behave in this supportive manner and as they see themselves through the eyes of these significant others, their self-images are enhanced. As they become more dependent upon their parents to maintain their self-esteem, the bonds between parents and children are strengthened. Thus, the more adolescents perceive parents as sources of supportive behavior, the more likely they are to comply with parental expectations, and the less likely they will be to engage in socially deviant behavior. Parental control has been divided into at least two types: inductive control and coercion. Inductive control includes such behavior as explanations of limits, attempts to make children aware of the consequences of their acts for themselves or others, and other such persuasive methods that place demands on children's reasoning abilities. Peterson and Rollins (1987) argue that "induction encourages role taking in children by providing them with information about parents' inner experiences, their expectations, and their rationale for child-rearing actions," which encourages the internalization of role expectations (p. 474). On the other hand, coercion, which is the direct and arbitrary use of force, communicates rejection of the child's "self" and does not allow the child to grasp the logic underlying parents' expectations. Thus, the more inductive control used by parents, the more compliance and socially acceptable behavior children will show--but the more coercion, the less compliance and the more problem behavior.

In addition to being influenced by parents, adolescent behaviors and attitudes are also influenced by peers (e.g., Coleman, 1961; Youniss and Smollar, 1985). The interpretation of the parental support and control findings within symbolic interaction theory provides a conceptual bridge to the research on peer group influence on drinking and other deviant behavior. To a varying degree, peers become significant others to adolescents, and the meaning that peers attribute to drinking behavior and deviance is often different from that of parents. To the extent that the adolescents' self-concept becomes anchored in peer group norms, they become more likely to increase drinking behavior and deviant acts. However, the strength of the peer group as a referent group will be influenced by the degree to which parents have built and maintained ties as significant others to their children. Thus, we would expect that the more parents are perceived as a source of support and inductive control, the less peers will be seen as a significant referent group for important decision making by the adolescent. The less peers are seen as significant others, the less likely the adolescent will be to engage in alcohol abuse and other socially deviant acts.

A variety of methodological problems have limited the generalizability of studies relating parent-child interactions to sub-

stance abuse and other related problem behaviors in adolescence.
For instance, there have been problems with operationalizing and
measuring constructs such as parental support and control. Within
the domain of parental support, for example, Barber and Thomas
(1986) have convincingly shown that investigators have overlooked important aspects of physical affection in the parent-child
relationship.

An additional problem with most studies of psychosocial and
biological influences of the family on various childhood outcomes
is that they have used samples of convenience rather than representative samples of the population at large. Studies of alcohol
problems and other related problems in adolescence have often
used samples of "deviant" youth or clinical populations. This
work has been important in identifying precursors and correlates
of maladaptive behaviors for these samples and for defining issues
for future study; yet it is also important to determine what types of
families are effective in socializing children for nonproblem behavior patterns. School samples have also provided useful findings with regard to parent-child relations, but these samples do not
include certain high risk young people such as school dropouts.
Furthermore, typically school samples do not allow investigators
to obtain independent information from parents as well as from
adolescents. General population samples have the advantage of
identifying young people with a full-range of drinking and other
behavioral patterns as well as a variety of family structural and interpersonal characteristics.

The present study uses a general population sample of families
with adolescents to assess parent-child relations and identifies a
model for describing the relationships between parental socialization factors and adolescent alcohol abuse and other deviant behaviors. More specifically, structural equation modeling
procedures are used to specify and test hypothesized patterns of interrelationships among the multiple-indicator latent variables of
parental support, parental inductive and coercive control attempts,
parent/peer orientation and adolescent substance abuse and other
problem behaviors. The use of structural equation modeling per-
mitted the simultaneous assessment of the influences of parental
support and parental control on problem behaviors, as well as the
moderating influence of peer reference group orientation on
problem behaviors in adolescence.

METHODS

Sample

A random-digit-dial (RDD) telephone procedure was used to select a representative household sample of adolescents, their parents, and their adolescent siblings in a Western New York State Standard Metropolitan Statistical Area. Households were included in the sample if they contained at least one adolescent between the ages of 12 and 17 years old and one parent (biological or surrogate). Details of the telephone sampling procedure are provided elsewhere (Barnes, 1984; Barnes et al., 1986). Family interviews were completed in approximately half of all eligible families containing an adolescent. Analysis of the sample characteristics with regional census data revealed that the sample closely matched the distribution of the population in terms of age, sex, race, marital status of parents, family composition, and socioeconomic status (Barnes and Cairns, 1982; Barnes et al., 1986).

Interviewing

In-person interviews were carried out with 124 adolescents (70 male and 54 female adolescents) and their families. A team of two interviewers was assigned on a random basis to the individual family respondents. Families ranged in composition from two-person families (i.e., a target adolescent and one parent) to four-person families (i.e., a target adolescent, an adolescent sibling, a mother, and a father). Separate interviews with multiple family members were accomplished by having two parts to each instrument--a self-administered questionnaire and a face-to-face interview. Thus, in the maximum four-person family, one interviewer gave brief instructions to the two adolescents who went to separate areas of the house to complete a self-administered questionnaire. That interviewer then gave one parent a face-to-face interview while the second interviewer spoke with the other parent. Upon completion of this first interviewing phase, each parent was given a self-administered questionnaire while the two interviewers spoke with adolescents in separate areas of the home. Even though interviews occurred in separate areas of the living quarters, sensitive questions such as drinking, deviance, and parental support and con-

trol were placed in the self-administered questionnaires, which
were sealed in envelopes upon completion by the respective
respondents. The family interviewing session required approximately 90 minutes to complete. Families were paid $25 for
their time in participating in the study. For purposes of this paper,
adolescents' reports of their own behaviors and their parents'
socialization behaviors are analyzed since the data for parental
socialization was more comprehensive in the adolescent instruments.

Measures

Parental support. The parental support construct was defined in
a manner consistent with Rollins and Thomas' work (1979) as
parental behaviors toward the child such as praising, encouraging,
and giving physical affection, which indicate to the child that
she/he is accepted, approved of, and loved.

Separate mother and father nurturance scales were derived for
each parent based on the adolescent's perceptions of the frequency
of recent parental praise, reliance on parent for advice and
guidance, physical affection (hug, kiss), doing things together,
decision making, discussion of future plans, discussion of personal
problems, and knowledge of parental expectations. For example,
the first nurturance item asked, "When you do something well,
how often does your mother give you praise or encouragement for
what you do?" Response categories were: never, hardly ever,
sometimes, frequently, and always. A numerical value of 1 to 5
was assigned to each response category. The same procedure was
used for other nurturance items, and the scores from each item
were totaled together for a mother nurturance score.

As a second indicator of support, adolescents were asked to rate
both their mothers and fathers on the positive-negative dimension
of Bales and Cohen's SYMLOG scale (Bales and Cohen, 1979).
Parke's (1985) adaptation of the SYMLOG adjective rating form
was used, which was developed to be suitable for use with
children. Reliability ranges were over .80 (Parke, 1985). The
overall rating form includes 26 items with a 3-item frequency
range. In the positive direction, the positive-negative dimension
includes ratings of the parents as sociable, helpful, friendly,
cooperative, appreciative, and happy. In the negative direction,

the dimension includes ratings of them as disapproving, angry, difficult to please, unfriendly, and discouraged.

Parental control. The control constructs were defined as parental behaviors toward the child--ranging from explaining rules to physical punishment--which are intended to direct the child's behavior in a manner acceptable to the parent (Rollins and Thomas, 1979). Two separate scale scores for control attempts were developed based upon work of Rollins and Thomas (1979) and Peterson and Rollins (1987). A coercive control attempts scale was derived for each parent using adolescent's responses to the following punishment techniques: slaps or hits, takes away privileges (TV, movies, dates), yells or screams. As in the nurturance scale described above, adolescents rated the frequency of recent control attempts along a 5-point scale (never to always), and the values for all of the coercive items were totaled together. In a similar manner, an inductive control attempts scale was derived based on adolescent's responses to the items: parent warns you not to do the same thing again, parent tells you why you shouldn't have done something and tells you how she/he expects you to act in the future.

An additional dimension was added to assess overall parental control attempts based upon the adolescent's understandings of explicit parental rules for his/her behavior. More specifically, adolescents were asked whether or not their parents had definite rules for their behaviors in 12 specific categories: time for being in at night, homework, dating, dress, watching television, eating with the family, helping around the house, against being with certain boys or girls, against smoking, alcohol, or other drugs. The total number of rules was calculated by summing the "yes" responses for the 12 individual items.

Parent/peer orientation. A peer reference group construct was derived by summing two items regarding parental and peer influences on decision making and life outlook. The questions were as follows: (1) If you had a serious decision to make, like whether or not to continue in school, or whether or not to get married, whose opinion would you value most? Response alternatives were: parents most, parents and friends equally, and friends most. (2) With regard to your present outlook on life--what's important to do and what's important to be--whose views have had a greater im-

pact on you? Adolescents again chose between the same three
response alternatives.

Substance use. The number of times adolescents reported being
drunk or very high from alcohol during the previous year was used
as a measure of alcohol abuse. There were eight response alternatives ranging from never to once a week or more often. Lifetime
cigarette smoking was assessed by using a 5-response alternative
variable ranging from never smoked to smoke regularly now. The
frequency of marijuana use during the past year was also included
among the substance use items based on six response alternatives.

Deviance. Adolescents indicated the frequency with which they
have done a series of nine problem behaviors during the past year.
The deviance scale has been developed and condensed based on
previous work in this area (cf., Bachman, 1970; Gold and Mann,
1972; Johnston, 1973). The nine items included were: stayed out
later than parents said, argued or fought with mother, skipped a
day of school without a real excuse, argued or fought with father,
ran away from home, purposely damaged or messed up something
not belonging to you, tried to get something by lying to a person
about what you would do for him or who you were, took something of value that did not belong to you, and beat up someone on
purpose. The responses to the individual items, each containing
six response alternatives, were totaled together for the number of
deviant acts committed in the past 12 months.

RESULTS

The results are presented in two sections. The first section is a
summary of the bivariate relationships among parent and child
variables using correlational analysis. In the second section, structural equation modeling procedures are used to evaluate alternative models of parental and peer socialization predictor variables
and adolescent problem behaviors.

Correlational Analysis

Table 1 provides the intercorrelation matrix of individual parent-
child variables measured in this study. Labels for the domains
being measured by the individual variables are underlined and
presented above the individual variables (e.g., Parental Support for

Table I

Intercorrelations Among Parent-Adolescent Variables

Variable	1	2	3	4	5	6	7	8	9	10	11	12	13	14	15	16
Parental Support																
1. Mother Nurturance																
2. Father Nurturance	.51***															
3. Mother Sociability	.66***	.33***														
4. Father Sociability	.27**	.53***	.39***													
Parental Control Attempts																
5. Mother Inductive Control	.33***	.29***	.18*	-.05												
6. Father Inductive Control	.23**	.41***	.08	.08	.66***											
7. Number of Parental Rules	.22**	.16	.04	.00	.37***	.35***										
8. Mother Coercive Control	-.16	-.05	-.38***	-.19*	.20**	.19*	.08									
9. Father Coercive Control	.12	-.03	-.10	-.27**	.18	.35***	.03	.45***								
Parent/Peer Orientation																
10. Parent/Peer Influence on Decision-Making	-.31***	-.09	-.21*	-.16	-.06	-.06	-.14	.17	-.07							
11. Parent/Peer Influence on Life View	-.23**	-.16*	-.07	-.23*	-.20*	-.16	-.08	-.06	-.04	.47***						
Problem Behaviors																
12. Time Drunk	-.20*	-.15	-.10	-.11	.02	.03	-.15	.07	.02	.21**	.30***					
13. Cigarette Smoking	-.31***	-.30***	-.23**	-.21*	-.06	-.12	-.17*	.15	-.03	.19*	.24**	.53***				
14. Marijuana Use	-.35***	-.24**	-.17*	-.18*	-.10	-.12	-.24**	.16	-.05	.16	.21*	.51***	.69***			
15. Deviance Other Than Substance Use	-.27**	-.26**	-.23**	-.32***	.05	.00	-.17	.29**	.15	.29***	.24**	.43***	.42***	.32***		
16. Adolescent's Sex (M-F)	.02	-.08	-.03	.05	-.02	-.04	.02	.06	-.10	.15	.08	.05	.19*	.10	-.08	

* p < .05
** p < .01
*** p < .001

variables 1-4). Bivariate relationships within and between
domains are now discussed.

Parental support. The four variables making up the parental
support construct are all highly correlated. These significant correlations hold for the relationships between variables for each
parent separately as well as for the correlations between father and
mother nurturance and father and mother sociability. This finding
is consistent with family systems theory or other more holistic
family culture theories that argue that the behavior of parents con-
stitutes an interdependent syndrome.

With regard to the relationships between parental support variables and other variables in the study, there are scattered significant relationships between parental support and parental
control variables. Mother and father nurturance are both significantly correlated with mother and father inductive control attempts. These relationships hold for each parent separately as well
as between mother and father variables. However, mother and
father nurturance are not correlated significantly with mother and
father coercive control attempts. Nonetheless, three of the four
correlations between parental sociability from the SYMLOG
rating scale and parental coercive control attempts do show significant negative correlations. Mother nurturance is positively correlated with the number of parental rules reported by adolescents
while the relationship between father nurturance and the number
of rules is in the same positive direction, but does not reach statistical significance.

Consistent with our hypothesis derived from symbolic interaction theory, parental support has a negative relationship with
parent/peer orientation; that is, where parental support is high,
reliance upon peers for important life decisions and life view is
low.

Most of the intercorrelations between the four parental support
variables and the four adolescent substance use/problem behavior
variables are statistically significant, and all the relationships are
negative. Mother nurturance shows the highest negative correlations for all four problem behavior categories, clearly indicating
that as mothers are perceived by their adolescents to be more nurturant, adolescents are less likely to abuse alcohol, smoke cigarettes, use marijuana, or engage in other deviant behaviors.

It is also interesting to note that none of the mother or father support variables is related to the sex of the adolescent in this general population study.

Control attempts. There are high correlations between mothers and fathers in control attempts. Adolescents who have mothers who are high on inductive control also are likely to have fathers who are high on inductive control attempts ($r = .66$). Mother's and father's coercive control attempts are also highly correlated. Furthermore, mother's and father's inductive control attempts are each positively correlated with their respective coercive control attempts. On the other hand, the number of parental rules an adolescent has is positively correlated with both mother and father inductive control attempts, but not with coercive control attempts by either parent.

While coercive control and inductive control are positively correlated, they show opposite relationships with parental support as noted above. Only one of the control variables--mother inductive control--is significantly related to peer orientation in decision making, and that relationship is negative. Neither mother nor father inductive control attempts are significantly related to any of the adolescent problem behavior outcome variables. General deviance is the only problem behavior outcome measure that shows a significant positive correlation with mother's coercive control attempts, and no problem behavior variables are significantly correlated with father's coercive control attempts. As the number of rules increases, there is a tendency for problem behaviors to decrease, particularly marijuana use. Once again none of the five parental control variables is significantly related to adolescents' gender.

Peer orientation. The intercorrelations of peer orientation variables with problem behaviors are consistent. As hypothesized, the more adolescents rely upon their peers for important life decisions and life orientations, the more likely the adolescents are to be involved in a variety of problem behaviors.

Problem behaviors. The data from the present study clearly demonstrate that alcohol abuse, smoking, marijuana use, and general deviance are highly interrelated behaviors. Furthermore, these problem behaviors have common correlates in parent and peer relations. The only significant relationship between various problem behaviors and gender is for cigarette smoking, where females are more likely to smoke cigarettes than are adolescent males.

Structural Equation Modeling

Since the independent variables are intercorrelated and our theory argues that peer influence is an intervening variable, the bivariate correlational analysis was supplemented by using structural equations to model multivariate patterns of covariation/correlation between parent and adolescent factors as they relate to substance abuse and other problem behaviors.

The initial model specified included hypotheses about the following three substantive relations:

1. That parental support would be significantly, inversely related to problem behaviors both by a direct effect and by an indirect effect via its influence on the reference group variable subsequently referred to as parent/peer orientation.

2. That parent/peer orientation would be significantly related to problem behaviors such that increasing reliance upon peers as a preferred reference group would be associated with increases in problem behaviors.

3. That parental control attempts would be significantly related to problem behaviors such that inductive control attempts would be inversely related to problem behaviors, and coercive control attempts would be positively related to problem behaviors.

In order to test these predictions, the EQS structural equations program (Bentler, 1985) was used to model the hypothesized interrelationships. Latent variables were derived for each of the psychological constructs specified for the model by using the manifest variables measured for the respective domains[1]. Figure 1, which is discussed in more detail subsequently, illustrates the selection of manifest variables that served as reflective indicators

---

[1] Preliminary descriptive statistical information regarding univariate and multivariate distributional features of the observed data (e.g., skewness, kurtosis) indicated that the observed data did not deviate from normality assumptions. Therefore, normal theory maximum likelihood estimators were used in the substantive models specified, rather than one of the nonnormal theory estimation procedures available optionally with EQS. Additionally, the equality of the male and female covariance matrices was tested using Box's M statistic, and the results indicated that there were no statistically significant differences between the two samples (X^2=85.41, df=91, p=64), thus justifying pooling across the two gender groups.

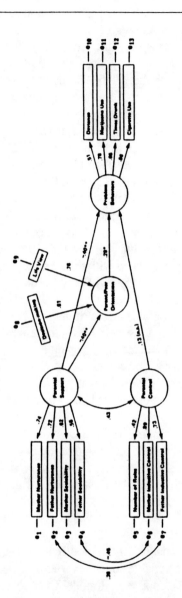

Figure 1. Standardized Solution of Final Model Representing Interrelationships Among Parental Factors, Parent/Peer Orientation, and Problem Behaviors Among Adolescents. All Factor Loadings for the Manifest Variable Indicators Are Significant by Univariate Two-tailed Tests ($p < .001$). As Are the Two Correlated Residuals.

of the latent variables. The representation of a general construct
(or latent variable) of problem behaviors--as indicated consistently
by empirical findings regarding high intercorrelations among alcohol abuse, illicit drug use, and delinquency--has often been
referred to as a problem behavior syndrome in adolescence (e.g.,
Barnes, 1984; Barnes and Welte, 1986; Jessor, 1987; Jessor et al.,
1968). In this study, it is measured by common sources of
variance among the four manifest variables of deviance, marijuana
use, times drunk, and cigarette use. The other latent variables are
similarly defined by their respective manifest variables.

The initial model specified focused on the interrelationships
among the four latent constructs displayed in figure 1. A coercive
control latent variable, with the manifest indicators of mother coercive control and father coercive control, was not included in this
model specification for three reasons. First, the bivariate correlational data did not suggest that the coercive control dimensions
were consistently highly correlated with the problem behavior indicators. Second, there was concern with the influence of col-
linearity effects on estimated parameters given the correlational
pattern among parental support, parental inductive control, and
parental coercive control dimensions. Third, there was concern
with the stability of the parameter estimates given the ratio of the
sample size to the number of parameters estimated. As is mentioned subsequently, a separate model was specified and tested
using the coercive control latent variable *instead of the parental inductive control latent variable.*

The initial substantive model specified was identical to the one
illustrated in figure 1, with the exception that the two residual
covariances between e2 and e7, and e4 and e6, were not freely estimated. Goodness of global model fit statistics for the initial
model are provided in table 2, along with fit statistics for the null,
or no association, baseline model that is used in deriving practical
fit indices (Bentler and Bonett, 1980).

The goodness of fit statistics for the modified, final model,
which included two correlated residual covariances, are also
presented in table 2. The goodness of model fit statistics for the initial model indicated that an improvement in fit could be obtained
by freeing parameters corresponding to the residual covariances of
e2 and e7, and e4 and e6. Substantively, the freeing of these
residual covariances suggests that statistically significant relation-

Table 2

Goodness-of-Fit Indices for Stuctural Equation
Models of Parent-Child Interactions (N = 124)

Model	dF	2	NFI[a]	NNFI[b]
1. Null (No Association)	78	552.25	--	--
2. Initial Model	60	118.12	.79	.84
3. Final Model	58	97.50	.82	.89
(Two correlated residuals)				

[a]Normed fit index
[b]Non-normed fit index

ships exist between father nurturance and father inductive control, and between father sociability and mother inductive control, over and above the significant contribution that the indicators have in relation to their referent latent variables and, by extension, in relation to the interrelationships among the latent variables. A hierarchical comparison of the initial model with the final model indicates that the freeing of the two residuals significantly improved the statistical fit of the model in accounting for the observed data ($X^2 = 20.62$, $df = 2$, $p < .001$). Further, both of the individual parameter estimates corresponding to the two residual covariances specified were statistically significant, indicating that residual relations existed in which father nurturance and father inductive control were positively related, and father sociability and mother inductive control were negatively correlated, the latter relationship possibly suggesting some kind of compensatory mechanism.

The indices of practical fit (i.e., the normed and nonnormed fit indices) for the final model were, from a purely statistical perspective, somewhat lower than desired (Bentler and Bonett, 1980). That is, Bentler and Bonett have proposed that a normed fit value of .90 or above should be used to determine whether a model adequately "fits" the data, and our value is somewhat below this proposed value. While the .90 or above value provides a useful guideline for evaluating model fit, it is not an absolute criterion and must be considered in conjunction with substantive meaningfulness in making a comprehensive evaluation of a hypothesized model. Our model modification, i.e., the freeing of two residual covariances, was based upon the substantive meaningfulness of freeing these parameters in conjunction with knowing (from the output of the initial model) that the model fit would be improved.

An examination of the residual covariation indicated that the further freeing of parameters would not be meaningful from a substantive perspective, and therefore, we stopped modifying the model at this point.

With regard to the specific predictions hypothesized for the data, two of the three were confirmed. Parental support was inversely related to problem behaviors, suggesting that increases in parental support were associated with decreases in problem behaviors. Parental support was also indirectly related to problem behaviors via parent/peer orientation, as increases in parental support were associated with increases in using parents as a reference group. Parent/peer orientation was positively associated with problem behaviors, indicating that primary reliance upon peers as a reference group is associated with increases in problem behaviors.

Parental control attempts were not significantly related to problem behaviors as predicted. This was the case both for the inductive control dimensions used to specify the parental control latent variable in figure 1, as well as an alternative latent variable (not shown) defined by the coercive control dimensions.[2] Part of the failure to find statistically significant relationships between the parental control constructs and problem behaviors may be due to the intercorrelation between the parental support and parental control constructs. That is, once parental support is taken into account in the model, parental control attempts have no unique contribution to make to the explanation of problem behaviors.

DISCUSSION

The findings from this study lend some support to Peterson and Rollins' (1987) symbolic interaction theory of socialization. As the theory predicts, the more the adolescent perceives parents as providers of support and nurturance, the less he or she regards peers as more important than parents as significant others, and the less he or she engages in deviant behavior. It is reasonable to propose that supportive parental behavior leads to internalization of parental norms and to the use of these norms as reference points in evaluating the self and in making decisions about whether or

---

2 The separate control variables were examined for curvilinearity using regression-based procedures, but the curvilinear pattern was not indicated.

not to engage in heavy drinking or other deviant behavior. Contrary to some theories of adolescent deviance (e.g., Olson et al., 1983), we did not find a curvilinear relationship between support and deviance. Clearly, high parental support is associated with the lowest degree of adolescent deviance. Furthermore, these findings hold consistently for both male and female adolescents.

Contrary to Peterson and Rollins' theory, after statistically controlling for parental supportiveness, we do not find a significant relationship between either inductive control or coercive control and problem behaviors. We also did not find a curvilinear relationship between these variables and deviance, as some theorists have suggested. Our bivariate analysis shows that inductive control is positively correlated with supportiveness; thus, the fact that the influence of inductive control is negligible after support is considered is not surprising. At least in this general population study, induction seems to be another manifestation of supportiveness.

It is noteworthy that parental induction and parental coercion are moderately positively correlated, yet it is generally accepted that these two types of control have opposite effects on child outcome variables (e.g., Peterson and Rollins, 1987). However, there is a lack of systematic, empirical research on the relationships between types of parental control and substance abuse and related adolescent problem behaviors. Thus, until there is additional empirical research, generalizations regarding parental control and substance abuse cannot be made with certainty. It is also conceivable that parental induction and parental coercion both may reflect *active* strategies on the part of parents to influence or control adolescent behaviors, in contrast to *passive parental* styles and strategies such as avoidance or neglect. Because parental induction and parental coercion share common features of activity (thus contributing to the moderate positive correlations), it does not necessarily follow that their respective application would or should result in common effects upon adolescent behavior. More specifically, the respective active strategies may have vastly different influence on adolescent outcomes because of positive or negative meanings that the adolescent assigns to these parental actions. Thus, parental inductive strategies, like parental support, may foster positive appraisals by adolescents of parental concern, caring, and openness, whereas coercive attempts may foster negative appraisals of parental unfairness, arbitrariness, and hostility. These issues need further empirical elaboration. There are other questions left unanswered by this research. The model tested here is drawn from the "social mold" perspective, which sees child outcomes as a consequence of parental behaviors. Our measures are indicators of current adolescent perceptions of parents. It may be that these perceptions do not reflect past behavior of parents, either because of recall problems or because adolescent behavior has influenced parental socialization behaviors. This latter question is an important one that can only be answered with longitudinal research. Longitudinal designs are critically important in attempting to understand the time sequence or "causal links" in the development of adolescent behaviors. While direct parental influences are undoubtedly important in adolescent development, it is also recognized that the parent-child system may be bi-directional in terms of parental influence processes (Belsky et al., 1986). It is important that models are able to take into account that some children may initiate problem behaviors that lead to negative parental socialization practices and family environments. Only through longitudinal designs can we begin to untangle the cause and effect relationships. This applies to the area of peer influences on adolescent drinking as well. We have argued that peer influences have an effect on drinking and deviance after family influences have come into play; however, in a longitudinal design this assumption can be tested as to whether or not negative peer influences occurred first and, if so, whether they contribute to a deterioration in family relations and subsequent adolescent alcohol abuse and other problem behaviors.

REFERENCES

Bachman, J. G. Youth in Transition, Vol. 2. The Impact of Family Background and Intelligence on Tenth Grade Boys. Ann Arbor, MI: Institute for Social Research, 1970.

Bales, R. F., & Cohen, S. P. SYMLOG--A system for the multiple level observation of groups. New York: The Free Press, 1979.

Barber, B. K., & Thomas, D. L. Dimensions of fathers' and mothers' supportive behavior: The case for physical affection. *Journal of Marriage and the Family*, 1986, *48*, 783-794.

Barnes, G. M. Adolescent alcohol abuse and other problem behaviors: Their relationships and common parental influence. *Journal of Youth and Adolescence*, 1984, *13*(4):327-348.

Barnes, G. M., & Cairns, A. L. The development of a new methodological approach for determining family influences on adolescent drinking. *Alcoholism: Clinical and Experimental Research,* 1982, *6*(1):136.

Barnes, G. M., Farrell, M. P., & Cairns, A. L. Parental socialization factors and adolescent drinking behaviors. *Journal of Marriage and the Family,* 1986, *48,* 783-794.

Barnes, G. M., & Welte, J. W. Adolescent alcohol abuse: Subgroup differences and relationships to other problem behaviors. *Journal of Adolescent Research,* 1986, *1*(1), 79-94.

Barnes, G. M., & Windle, M. Family factors in adolescent alcohol and drug abuse. *Pediatrician,* 1987, *14,* 13-18.

Baumrind, D. New directions in socialization research. *American Psychologist,* 1980, *35,* 639-652.

Belsky, J., Hertzog, C., & Rovine, M. Causal analysis of multiple determinants of parenting: Empirical and methodological advances. In M. Lamb, A. Brown, & B. Rugoff (Eds.), *Advances in developmental psychology* (Vol. 4). Hillsdale, NJ: Erlbaum, 1986.

Bentler, P. M. *Theory and implementation of EQS: A structural equations program.* Los Angeles: BMDP Statistical Software, 1985.

Bentler, P. M., & Bonett, D. G. Significance tests and goodness of fit in the analysis of covariance structures. *Psychological Bulletin,* 1980, *88,* 588-606.

Coleman, J. S. *The adolescent society.* New York: The Free Press, 1961.

Gold, M., & Mann, D. Delinquency as defense. *American Journal of Orthopsychiatry,* 1972, *42(3), 463-479.*

Goodwin, D. W. Studies of familial alcoholism: A growth industry. In D. W. Goodwin, K. T. Van Dusen, & S. A. Mednick (Eds.), *Longitudinal research in alcoholism.* Boston: Lkuwer-Nijhoff Publishing, 1984.

Jessor, R. Problem-behavior theory, psychosocial development, and adolescent problem drinking. *British Journal of Addiction,* 1987, *82*(4), 331-342.

Jessor, R., Graves, T. D., Hanson, R. C., & Jessor, S. L. *Society, personality and deviant behavior--a study of a tri-ethnic community.* New York: Holt, Rinehart and Winston, Inc., 1968.

Johnston, L. D. *Drugs and american youth: A report from the youth in transition project.* Ann Arbor, MI: Institute for Social Research, University of Michigan, 1973.

Kandel, D. B., & Andrews, K. Processes of adolescent socialization by parents and peers. *The International Journal of the Addictions,* 1987, *22*(4), 319-342.

Maccoby, E. E., & Martin, J. A. Socialization in the context of the family: Parent-child interaction. In E. Mavis Heatherington (Ed.), *Handbook of child psychology,* Vol. 4. New York: Wiley, 1983.

Olson, D. H., McCubbin, H. I., Barnes, H., Larsen, A. S., Muxen, M. J., & Wilson, M. A. *Families, what makes them work?* Beverly Hills, CA: Sage Publications, 1983.

Parke, B. A field adaptation to the SYMLOG adjective rating form suitable for children. *International Journal of Small Group Research*, 1985, March, 89-95.

Peterson, G. W., & Rollins, B. C. Parent-child socialization. In M. B. Sussman, & S. K. Steinmetz (Eds.), *Handbook of marriage and the family*. New York: Plenum Press, 1987.

Rollins, B. C., & Thomas, D. L. Parental support, power, and control techniques in the socialization of children. In W. R. Burr, R. Hill, F. I. Nye, & I. L. Reiss (Eds.), Contemporary Theories about the Family (Vol. 1). New York: The Free Press, 1979.

Schuckit, M. Biological vulnerability to alcoholism. *Journal of Consulting and Clinical Psychology*, 1987, *55*(3), 301-309.

Youniss, J., & Smollar, J. Adolescent relations with mothers, fathers, and friends. Chicago: University of Chicago Press, 1985.

The main purpose of the present research was to construct and empirically test a model of family religiosity and socialization factors and adolescent substance abuse. The study tested the independent and additive influence of religion and the family as predictors of adolescent substance abuse. The sample included data from 143 fathers, mothers, and adolescent children. Adolescent religious practice, mother's companionship with her children (from her own perception), teen's perception of father's coercive and/or inconsistent control attempts, and father's approval or disapproval of his children's use of tobacco, alcohol, marijuana, and/or drugs (from his own perception) appear to be central factors in the model that accounts for up to 51% of the variance in adolescent substance abuse. Religious practice and family factors show strong independent effects, with some overlap. This simultaneous analysis of religion and parent/child factors from family data gives a clearer picture of the substance abuse problem than when they are treated separately and from the single perception of the abuser.

7

The Religiosity and Parent/Child Socialization Connection with Adolescent Substance Abuse

RICKY R. KENT

During the past decade or so, adolescent illicit substance abuse has been a focus of social research on a local, regional, and national level. Macdonald (1984) refers to adolescent substance abuse as a national disaster because of the high proportion of adolescents who use drugs and alcohol, and because of the consequences associated with their use. Others have referred to alcohol and drug use as an "American epidemic" (Barnes, 1977; Lavenhar, 1979; Napier et al., 1984; Norem-Hebeisen and Hedin, 1983; Robins, 1984). It is clear that action must be taken to reverse the trend of alcohol and drug abuse among youth, yet society lacks a definitive understanding of the antecedents and developmental processes associated with the problem. Before any decisive action can be taken, the factors that influence adolescent substance abuse must be identified. Two important factors that have been linked with substance abuse by teenagers are religiosity and the parent/child relationship (Albrecht et al., 1977; Bahr and Marcos, 1985; Brook et al., 1977; Brook et

Ricky R. Kent • LDS Institute of Religion, Marysville, California 95901.

al., 1984; Burkett, 1977; Currie et al., 1977; Hadaway et al., 1984;
Penning and Barnes, 1982; Potvin and Lee, 1980).

RELIGIOSITY

Religiosity has consistently been found to be negatively related
to adolescent substance abuse (Albrecht, et al., 1977; Amoateng
and Bahr, 1986; Beigel and Chertner, 1977; Bry et al., 1982; Mc-
Lukie et al., 1975; Peele, 1984; Rachel et al., 1980; Tittle and
Welch, 1983; Zucker and Harford, 1983). Substance abusers are
significantly less likely to have attended church or temple with
their families than nonabusers (Blum and associates, 1972; Gossett
et al., 1972; Streit, 1978). Crumpton and Brill (1971) report that
marijuana users have notably fewer religious beliefs than do non-
marijuana users. Religiosity is positively related to low alcohol
use in the national adolescent studies for both 1974 and 1978 completed by Rachel et al. (1980). Gersick et al. (1981), Jessor et al.
(1980), and Kandel (1982) have also suggested that religiosity is
inversely related to substance use.

In summary, religiosity is viewed as an important deterrent
against deviance, particularly with what Albrecht et al. (1977)
have termed "victimless deviance" as measured, in part, by smoking cigarettes, drinking beer and/or hard liquor, smoking
marijuana, and/or taking hard drugs. There are a number of different definitions and conceptualizations of religiosity. One of the
ways the present study will contribute to the literature on
religiosity and adolescent deviance will be by utilizing measures
of multiple dimensions of religiosity, e.g., practice, belief, and affiliation.

PARENT/CHILD SOCIALIZATION PROCESS

Parent/child socialization factors are strongly implicated in the
etiology of adolescent substance abuse. The literature supports the
idea that positive family relationships, involvement, and attachment discourage youths' initiation into drug and alcohol use
(Adler and Lotecka, 1973; Bahr and Marcos, 1985; Barnes et al.,
1986; Brook et al., 1981, 1984; Jessor and Jessor, 1977; Kim,
1979; Lassey and Carlson, 1980; Potvin and Lee, 1980; Search Institute, 1984; Shibuya, 1974; Wechsler and Thum, 1973). Sub-

stance abusers are less likely to feel "very close" to their families (Wechsler and Thum, 1973); they are more likely to feel loosely controlled, specifically by the mother, and to feel rejected, especially by the father, along with perceiving a great deal of psychological tension in the relationship with the father (Prendergast, 1974). Thus, substance abusers distinguish themselves from other youth in that their homelife is reported to be unhappy and inadequate in terms of the adolescent socialization process (Barnes et al., 1986).

In summary, adolescent substance users describe the relationships with their parents as conflictual rather than harmonious, cold rather than warm, distant rather than supportive, permissive or authoritarian rather than authoritative. Moreover, substance abusers report a lack of contact with their parents, hostility in their relations, negative communication patterns, inconsistent and unclear behavioral limits, unrealistic parental expectations, and, at times, parental indifference (Reilly, 1979; Tudor et al., 1980).

THE RELIGIOSITY AND PARENT/CHILD SOCIALIZATION CONNECTION

An appreciation of the complexity of the antecedents, processes, and developmental issues argues for a multidimensional analysis of religiosity and parent/child socialization in understanding adolescent substance abuse. Some important recent empirical and theoretical works are arguing for the multidimensional approach in the study of the human condition. Thomas and Henry (1985) feel that such an approach can clarify the interface between religion and the family. They argue that good research and theory of the future will be that which is conducted in multiple institutions simultaneously to better address the similarities and differences between those institutions.

Hadaway et al. (1984:111) have noted, "Religion has seldom been examined as a social control factor relative to drug use within a multivariate context that incorporates . . . parental influences, all of which are considered important factors in creating a social bond and thus limiting or precluding deviant acts," such as illicit substance abuse. Elifson et al. (1983:112) conclude that

Religion is so intertwined with the family that its direct contribution is almost totally negated . . . religious young people are less

likely to be delinquent; however, the apparent source of this tendency seems to be found in the type of families and friends that religious young people have.

This notion of a combined effect of religion and family is supported by other researchers investigating deviant behavior (Albrecht et al., 1977; Bahr and Marcos, 1985; Hadaway et al., 1984). The present study allows for this combined effect in simultaneously measuring multiple dimensions from both of these institutions of socialization.

Source of Data

Another important issue in the study of the relationship between religion and family and adolescent drug use, as well as socialization studies in general, has to do with the source of the data used. Most of the alcohol and drug use studies that incorporate measures of the parent/child relationship utilize data from the adolescents' perceptions of their parents' behavior. Barnes (1981:212) observes that

A major limitation of most of these studies is that they have relied on reports of parental behaviors as provided by the adolescent. Parents' perceptions of their own behavior may be different from adolescent reports of their parents' behavior.

At present we do not know whether what mothers and fathers perceive to be their supportive, affectionate, and/or controlling childrearing techniques are predictive of adolescent substance abuse. Barnes calls for

intensive studies of the adolescent's relationships within the family. There are no studies which focus on adolescent substance abuse behavior while obtaining independent information from both mothers and fathers. There is little systemic study of the dynamic interaction patterns of adolescents in the family as they relate to the "socialization" of substance abuse behavior. It is suggested that whole family methodological approaches could be very useful in filling many of these informational gaps. . . . Furthermore, a great deal of literature we have available has been on deviant populations. . . . We need intensive studies within "normal populations," populations that are representative of that large body of modal American adolescents. [Barnes, 1977:585-586]

In addressing this need, the present study will measure relevant variables from the fathers', the mothers', and the adolescents' perceptions.

METHODOLOGY

The Data

The present research utilizes two independent sets of data from two rather different geographical areas: Utah (Salt Lake, Carbon, and Cache counties), and Seattle (King County), Washington. Four independent systematic random samples of households were selected from the phone books for each of the counties in Utah and Washington. An attempt was made to draw 500 families from each Utah county and 3000 families from Seattle. The actual numbers were 524 for Salt Lake, 492 for Carbon, 509 for Cache, and 3,248 for Seattle.

The procedures followed are widely used in mail questionnaire studies (Dillman, 1978); therefore, it was expected there would be a reasonable response rate. The response rates were 49.2% for the Utah data and 28.0% for the Seattle data. One hundred and six complete families (husband, wife, and teenager) responded in Utah, while 37 did so in Seattle. The relatively low response rates can be partially attributed to the fact that the questionnaires were sent to random samples of *households*, many of which were ineligible for participation in the study. Singles, widows, widowers, and divorced persons could not report interaction patterns with a spouse and children. Also, it appears that many married couples felt that if they did not have a teenager living at home they were not to participate. Efforts were made to make it clear that we wanted data from families without teenagers as well as from those with one. Despite these efforts, at least 25 families in each sample sent back a blank questionnaire with a notation that they have no teenager at home. It is unknown how many of the households surveyed were ineligible to participate, but it is clear that the low response rates were largely the consequence of such individuals not responding.

Instrumentation

Adolescent substance abuse was measured by self-report attitudes concerning self-use and actual frequency of use of seven types of drugs: tobacco (cigarettes, snuff, chewing, etc.), alcoholic beverages, marijuana, amphetamines (uppers, etc.), barbiturates (downers, etc.), cocaine (coke, crack, etc.), and psychedelics (LSD, PCP, etc.).

The substance abuse items were taken from the Bahr and Marcos (1984, 1985) instrument used in their study of Arizona and Utah high school students not residing in institutional arrangements. They conclude that valid and reliable data can be obtained concerning substance use through voluntary and anonymous survey methods.

Overall, there is a substantial amount of evidence that the responses of high school students to questions regarding drug use are valid. Given the limitations of official or clinical records, self-reports may be the best single measure of adolescent drug use. [Bahr and Marcos, 1986:262]

Religiosity was defined as a multidimensional construct made up of practice and belief items from all three family respondents. In both data sets, fathers, mothers, and adolescents were asked to respond to the same religious practice and religious belief items.

The religiosity practice and belief items were adopted from Glock and Stark's (1966) Dimensions of Religious Commitment and from Putney and Middleton's (1961) Dimensions and Correlates of Religious Ideology. As reported in Robinson and Shaver's (1969) *Measures of Social Psychological Attitudes*, Glock and Stark's instrument shows substantial association and high correlations with answers to other items designed to measure the same dimension (religious practice). The five religious belief items are from Glock and Stark's (1966) belief dimension (orthodoxy index) and Putney and Middleton's (1961) orthodoxy scale, which appears to be a good measure of what has been called the "belief component" of religiosity (Robinson and Shaver, 1969).

The *parent-child relationship* was measured using the following dimensions: parental support, parental physical affection, and parental coercion and parental inconsistent control attempts. Items measuring these dimensions were answered by each father, mother, and teenager. The items used to measure these dimensions of the parent-child relationship have been consistently found to comprise valid and reliable measures (Barber and Thomas, 1986; Peterson, 1986).

In order to construct the best-fitting model possible, fathers' and mothers' substance use behavior and attitudes concerning their children's substance use behavior were included in the study to estimate the impact each variable has on adolescent substance abuse. As reviewed, parental substance abuse behavior has been shown to be a good predictor of adolescent substance abuse. These items were also adopted from the Bahr and Marcos (1984, 1985, 1986) instrument, and they show the same level of validity and reliability as do the adolescent substance attitude and frequency use items.

Analysis

The primary method of analysis used in this study is LISREL. LISREL is a linear structural equation model that makes use of latent variables indexed by one or more observed indicators. LIS-REL is thus particularly useful for data sets that utilize constructs measured by a series of individual items as dimensions. LISREL tests the measurement model by performing a confirmatory factor analysis on the items indicating each latent variable. Simultaneously, the program tests the structural model by estimating coefficients between the independent and dependent latent variables.

In confirmatory factor analysis the dimensions are defined in advance with respect to theoretical reasoning and previous empirical results. The main question is whether the model specified fits the data. There are two indications generated by LISREL to answer this question: a chi-square value informs about "goodness of fit," and maximum likelihood estimates are elicited from the factor loadings, with all other parameters that are specified being free.

Long (1983) notes that researchers may not have a single, compelling model. Instead, several equally reasonable models may be suggested by theory and substantive research. Also, the researcher may find that the single model derived from theory does not fit. In either case he suggests that a confirmatory factor model can be used in an exploratory fashion. "A specification search can be conducted in which the selection of a model is based on prior examination of the data" (p. 15). This is the general procedure used in this research.

150   Ricky R. Kent

In summary, the objective of this research was to conduct the type of confirmatory factor (specification) search discussed by Long (1983) and Leamer (1978) and formulate the best-fitting model possible, given the data and sample, based on symbolic interaction and socialization theory and the extant empirical evidence that links the various dimensions of socialization with adolescent substance abuse.

RESULTS

The first step in the analysis was to test a model that included all of the indicators for each of the variables depicted in the theoretical model in figure 1. This run indicated that some of the variables had no meaningful relationship with the dependent variable and thus the model did not fit the data well. Since there appeared to be little theoretical reasoning to guide decisions to modify the model, two empirical steps were taken to reduce the

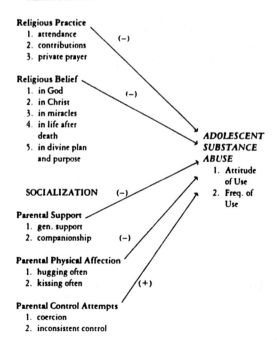

Figure 1. Religious and Parent/Child Socialization Factors as Predictors of Adolescent Substance: A Theoretical Model (Father, Mother, and Adolescent Perceptions).

number of parameters so that the model would fit better: (1) decreasing the number of observed variables by creating scale scores from varimax factor analyses, and (2) by investigating simple zero-order correlations of all of the new scale scores with the dependent variable.

Correlation Analysis

Bivariate correlations were run between each of the two dimensions of father, mother, and adolescent religiosity and each of the dimensions of parental support, parental affection, and parental control attempts from all three perceptions, and each of the two dimensions of adolescent substance abuse (attitude toward self-use and frequency of self-use). Also, parental attitude concerning their children's use and parental substance use variables were included in the bivariate analysis. This was done to clarify how the various dimensions of religion and family are related to adolescent substance abuse. Table 1 presents each of these correlations. Variables significantly related to the dependent variables were ($p <$ .01): mother's religious practice, teen religious practice, teen religious belief, father's inconsistent control attempts, father's and mother's attitude concerning children's use, and father's and mother's use of tobacco and alcohol--all with adolescent attitude toward self-use; and father, mother, and teen religious practice, mother and teen religious belief, mother's companionship, teen's perception of father's coercive and inconsistent control attempts, father's and mother's attitude concerning children's use, and father's and mother's use--all with adolescent frequency of use. These are the items used in various confirmatory models in conducting the specification search for the parameters that have significant relationships with the dependent variable. One further step was to validate these items by using them in simple stepwise regression equations with each of the two dimensions of adolescent substance abuse. Each of these parameters were then used in the model, relaxing or eliminating various ones, until an adequate fit was found or no further improvement in fit appeared possible.

Using this exploratory approach, the items identified as significant for the measurement model were: teen's religious practice, mother's perception of her companionship behavior, teen's perception of father's coercive and inconsistent control attempts, and father's attitude concerning his children's use of illicit substances. The others dropped out of the model.

Table 1

Zero-Order Correlations Between Religiosity and Parent/Child Socialization
Variables and Adolescent Attitude of Self-Use and Frequency of Self-Use

SUBSTANCE	ATTITUDE OF USE	FREQUENCY OF USE
Adol. attitude	1.00**	.66**
RELIGION		
practice		
father	-.19	-.32**
mother	-.26*	-.32**
teen	-.34**	-.41**
belief		
father	-.08	-.15
mother	-.15	-.26*
teen	-.31**	-.26*
SOCIALIZATION		
general support		
father	-.08	-.09
mother	-.16	-.19
teen of father	-.07	-.05
teen of mother	-.04	.03
companionship		
father	.08	.07
mother	-.19	-.23*
teen of father	-.03	-.02
teen of mother	.01	.05
physical affection		
father	-.10	-.10
mother	-.08	-.17
teen of father	-.04	-.02
teen of mother	.06	.19
coercive control		
father	.13	.03
mother	-.04	-.09
teen of father	.17	.24*
teen of mother	.04	.05
inconsistent control		
father	.23*	-.003
mother	.20	-.12
teen of father	.18	.23*
teen of mother	.11	.05
parental attitude		
father	-.35**	-.45**
mother	-.32**	-.36**
parental use		
father	-.24*	-.34**
mother	-.28**	-.36**

*p < .01
**p < .001

Teen's Religious Practice as a Predictor of Adolescent Substance Abuse

Having determined the list of independent variables to be used in predicting substance abuse, the next step in the analysis was to test a partial model. This partial model included teen's religious practice as a predictor of adolescent substance abuse. The results of this model are found in figure 2. The fact that attendance, donations, and prayer remained in the model as reliable indicators of the latent variable teen religious practice confirms the theoretical and empirical evidence that as religious attendance increases, the more likely an individual is to make contributions to his/her church and the more likely he/she is to have private prayers. Twenty-three percent of the variance in substance abuse (indicated by attitude toward use and actual frequency of use) was explained by teen religious practice. The negative gamma coefficient (to be interpreted similarly to standardized regression coefficient) of -.44 indicates that for this sample, as teen religious practice increased, the lower the level of substance abuse. The goodness of fit of the model was .977, suggesting that the model fit the data well.

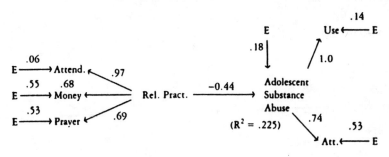

Key: Attend. = Church Attendance
      Money = Church Donations
      Prayer = Personal Private Prayer
      Use = Frequency of Self-Use
      Att. = Attitude Concerning Self-Use
      Rel. Pract. = Religious Practice
      Chi-Square = 8.39
      df = 5
      Goodness of Fit = .977

Figure 2. Measurement Model of Teen's Religious Practice and Adolescent Substance Abuse.

In summary, the partial model appears to fit the population, given the data. The observed items load quite heavily as measures of teens' religious practice, which in turn appears to be a fairly strong predictor of adolescent substance abuse. The partial model seems to substantiate the theoretical and empirical notions concerning the negative relationship between religious involvement and substance abuse behavior.

RELIGION AND FAMILY VARIABLES AS PREDICTORS OF ADOLESCENT SUBSTANCE ABUSE

In order to make the case that religion and family together can provide a more complete understanding of adolescent substance abuse, an integrated model consisting of teen's religious practice and parent/child socialization factors was specified and tested. Indicators of teen's religious practice, mother's companionship, teen's perception of father's control, and father's attitude concerning his children's use were tested in a model predicting substance abuse. The results of this model are found in figure 3.

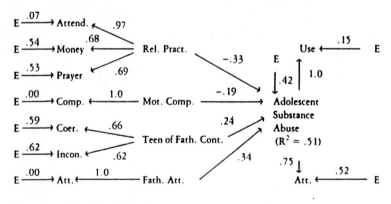

Key: Attend. = Church Attendance
      Money = Church Donations
      Prayer = Personal Private Prayer
      Rel. Pract. = Religious Practice
      Mot. Comp. = Mother's Perception of Her Companionship
      Teen Fath. Cont. = Teen's Perception of Father's Control
      Fath. Att. = Father's Attitude About Children's Use
      Coer. = Coercion
      Incon. = Inconsistent Control Attempts
      Chi-Square = 18.51
      df = 23
      Goodness of Fit = .97

Figure 3. Measurement Model of Teen's Religious Practice and Parent/Child Factors as Predictors of Adolescent Substance Abuse.

Fifty-one percent of the variance in substance abuse was accounted for by the religion and family variables. The path coefficients indicate a negative relationship between religious practice and mother's companionship, and abuse. In other words, as a teen's religious practice and companionship with mother increases, the chances that an adolescent will abuse illicit substances decreases. The coefficients also indicate a positive relationship between teen's perception of father's coercive and/or inconsistent control attempts and father's supportive attitude of his children's use of tobacco, alcohol, marijuana, and drugs, and abuse. In other words, as father's negative control (as perceived by the child) and as his positive attitude about his children using alcohol and drugs increases, the more the likelihood that an adolescent will engage in substance abuse.

In comparing the partial model and the complete integrated model, the case is made for the additive effect of religion and family in better understanding adolescent substance abuse. The total variance accounted for by the partial model was 23%, and for the complete model it was 51%. Using religion and family variables together gives a clearer picture concerning the nature of the adolescent substance abuse problem. The case is also made by comparing the teen's religious practice path coefficient of the partial model (-.44) with the same coefficient of the whole model (-.33). It appears that a portion (.11) of the teen's religious practice influence is accounted for or absorbed in the dynamics of the family.

FINDINGS AND DISCUSSION

The results of this study indicate that up to 51% of the variance in self-reported adolescent illicit substance abuse can be accounted for with measures of religion and family variables. This percentage is substantially higher than other studies that report variance accounted for between 10% to 25% (e.g., Barnes et al., 1986; Hundleby and Mercer, 1987; Jessor and Jessor, 1977; Marcos, 1985). This is probably due to the fact that multiple perceptions of family variables were used and that religious and family variables were analyzed simultaneously. In broad terms, the results support (1) the utility of "normal" population samples, (2) the contribution made by the dynamics of family in light of multiple perceptions,

and (3) the notion of a religion and family connection in understanding the nature of adolescent substance abuse.

Religiosity and Adolescent Substance Abuse

The results indicate that teen's religious practice accounts for up
to 23% of the variance in self-reported tobacco, alcohol, and drug
abuse. The negative coefficient between religious practice and
drug abuse (-.44) supports the theoretical and empirical notion that
the more a teen is involved in practicing ritual religious behavior,
the less likely that teen is to be involved with illicit substances.
The study failed to find evidence that religious beliefs are good
predictors of adolescent substance abuse. It appears that whether
an adolescent believes in the traditional principles of religion or
not, there is a chance that he/she may still experiment with and
subsequently use illicit substances. The possibility is evident that
one can believe in God, etc., and still be influenced and motivated
to use illicit substances, possibly because the believing individual
may be involved in an environment (peers, etc.) that supports the
use of illicit substances. However, those adolescents who are involved in religious activities and whose parents did not approve of
their use are much less likely to become involved with substance
abuse.

The study failed to give evidence supporting the idea that parental religious beliefs and/or practices are good predictors of their
children's substance abuse behavior or attitudes. It appears that
the religious world of parents and their children are two different
phenomena, predicting different parent and child outcome variables.

The Family and Adolescent Substance Abuse

The results suggest that a group of variables including mother's
perception of her companionship with her children, teen's perception of father's control attempts, and father's attitude concerning
his children's use of illicit drugs accounts for some 29% of the
variance of self-reported adolescent substance abuse.

Mother's companionship (-.19) indicates a relatively weak
relationship with adolescent substance abuse; however, it is statistically significant and supports the theoretical notion of a negative
relationship with substance abuse. It appears that mothers who

perceive that they spend time with and do things with their children are less likely to have adolescents who abuse illicit substances. Companionship, as perceived by fathers, and companionship with mothers and fathers as perceived by the teenager were not found to be related to adolescent substance abuse. Likewise, general support and physical affection, from all three perceptions, were not found to be good predictors of abuse.

Teen's perception of father's coercive and/or inconsistent control attempts has a somewhat stronger relationship (.24) with adolescent substance abuse. It appears from the findings that teenagers who perceive their fathers' to be coercive and/or inconsistent in their control methods are more likely to abuse drugs and alcohol. Control as perceived by mothers and fathers was not found to be predictive of adolescent substance abuse.

A father's attitude concerning his children's substance use had a moderately strong relationship with adolescent substance abuse (.34). In fact, this appears to be the best predictor among the independent variables. As father's approval of or indifferent attitude concerning his children's use of tobacco, alcohol, and/or marijuana increases, the more likely an adolescent is to be involved in illicit substance abuse behavior. Mother's attitude was not found to be related to or a predictor of her children's use of illicit drugs.

Preliminary models tested whether or not fathers and mothers used tobacco or drank alcoholic beverages. Unlike most other studies, this analysis failed to support the notion that parental substance use behavior was related to their children's substance use behavior. It appears, from this study at least, that what parents teach their children, via attitudes and values concerning the use of chemical substances, is more important and powerful than the behavior they model. The old adage "Do what I say, rather than do what I do" may have some validity in regards to the adolescent substance abuse phenomenon. It may be possible that if parents are teaching the negative consequences of drug and alcohol use and yet are modeling use, their children are less likely to use similar substances. There appears to be hope for parents, particularly fathers, who use tobacco, alcohol, and/or illicit drugs to have an impact on their children's use by teaching and demonstrating their disapproval of such behavior. *Parents can teach the opposite of what they do, and still elicit positive results in their children.* Further research is needed to substantiate such a possibility. However, the findings of this research may add support for the interactional/socialization model in dealing with the substance abuse problem over the social learning model.

The Religiosity and Family Connection with Adolescent Substance Abuse

The current findings come down clearly on the side calling for the independent effects of religion and the family in understanding the human condition, at least in regards to adolescent substance abuse behavior. When the partial model of this study is compared with the complete integrated model, it is fairly clear that some overlap does take place, but it is relatively small. The partial model yielded a -.44 coefficient for teen's religious practice, accounting for 22% of the variance and a goodness-of-fit index of .977. The whole model yielded a -.33 coefficient for teen's religious practice, and when the family variables were added, the model then accounted for 51% of the variance and had a goodness-of-fit index of .972 with a probability level equal to .730.

In summary, in this sample religion and family variables do have significant influence on adolescent substance abuse independent of each other, but do give a clearer and more complete picture when used in an additive manner. This is clearly different from the findings reported by Stack (1985), who measured suicide. The connection between these two institutions appear to have a different relationship with suicide than with substance abuse.

In order to validate the independent effects model of this study, the religious practice variable and the parent/child variables were entered in multiple regression equations to test for intervening effects. This procedure failed to indicate that an intervening model might prove to be better fitting than the one presented in this study.

It should be noted that approximately 62% of the families of the sample belong to a specific religious denomination, namely, The Church of Jesus Christ of Latter-day Saints (Mormon). This posed a methodological question: "Are the results of this study unique to a Mormon population?" In order to answer this question, the variable Religious Preference was recoded into a dummy variable, with those responding as LDS being equal to one, and all other religious preferences being zero. This new independent variable was entered into the complete model to test the effects of being a

Mormon would have on the model. The new variable, LDS affiliation, did not improve the goodness-of-fit of the model; in fact, it decreased slightly, from .972 to .970. These results appear to support the notion that it is religious practice, not affiliation, that is critical in accounting for consequent effects. The path coefficient for this variable was nonsignificant at -.15.

LIMITATIONS

There are some limitations to this study that deserve mention. The first concerns the sample size. While the sample used is by no means small considering other family studies, especially considering that data was collected from three family members, there are naturally limits to the generalizability of the findings. The second limitation regards the use of a specification model rather than a pure confirmatory factor model. While the specification search and model posited in this study provides useful information, it is important to realize that since the sample data are used to select a model, the same data cannot be used to formally assess the fit of that model (Leamer, 1978). Therefore, the model selected in this study must be viewed as tentative, in need of verification in subsequent research. With this caution in mind, the results of this study can be useful in further research concerning the religion and family connection with adolescent substance abuse.

Finally, a third limitation of this and other research on substance abuse regards causal direction. Most drug and alcohol-oriented studies, including this one, test their proposed theoretical models utilizing cross-sectional data, and, therefore, causal relationships cannot be absolutely determined. In the present case, direction of effects were predicted theoretically and then tested to see if the model fit the data. Such a test, however, does not provide confirmation of causal direction. It is possible, for example, that substance abusing behavior on the part of adolescents determines the extent to which they participate in religious practices and the nature of the parent/child relationship instead of the reverse. There is much need for research to investigate these types of possibilities.

IMPLICATIONS OF THE STUDY

The findings of this research suggest fairly strong support for the interactional/socialization model (Barnes, 1977; Barnes et al., 1986; Kandel, 1978; Utada and Friedman, 1986) that suggests that social institutions (such as religion and family) serve as the means whereby individuals learn the morals, values, and relationships necessary in becoming acceptable social beings. The findings also add to the current empirical literature that forms a basis of support for the theoretical assumptions and generalizations found in the framework of symbolic interaction and the socialization process, and for the simultaneous analysis of the two primary institutions and agents of socialization (religion and the family) in developing social competence in children (D'Antonio, 1980; Rollins and Thomas, 1979; Thomas and Henry, 1985).

If parents, educators, helping professionals, and researchers want to have a good understanding of adolescent alcohol and drug abuse, they should realize the tremendous importance and dynamics of religiosity and family relationships as agents or transmitters of moral principles, social norms, and personal values. Educative approaches should instill the notions that (1) if mothers perceive themselves as not spending time or doing things with their children, this can have an impact on their children's behavior, particularly related to tobacco, alcohol, and/or drug use; (2) if teenagers perceive their fathers as being coercive or inconsistent in their control attempts, regardless of what fathers think, they are more likely to use drugs; (3) parents, particularly fathers, can teach socially acceptable behavior that impacts on their children, regardless of parental use patterns; and (4) having strong religious and moral beliefs is not sufficient for adolescents to avoid illicit substances, they must practice and be involved in religious activities.

These findings have important implications for education and prevention, particularly for those families that have adolescents who are currently abusing drugs. Substance Abuse Volunteer Efforts (S.A.V.E.), is an example of a religious and family-centered approach to adolescent drug use. SAVE is a nonprofit corporation that provides an approach linking religion and family together in dealing with substance abuse in Mormon families. It is the goal of

SAVE to bring into congruence the family and religious values and behaviors of all members. SAVE's unique religious and family approach has implications and benefits for all religious and special interest groups in society at large, not just the LDS abusing family. If the findings cited in this and other studies have validity and utility, then they should be applied to all families from a variety of religious backgrounds. It is possible that such a religious and family-centered program as SAVE will prove more effective than current conventional approaches.

SUGGESTIONS FOR FUTURE RELEVANT RESEARCH

The findings provided by the specification search and the structural equation models of this study call for additional research to confirm and integrate the theoretical perspectives of the socialization model connecting religious and family influences with adolescent substance abuse. Specifically, the model specified and tested in this study needs to be confirmed using a different and independent data set.

Future research needs to use a similar integrated model on clinical, intact family samples. In other words, family data of adolescents who are more intensely involved with alcohol and drugs needs to be analyzed in determining the utility of religiosity and socialization factors in predicting drug use in clinical populations.

Finally, longitudinal studies utilizing integrated models need to be conducted to better pin down causal direction.

REFERENCES

Adler, P. T. and Lotecka, L. Drug use among high school students: patterns and correlates. *International Journal of the Addictions*, 1973, *8*, 537-548.

Albrecht, S., Chadwick, B. A., & Alcorn, D. S. Religiosity and deviance: Application of an attitude-behavior contingent consistency model. *Journal for the Scientific Study of Religion*, 1977, *16*(3), 263-274.

Amoateng, A. Y. and Bahr, S. J. Family, religion, and adolescent drug use. *Sociological Perspectives*, 1986, *29*(1), 53-76.

Bahr, S. J., & Marcos, A. C. *Drug use among Utah secondary students.* Utah Division of Alcoholism and Drugs: Utah Department of Social Services. Utah State Office of Education, Salt Lake City, UT, 1984.

Bahr, S. J., & Marcos, A. C. Adolescent drug use: Utah and United States comparisons. Paper presented at the annual meeting of Utah Academy of

Sciences, Arts, and Letters, Brigham Young University, Provo, UT, May 3, 1985.

Bahr, S. J., & Marcos, A. C. Adolescent drug use. In T. K. Martin, T. B. Heaton & S. J. Bahr (Eds.), *Utah in demographic perspective*. Salt Lake City, UT: Signature Books, 1986.

Barber, B. K., & Thomas, D. L. Dimensions of fathers' and mothers' supportive behavior: The case for physical affection. *Journal of Marriage and the Family*, 1986, *48*, 783-794.

Barnes, G. M. The development of adolescent drinking behavior: An evaluative review of the impact of the socialization process within the family. *Adolescence*, 1977, *12*, 571-591.

Barnes, G. M. Adolescent alcohol abuse and other problem behaviors: Their relationships and common parental influences. *Journal of Youth and Adolescence*, 1981, *13*, 327-346.

Barnes, G. M., Farrell, M. P., & Cairns, A. Parental socialization factors and adolescent drinking behaviors. *Journal of Marriage and the Family*, 1986, *48*, 27-36.

Beigel, A., & Chertner, S. Toward a social model: an assessment of social factors which influence problem drinking and its treatment. In B. Kissin & H. Begleiter (Eds.), *Treatment and rehabilitation of the chronic alcoholic*. New York: Plenum, 1977.

Bentler, P. M., & Bonett, D. G. Significance tests and goodness-of-fit in the analysis of covariance structures. *Psychological Bulletin*, 1980, *88*, 588-606.

Blum, R. H., & associates *Horatio Alger's children: Role of the family in the origin and prevention of drug risk*. San Francisco: Jossey-Bass, 1972.

Brook, J. S., Lukoff, I. R., & Whiteman, M. Peer, family, and personality domains as related to adolescents' drug behavior. *Psychological Reports* 1977, *41*, 1095-1102.

Brook, J. S., Whiteman, M., Gordon, A. S., & Brook, D. W. 1981 The role of the father in his son's marijuana use. *Journal of Genetic Psychology*, 1981, *138*, 81-86.

Brook, J. S., Whiteman, M., Gordon, A. S., & Brook, D. W. Paternal determinants of female adolescent's marijuana use. *Developmental Psychology*, 1984, *20*(6), 1032-1043.

Bry, B. H., McKeon, P., & Pandina, R. J. Extent of drug use as a function of number of risk factors. *Journal of Abnormal Psychology*, 1982, *91*(4), 273-279.

Burkett, S. R. Religion, parental influence, and adolescent alcohol and marijuana use. *Journal of Drug Issues*, 1977, *7*, 263-273.

Crumpton, E., & Brill, N. Q. Personality factors associated with frequency of marijuana use. *California Medicine*, 1971, *115*, 11-15.

Currie, R. F., Perlman, D., & Walker, L. Marijuana use among Calgary youths as a function of sampling and locus of control. *British Journal of Addictions*, 1977, *72*(2), 159-165.

D'Antonio, W. V. The family and religion: Exploring a changing relationship. *Journal for the Scientific Study of Religion*, 1980, *19*(2), 89-104.

Dillman, D. A. *Mail and telephone surveys: The total design method*. New York: John Wiley, 1978.

Durkheim, E. *The division of labor in society*. Translated by George Simpson. New York: Macmillan, The Free Press, 1933.

Elifson, K. W., Peterson, D. M. & Hadaway, C. K. Religion and delinquency: A contextual analysis. *Criminology*, 1983, *21*, 505-527.

Ellis, G. J., Thomas, D. L. and Rollins, B. C. Measuring parental support: The interrelationship of three measures. *Journal of Marriage and the Family*, 1976, *38*(4), 713-722.

Gersick, D. E., Grady, K., Sexton, E., & Lyons, M. Personality and sociodemographic factors in adolescent drug use. In D. J. Lettieri & J. P. Ludford (Eds.), Drug Abuse and the American Adolescent. National Institute on Drug Abuse Research Monograph 38, DHEW Pub. No. (ADM) 81-1166. Washington, D.C.: U.S. Government Printing Office, 1981.

Glock, C. Y., & Stark, R. Christian Beliefs and Anti-Semitism. New York: Harper and Row, 1966.

Gossett, J. T., Lewis, J. M., & Phillips, V. A. 1972 Extent and prevalence of illicit drug use as reported by 56,745 students. *Journal of the American Medical Association*, 1972, *216(9)*, 1464-1470.

Hadaway, K. C., Elifson, K. W., & Peterson, D. M. Religious involvement and drug use among urban adolescents. *Journal for the Scientific Study of Religion*, 1984, *23*, 109-128.

Heilbrun, A. B. Parental model attributes, nurturant reinforcement, and consistency of behavior in adolescents. *Child Development*, 1964, *35*, 151-167.

Hollender, J. W. Parental Contact Scale. Atlanta, GA: Emory University, 1973.

Hundleby, J. D., & Mercer, G. W. Family and friends as social environments and their relationships to young adolescents' use of alcohol, tobacco, and marijuana. *Journal of Marriage and the Family*, 1987, *49*(1), 151-164.

Jessor, R., Chase, J. A., & Donovan, J. E. Psychosocial correlates of marijuana use and problem drinking in a national sample of adolescents. *American Journal of Public Health*, 1980, *70*, 604-613.

Jessor, R., & Jessor, S. L. *Problem behavior and psychosocial development: A longitudinal study of youth*. New York: Academic Press, 1977.

Joreskog, K. G., & Sorbom, D. *LISREL IV. user's guide*. Chicago: National Educational Resources, 1978.

Joreskog, K. G., & Sorbom, D. 1979 Author's addendum to a general approach to confirmatory maximum likelihood factor analysis. In K. G. Joreskog and D. Sorbom (Eds.), *Advances in factor analysis and structural equation models*. Cambridge, MA: Abt Books.

Kandel, D. B. Longitudinal research on drug use: Empirical findings and methodological issues. New York: John Wiley and Sons, 1978.

Kandel, D. B. Epidemiological and psychosocial perspectives on adolescent drug use. *Journal of American Academic Clinical Psychiatry*, 1982, *21*, 328-347.

Kim, S. *An evaluation of ombudsman primary prevention program on student drug abuse*. Charlotte Drug Education Center, Inc., 1979.

Lassey, M. L., & Carlson, J. E. Drinking among rural youth: The dynamics of parental and peer influence. *International Journal of the Addictions*, 1980, *15*(1), 61-75.

Lavenhar, M. A. Methodology in youth drug-abuse research. In G. M. Beschner, & A. S. Friedman (Eds.), Youth drug abuse: Problems, issues and treatment. Lexington, MA: D.C. Heath and Company, 1979.

Leamer, E. E. Specification searches. New York: John Wiley, 1978.

Long, J. S. *Confirmatory factor analysis. Series: Quantitative applications in the social sciences*. Beverly Hills, CA: Sage Publications, 1983.

Macdonald, D. I. *Drugs, drinking, and adolescents*. Chicago, IL: Year Book Medical Publishers, 1984.

Marcos, A. *Causal models of adolescent drug use in Arizona and Utah*. Unpublished dissertation, Brigham Young University, Provo, UT, 1985.

McLukie, B. F., Zahn, M., & Wilson, R. A. Religious correlates of teenage drug use. *Journal of Drug Issues*, 1975, (Spring):129-139.

Napier, T. L., Goe, R., & Bachtel, D. C. An assessment of the influence of peer association and identification on drug use among rural high school students. *Journal of Drug Education*, 1984, 14, 227-248.

Norem-Hebeisen, A., & Hedin, D. P. Influences on adolescent problem behavior: causes, connection, and contexts. *Child and Youth Services*, 1983, *6*, 35-56.

Peele, S. The cultural context of psychological approaches to alcoholism: Can we control the effects of alcohol? *American Psychologist*, 1984, *39*(12), 1337-1351.

Penning, M., & Barnes, G. E. Adolescent marijuana use: A review. *International Journal of the Addictions*, 1982, *17*, 749-791.

Peterson, G. W. Family conceptual frameworks and adolescent development. In G. K. Leigh & G. W. Peterson (Eds.), *Adolescents in families*. Cincinnati, OH: South-Western Publishing Co, 1986.

Peterson, G. W., & Rollins, B. C. Parent-child socialization: A review of research and application of symbolic interaction concepts. In M. B. Sussman & S. K. Steinmetz (Eds.), *Handbook of marriage and the family*. New York: Plenum, 1987.

Potvin, R. H., & Lee, C. Multistage path models of adolescent alcohol and drug use. *Journal of Studies of Alcohol*, 1980, *41*(5), 531-542.

Prendergast, T. J., Jr. Family characteristics associated with marijuana use among adolescents. *International Journal of the Addictions*, 1974, *9*, 827-839.

Putney, S., & Middleton, R. Dimensions and correlates of religious ideologies. *Social Forces*, 1961, *39*, 285-290.

Rachel, J. V., Maisto, S. A., Guess, L. L., & Hubbard, R. L. Alcohol use among youth. In *Alcohol consumption and related problems*, 55-95. Alcohol and health monograph No. 1, DHHS Pub. No. (ADM) 82-1190. Washington D.C.: Government Printing Office, 1980.

Reilly, D. M. Family factors in the etiology and treatment of youthful drug abuse. *Family Therapy*, 1979, *11*, 149-171.

Robins, L. N. The natural history of adolescent drug use. *American Journal of Public Health*, 1984, *74*, 656-657.

Robinson, J. P., & Shaver, P. R. *Measures of social psychological attitudes: Appendix B to measures of political attitudes.* Institute for Social Research, University of Michigan, Ann Arbor, MI, 1969.

Rollins, B. C., & Thomas, D. L. Parental support, power, and control techniques in the socialization of children. In W. R. Burr, R. Hill, F. I. Nye & I. L. Reiss (Eds.), *Contemporary theories about the family* (Vol. 1). New York: Free Press, 1979.

Schaefer, E. S. Children's report of parental behavior: An inventory. *Child Development*, 1965, *36*, 413-424.

Search Institute *Young adolescents and their parents, project report.* Minneapolis, MN: Search Institute, 1984.

Shibuya, R. R. Categorizing drug users and nonusers in selected social and personality variables. *Journal of School Health*, 1974, *44*, 442-444.

Stack, S. The effect of domestic/religious individualism on suicide, 1954 through 1978. *Journal of Marriage and the Family*, 1985, *47*(2), 431-447.

Streit, F. Parents and problems: Through the eyes of youth. Highland Park, NJ: Essence Publications, 1978.

Thomas, D. L., & Henry, G. C. The religion and family connection: Increasing dialogue in the social sciences. *Journal of Marriage and the Family*, 1985, *47*(2), 369-379.

Tittle, C. R., & Welch, M. R. Religiosity and deviance: Toward a contingency theory of constraining effects. *Social Forces*, 1983, *63*, 653-682.

Tudor, C. G., Peterson, D. M., & Elifson, K. W. An examination of the relationship between peer and parental influences and adolescent drug use. *Adolescence*, 1980, *15*, 783-798.

Utada, A., & Friedman, A. S. The family scene when a teenager uses drugs: Case vignettes and the role of family therapy. In G. Beschner & A. S. Friedman (Eds.), *Teen drug use.* Lexington, MA: D.C. Heath and Company, 1986.

Wechsler, H., & Thum, D. Teenage drinking, drug use, and social correlates. *Journal of Studies on Alcohol*, 1973, *34*, 1220-1227.

Zucker, R. A., & Harford, T. C. National study of the demography of adolescent drinking practices in 1980. *Journal of Studies on Alcohol*, 1983, *6*, 974-985.

Studies investigating family variables and their relationship to parent-adolescent agreement on religious values were reviewed. Several findings are consistent across studies. Adolescents are strongly influenced by their perceptions of their parents' values; thus, accurate transmission of values depends on how parents act with their children. Mothers and fathers transmit religious values through different processes, fathers needing to be clearer and more direct than mothers. Beliefs and behaviors are transmitted differently, and high salience of the value within the home facilitates transmission. Family conflict, either between parent and child or between the spouses inhibits transmission of religious values. An atmosphere of intimacy within the home promotes the learning of values. Parental styles that balance control with emotional support for the adolescent also promote accurate transmission of religious values. Most of the studies are correlational investigations of demographic variables. Little attention has been given to causal designs in studying the transmission of religious values from parents to adolescents. Often studies have not been well controlled, and responses of adolescents throughout early, middle, and late adolescence have not been differentiated. Finally, there is a need for more conceptual clarity concerning theoretical terms such as religious salience and for more care in differentiating among stages of adolescence.

8

Family Variables Affecting the Transmission of Religious Values from Parents to Adolescents: A Review

CYNTHIA A. CLARK AND EVERETT L. WORTHINGTON, JR.

In our pluralistic society, parents are deeply concerned about whether values important to them can be transmitted accurately to their adolescent children. Numerous research studies have defined the conditions conducive to transmission of values. Of major import is the content of the values. Educational values (Smith, 1981, 1982), political values (Tedin, 1974; Thomas, 1971), and religious values have been found to be influenced by different variables.

An important factor in transmission of religious values to adolescents is the child's perception of parental values. Indeed, for transmission of values to occur successfully, (a) parental values must be detectable, and (b) children must perceive them accurately. For example, Acock and Bengtson (1980) compared ac-

Cynthia A. Clark and Everett L. Worthington, Jr. • Psychology Department, Virginia Commonwealth University, Richmond, VA 23284-0001.

tual parental values with parental values as perceived by the child. They administered a questionnaire of political and religious items to 416 youth from age 16 to 26, and to both parents. Acock and Bengtson (1980) found that the adolescents and young adults predicted their parents' responses with a low level of accuracy, perceiving them as being more conservative or traditional than they actually were. They also exaggerated the perceived similarity of theirs and their parents' values. Moreover, youths' perceptions of their parents' values were better predictors of the youths' values than were actual parental values.

From a broad social psychological perspective, behavior is the product of internal and external factors (Sherif, 1936). Research on the transmission of religious values to adolescents has concentrated on the external factors, especially examining the influences on adolescents of the major social institutions: the family, the church, the school, media, and the peers of the adolescents. The effects of each institution depend to some extent on who the adolescents perceive to be expert in a particular area, on the number of salient competing influences, and on conditions within the family, church, school, or peer group that facilitate or inhibit influence (Brittain, 1963). Religious beliefs have usually been nurtured within the home, so it has been hypothesized by a number of researchers that variables affecting the home environment will affect the success of transmission of religious values from parents to adolescents.

This paper examines empirical research on family variables affecting transmission of religious values from parents to adolescents. Three major topics are considered in the following review. In the first section, research findings that relate five family variables to successful transmission of religious values from parents to adolescent are summarized. The family variables are: (a) family conflict, (b) marital conflict, (c) similarity of parental beliefs, (d) family intimacy, and (e) parenting styles that demonstrate parental control and support. In the second section of the paper, methodological considerations are addressed because the interpretation of the findings depends on understanding the methodological limitations of current research. In the final section of the paper some implications of the review for future research and theory are drawn.

VARIABLES AFFECTING TRANSMISSION OF RELIGIOUS VALUES

Parent-Adolescent Conflict and Transmission of Religious Values

Conflict is usually present in families with adolescent and prepubertal children (Montemayor, 1983). The effect of parent-adolescent conflict on transmission of religious values must be understood against a backdrop of (a) age of the adolescent, (b) topic of conflict, (c) intensity of conflict, and (d) social class of the family.

After a review of research, Montemayor (1983) described parent-adolescent conflict as increasing as the child reaches puberty, remaining constant from about age 12 to 18, and decreasing after the adolescent leaves home. He also showed, using 17 studies since 1929, that adolescents are likely to argue with parents over "normal, everyday, mundane family matters such as school work, social life and friends, home chores, disobedience, disagreements with siblings, and personal hygiene" (p. 91). They rarely argue about topics such as sex, drugs, politics, or religion (see also Brittain, 1963; Hill, 1980; Lerner et al., 1972). The impact of conflict depends on its intensity. Montemayor found that only about one-fifth of the families of adolescents experience severe conflict. In the remaining families, conflict is occasional and mild relative to troubled families, even though *any.* conflict disturbs family harmony. Patterns of conflict also depend on the family's social class. In middle-class families, adolescents become more dominant at the expense of mothers. In lower-class families, adolescents gain influence at the expense of fathers (Jacob, 1974).

Four studies dealing with the impact of family conflict on transmission of religious values to adolescents were found (Dudley, 1978; Hoge and Petrillo, 1978; Hoge et al., 1982; LoSciuto and Karlin, 1972). Two of these demonstrate a direct association between parent-child relations and acceptance or rejection of religious beliefs. Dudley (1978) found that a poor-quality relationship between parents and 9th- and 12th-grade adolescents attending a school for Seventh-Day Adventists was strongly correlated with adolescent alienation from religion. LoSciuto and Karlin

(1972) found that 10th- to 12th-grade adolescents who reported high parent-child disagreement, in comparison with those reporting low parent-adolescent disagreement, tended to spend less time with parents, felt more separated from family members, and tended to reject religious beliefs as part of their everyday living.

Two other studies have found less support for the effect of family conflict on transmission of religious values to adolescents. Hoge and Petrillo (1978) studied 10th graders who were Catholic, Baptist, and Methodist. They found only a weak association between parent-adolescent conflict and transmission of religious values to adolescents. Hoge et al. (1982) found that agreement within the parent-adolescent relationship enhanced similarity of creedal beliefs between parents and 16-year-old adolescents from Catholic, Baptist, and Methodist congregations.

There are at least three possible explanations for these findings. First, the studies vary according to how family conflict was assessed. In studies that obtained a weak relationship between family conflict and transmission of religious values, conflict concerned lifestyle issues, such as choice of friends and dates, books, clothes, and music, which are particularly given to peer-conformity (Brittain, 1963; Hill, 1980). On the other hand, studies that obtained strong relationships between family conflict and transmission of religious values employed more general indices of family conflict: feelings of acceptance in the family, the degree to which parents "get along," and the degree of alienation or separation of adolescents from family members.

A second explanation for the findings involves the nature of the religious values measured. There appears to be a stronger association between conflict and transmission of religious beliefs and attitudes than transmission of religious behaviors or activities. For example, Dudley (1978) and LoSciuto and Karlin (1972) used attitudinal and belief measures of religious values and obtained conclusive results. Hoge et al. (1982) and Hoge and Petrillo (1978) considered both attitudinal and behavioral aspects and found weak correlations between family conflict and religious attitudes but no relationship between family conflict and religious behavior.

Third, the strongest effects were found for students in theologically conservative schools. One might infer a high commitment to religion in the parents who elected to send their child to a parochial school. Salience of religious commitment within the home has been shown repeatedly to facilitate the transmission of religious values (Bahr et al., 1971; Harris and Mills, 1985; Hoge and DeZulueta, 1985). In addition, the theological conservatism of the parents suggests that values might be more salient in the home (Harris and Mills, 1985; Jennings and Niemi, 1974; Smith, 1982) and more easily taught because they are less abstract than values of parents who are more theologically liberal (Smith, 1982).

Marital Interaction and the Transmission of Religious Values

Kleiman (1981) found evidence to suggest that parents' interactions with each other are important for optimal adolescent development. Ironically, marital satisfaction varies over the family life cycle and is at its lowest level while children are adolescents (Burr, 1970; Olson et al., 1983). Religion has been found to affect both marriage satisfaction and stability (e.g., Filsinger and Wilson, 1984; Hunt and King, 1978; Jernigan and Nock, 1983; Mosher and Hendershot, 1984; Shrumm, 1980). When marital conflict does occur within religious couples, it can affect the beliefs of adolescent children in the home.

Nelsen (1981) has examined the effect of marriage discord with still-married parents of fourth through eighth graders on early adolescent religiosity. A questionnaire measuring marriage discord, adolescent religiosity, and parental religiosity as perceived by the child was administered to 2,774 male and female fourth-through-eighth-grade students from intact families. Parental religiosity (high, low, or none) and marriage discord (high, low, or none) were both trichotomized, forming a 3 x 3 matrix. Adolescent religiosity focused on both religious beliefs and activities; parental religiosity was determined by children's perceptions of parents' church attendance and interest in religion. Children who perceived their parents as low in marital discord were apparently influenced the most by their parents' religiosity. When those parents had high religiosity, the adolescents were highest of the nine groups in religiosity. When parents had low religiosity, the adolescents had the lowest religiosity of the nine groups. For parents perceived to be highly religious, those who were perceived to have no marital discord had more religious children than those perceived to have high marital discord. For parents perceived low in religiosity, however, those perceived to have high marital discord had adolescents with higher religiosity than those perceived to have no marital discord. When marital harmony exists, adolescents' religious values mirror their parents' values, but when parents experience neither marital harmony nor religion, adolescents apparently seek solace in religion.

Clark et al. (1986) used a carefully controlled study to investigate the effects of numerous variables on parent-son similarity in religious beliefs and religious commitment to church attendance and devotional practices. Participants were 68 mother-father-son triads who met the following criteria: sons were firstborn, prepubertal Caucasian boys between 9 and 12 years old in families where mothers and fathers were first-time parents of middle socioeconomic status, Protestant, and agreeing on level of religious commitment and doctrinal beliefs. Canonical correlations were calculated to investigate the set of variables predicting mother-son agreement on religious beliefs (not significant) and mother-son agreement on religious commitment (one significant canonical root), as well as father-son agreement on religious beliefs (one significant root) and father-son agreement on religious commitment (two significant roots). Marital satisfaction was one predictor variable but was not involved significantly in prediction of any parent-son value agreement.

The difference in findings between Nelsen (1981) and Clark et al. (1986) might depend on differences in methodology. Nelsen measured children's perceptions of their parents' marriage and religiosity, whereas Clark et al. used direct measures by each parent. In addition, Clark et al. used a carefully controlled study that restricted the range of both marriage satisfaction and religiosity.

Similarity of Parental Beliefs and the Transmission of Religious Values

Similarity of mothers' and fathers' beliefs is important in the transmission of educational goals (Smith, 1981) and political values (Jennings and Niemi, 1974) as well as in the transmission of religious values to adolescents. Three studies involving transmission of religious values from parents to adolescents were reviewed (Hoge and Petrillo, 1978; Hoge et al., 1982; Putney and Middleton, 1961). Putney and Middleton (1961) found that on the whole, college students conformed to perceived parental religious ideologies when the parents were perceived as being in agreement on ideology. Hoge and Petrillo (1978) found similar results. If both parents belonged to the same denomination, children had higher rates of church attendance than when parents belonged to different denominations. Hoge et al. (1982) further found that denominational membership was more predictive of children's religious beliefs and practices than were parental beliefs and practices.

All three studies were correlational, cross-sectional, and differed in their sources of data. Both Hoge and Petrillo (1978) and Putney and Middleton (1961) obtained their data from adolescents and college students, and secured information about their families via the children's perceptions. On the other hand, Hoge et al. (1982) obtained data from both parents and children, finding that children perceived their parents to agree more closely than was actually the case.

Family Intimacy and the Transmission of Religious Values

Intimacy in relationships is defined differently by various writers (cf. Clinebell and Clinebell, 1971; Hatfield, 1979; Hinde, 1978). Generally, theorists and researchers agree that intimacy involves communication of aspects of value within an affectively positive context (Chelune and Waring, 1984).

Several studies have examined the relationship between family religiosity and feelings of intimacy among family members. Of the eight studies reviewed (Chartier and Goehner, 1976; Dudley, 1978; Hoge and Smith, 1982; Johnson, 1973; Landis, 1960; Lo-Sciuto and Karlin, 1972; Potvin, 1977; Wilkinson and Tanner, 1980), the major variables that were studied were feelings of closeness among family members and family affection. However, two studies, reasoning that children learn about their Heavenly Father by observing the earthly parent, focused on adolescents' images of God as a function of affection and quality of family communication. One study (Dudley, 1978) measured quality of relationships using scales such as family harmony, sincerity of parents, and relationship with parents.

The findings of these studies are relatively consistent, and several conclusions can be derived. First, children's feelings of warmth and closeness toward family members are associated with family religiosity--both belief and practice (Dudley, 1978; Johnson, 1973; Landis, 1960). The adolescents have frequent, strong disagreements with their parents, and they tend to reject their families' religious beliefs as a source of strength or comfort (LoSciuto and Karlin, 1972). Second, in Mormon families, parental religiosity (church attendance)--especially maternal religiosity-- had a direct effect on total affectional relationships independent of family activities (Wilkinson and Tanner, 1980). For Methodist youth, church attendance by the father was related to the adolescent having religious experiences normative for their denomination (Hoge and Smith, 1982). Third, family closeness in the form of talks between fathers and adolescents about religion were also associated with adolescents having normative religious experiences (Hoge and Smith, 1982). Finally, parental religiosity (church attendance), parental affection and control, and quality of family communication are associated with adolescents' development of their images of what God is like (Chartier and Goehner, 1976; Hoge and Smith, 1982; Potvin, 1977).

Although the eight studies present consistent findings, there are limitations regarding methodology and control of variables. Like most studies reviewed, all eight used cross-sectional questionnaire data; six used data based on children's perceptions of their parents'; only one study, Wilkinson and Tanner (1980), used data from parent-child triads. Studies defined both religiosity and affection differently.

As for the control of secondary variables, seven studies did not control for either social class or parental agreement on religious values. None separated families highly and weakly committed to religion. Five studies did not consider family stability or family conflict, and five did not make any distinction between maternal and paternal differences. Only one study, Potvin (1977), took parenting styles into consideration, and one other, Wilkinson and Tanner (1980), controlled for age and length of marriage. In summary, while the studies on family intimacy and religious value transmission are consistent in their findings, they are plagued with numerous limitations so that firm conclusions may not be drawn.

Parenting Styles and the Transmission of Religious Values

Parents might conflict little with each other or with their children, might agree on essential values, and might promote warm and intimate homes for raising children. Still, adolescents might reject parental values because the parents' childrearing beliefs and practices are aversive to adolescents. Baumrind (1971, 1980) has pioneered research on parenting styles and has particularly focused on parental control structures. She has defined and evaluated three models of parental control. The permissive parent stresses support but not control. The authoritarian parent stresses control but not support. The authoritative parent is the most effective style and stresses both control and support.

Several theoretical concerns have arisen concerning transmission of religious values to adolescents. Lewis (1981) has suggested that parental control is primarily responsible for adolescents' internalization of their parental values. Using the *overjustification hypothesis*, Lewis has suggested that high control will prompt adolescents to attribute compliance with parental demands (such as to attend church or profess beliefs consistent with parental beliefs) to the high levels of parental control rather than to internal beliefs. It should be expected, then, that as parent-adolescent ties loosen in late adolescence, many adolescents in homes using high control (such as physical or verbal coercion) should be expected to reject the religious beliefs and practices of their parents.

Baumrind (1983) has countered this attributional theory by suggesting that the context in which control occurs is more important than level of control alone. If control occurs within the context of warmth, intimacy, and nurturance, the effects are different than in homes characterized by indifference, conflict, and discord. She even argues that value internalization is impossible without clear parental control. Seven studies have focused on parenting styles as they relate to religious values (Clark et al., 1986; Dudley, 1978; Luft and Sorell, 1986; Potvin, 1977; Rosik and Gorsuch, 1985; Weigert and Thomas, 1970, 1972).

Weigert and Thomas (1970, 1972) found that high parental control and support were associated with high adolescent religiosity scores. The lowest scores on adolescent religiosity were obtained by adolescents who reported low parental control and support. Inconsistent findings exist regarding the mixed combinations of control and support. Weigert and Thomas (1970) found that support accounted for most of the variance in global religiosity, religious practice, and belief with a sample of Roman Catholics. Weigert and Thomas (1972), however, found that for Mormons, parental control was more strongly associated with adolescent religiosity

than was parental support. The discrepant findings in the two
studies by Weigert and Thomas may be due to the different
measures of the dependent variable, religiosity: beliefs and attitudes versus church attendance. Weigert and Thomas (1972) also
suggest that the discrepancy is due to *stronger family control and
family church-going among Mormons than among Catholics* (p.
391), or to the small-town nature of their 1972 sample as opposed
to the urban nature of their earlier sample.

Potvin (1977) investigated how parenting styles might influence
an adolescent's image of what God is like. Parental support was
positively related to belief in a personal God; parental control was
positively related to belief in a punishing God.

Dudley (1978) studied adolescents' alienation from religion in a
Seventh-Day Adventist sample. He found that parental harshness
and authoritarianism were related to adolescent alienation.

Luft and Sorell (1986) surveyed 222 college-age adolescent-
parent family units, 195 of which were triads. They found that for
fathers, control and nurturance interacted to influence agreement
on religious beliefs and devotional practice. For mothers, control
and communication style interacted to influence agreement on
religious beliefs and devotional practice. Generally, nurturance
was important for fathers but not for mothers. High levels of communication by mothers promoted value convergence, but high
levels of communication by fathers did not.

Parenting styles are generally expected to change as children
move from early to late adolescence (Hower and Edwards, 1979;
Rosik and Gorsuch, 1985; Sampson, 1977). Parents relinquish
control and also find fewer opportunities for nurturance as adolescents become more independent and physically mobile. All of the
foregoing studies investigated high school or college-age adolescents. Clark et al. (1986) investigated 68 early adolescents. They
found that early adolescents' ratings of parental control and support were unrelated to parent-child similarities in religious beliefs
or behavior.

Finally, Rosik and Gorsuch (1985) used entirely different
methods and measures to test the effects of parenting styles on
transmission of religious values from parents to early adolescents
(ages 11 to 13). Parental control was likened to dominance, and
support was likened to love using Leary's (1957) interpersonal
circle. Transmission of religious values was examined by parent-

adolescence similarity or intrinsic and extrinsic scales of Allport and Ross' (1967) Religious Orientation Scale. Rosik and Gorsuch found that fathers had less impact on sons' religious beliefs than did mothers. For daughters, mothers who spent time with their daughters and disciplined or protected them had more religiously similar daughters. Fathers generally weakened the influence of the mothers if the fathers were dominant.

In these studies, methodology differs substantially paralleling issues raised earlier: sample composition, operationalization of variables, and control of variables. In addition, few distinctions among parenting styles were drawn (cf. Rosik and Gorsuch, 1985), using very global measures of both control and support. Future research is needed to differentiate among types and levels of control and support.

METHODOLOGY

Currently, research on family variables that affect the transmission of religious values from parents to adolescents is largely correlational. Little attention has been given to experimental studies. Often this means that crucial variables have not been controlled. For example, religious values might be transmitted differently in homes in which a high commitment to religion, or high salience of religion, exists than in homes in which there is little interest in religion. Furthermore, religious beliefs might be involved in parenting styles, discipline techniques, and attitudes of the parents toward the nature of a "proper" home environment. Such variables are difficult to investigate using large sample correlational methods. In addition, the heavy reliance on correlational methods restricts the ability to establish causal relationships among variables.

Subject variables are often not controlled, even when past research has shown them to be significant. For example, socioeconomic status has been shown to affect the relative power of the father (Jacob, 1974), but few studies have considered it. Race effects have not been investigated. Age of the adolescent is crucial to the way the adolescent acts toward his or her mother and father, but most studies make little differentiation according to the adolescent's age. Most discussions are devoid of reference to changes in influenceability in adolescents as they age (cf. Clark et

al., 1986; Rosik and Gorsuch, 1985). In particular, disturbances in
both parent and adolescent behavior occur as the child enters
adolescence (Steinberg and Hill, 1978), yet most researchers have
not considered this, simply reporting on adolescents as a group or
treating early adolescents as if they were adolescents in their
precollege years. Research on religious denominations has shown
that Catholics differ substantially from Methodists, Baptists, or
non-Christian religions, yet many researchers lump diverse
religious groups together and try to study *religious values* as a
whole. Furthermore, there are important differences even within
denominational bodies (Gorsuch, 1984).

Studies in which family behavior is *observed* are nonexistent.
Studies that address behavior within families rely on self-report of
family behavior, usually by the adolescent (who might be the least
likely to report accurately). This suggests three needed improve-
ments in methodology.

a. Research that observes families in interaction tasks is needed
to investigate the validity of the findings about self-reports of family conflict, family intimacy, and parenting styles.

b. In measuring family variables, few researchers have used
standardized, validated measuring instruments. Most have relied
on either demographic data or questionnaires that were designed
for the purpose of their particular study.

c. Many researchers have operationalized variables similarly,
especially in early research. Failure to use independent measures
can lead to false confidence that effects are real when they may be
measure-dependent. Replication depends on use of a variety of
reliable and valid instruments for measuring theoretical constructs.
In recent studies (Clark et al., 1986; Luft and Sorell, 1986; Rosik
and Gorsuch, 1985), researchers have begun to operationalize variables differently than previous researchers. This trend needs to be
continued.

CONCLUSIONS

Adolescents are strongly influenced by the values of their
parents. Thus, how parents talk and behave in the presence of
their children is crucial to accurate transmission of religious
values. Mothers and fathers have different effects in the transmission of their religious values to sons and daughters. For instance,

five studies have found mothers to be more influential than fathers (Cooke, 1962; Hoge and Petrillo, 1978; Peck and Havighurst, 1960; Peterson et al., 1985; Rosik and Gorsuch, 1985). Three studies have found fathers more influential than mothers (Acock and Bengtson, 1978; Clark et al., 1986; Luft and Sorell, 1986). Three have found no difference (Fluegel, 1980; Hadaway, 1978; Hunsberger and Brown, 1984). The reasons for these disparate findings are unclear. Perhaps the answers lie in differing measures of value agreement, different participant characteristics, or different ages of adolescents. Certainly interactions between parents and sons must be treated separately from parent-daughter interactions.

The salience of a value within the family is crucial to the adolescent's learning the value (Bahr et al., 1971; Hoge and De-Zulueta, 1985). More conceptual clarity is necessary concerning the concept of religious salience as an explanatory variable in the transmission of religious values. For example, does high religious salience mean (a) some global characteristic of a family in which the family environment could be reliably evaluated as *religious*; (b) high frequency of religious behavior by mother, father, son, or daughter (or some combination of those); or (c) high *perception* of religiosity by some individual or combination of family members?

Even if the values are easily observable in the home, adolescents might still reject the beliefs of their parents. Factors responsible for the adolescents' acceptance or rejection of their parents' beliefs include several family variables. A high level of conflict in the home can lead to less agreement between parents and adolescents on religious values than does a low level of conflict. This is true whether the conflict is between parents and the child or between the spouses on religious values. When spouses agree on their religious values, adolescents tend to agree with them. Intimacy within the home and an atmosphere of warmth and acceptance can promote agreement between parents and their adolescents on religious values, but it may depend on the intensity of intimacy and on the presence of other family characteristics. Finally, parenting styles affect adolescents. Firm control undergirded by emotional support seems most conducive to agreement between parents and adolescents about religious values, but effects can vary widely within individual families.

REFERENCES

Acock, A. C., & Bengtson, V. L. On the relative influence of mothers and fathers: a covariance analysis of political and religious socialization. *Journal of Marriage and the Family*, 1978, *40*, 519-530.

Acocok, A. C., & Bengtson, V. L. Socialization and attribution processes: Actual versus perceived similarity among parents and youth. *Journal of Marriage and the Family*, 1980, *42*, 501-515.

Allport, G. W., & Ross, J. M. Personal religious orientation and prejudice. *Journal of Personality and Social Psychology*, 1967, *5*, 432-443.

Bahr, H. M., Bartel, L. F., & Chadwick, B. A. Orthodoxy activism and the salience of religion. *Journal for the Scientific Study of Religion*, 1971, *10*, 69-75.

Baumrind, D. Current patterns of parental authority. *Developmental Psychology Monographs*, 1971, *4*(1), 1-103.

Baumrind, D. New directions in socialization research. *American Psychologist*, 1980, *35*, 639-652.

Baumrind, D. Rejoinder to Lewis's reinterpretation of parental firm control effects: Are authoritative families really harmonious? *Psychological Bulletin*, 1983, *90*, 132-142.

Brittain, C. V. Adolescent choices and parent-peer cross-pressures. *American Sociological Review*, 1963, *28*, 385-391.

Burr, W. R. Satisfaction with various aspects of marriage over the life cycle: A random middle-class sample. *Journal of Marriage and the Family*, 1970, *32*, 29-37.

Chartier, M. R., & Goehner, L. A. A study of the relationship of parent-adolescent communication self-esteem and God image. *Journal of Psychology and Theology*, 1976, *4*, 227-232.

Chelune, G. J., & Waring, E. M. Nature and assessment of intimacy. In P. McReynolds (Ed.), Advances in Psychological Assessment. San Francisco: Jossey-Bass, 1984.

Clark, C. A., Worthington, E. L., Jr., & Danser, D. B. *Family and religious variables in the transmission of religious values from parents to firstborn early adolescent sons.* Paper presented at the meeting of the American Psychological Association, Washington, D.C., 1986.

Clinebell, H. J., & Clinebell, C. H. *The intimate marriage.* New York: Harper and Row, 1971.

Cooke, T. F. *Interpersonal correlates of religious behavior.* Unpublished doctoral dissertation, University of Florida, Gainesville, 1962.

Dudley, R. L. Alienation from religion in adolescents from fundamentalist religious homes. *Journal for the Scientific Study of Religion*, 1978, *17*, 389-398.

Filsinger, E. E., & Wilson, M. R. Religiosity, socioeconomic rewards, and family development: Predictors of marital adjustment. *Journal of Marriage and the Family*, 1984, *46*, 663-670.

Fluegel, J. R. Denominational mobility: Current patterns and recent trends. *Journal for the Scientific Study of Religion*, 1980, *19*, 26-34.

Gecas, V. Parental behavior and dimensions of adolescent self-evaluation. *Sociometry*, 1971, *34*, 466-482.

Gorsuch, R. L. 1984 Measurement: The boon and bane of investigating religion. *American Psychologist*, 1971, *39*, 228-236.

Hadaway, C. K. Denominational switching and membership growth: In search of a relationship. *Sociological Analysis*, 1978, *40*, 279-299.

Harris, R. J., & Mills, E. W. Religious values and attitudes toward abortion. *Journal for the Scientific Study of Religion*, 1985, *24*, 137-154.

Hatfield, E. Love, sex, and the marketplace. New York: Academic Press, 1979.

Hill, J. P. The family. In M. Johnson (Ed.), *Toward adolescence: The middle school years*. The Seventy-ninth Yearbook of the National Society for the Study of Education. Chicago: University of Chicago Press, 1980.

Hinde, R. A. Interpersonal relationships: In quest of a science. *Psychological Medicine*, 1978, *3*, 378-386.

Hoge, D., & DeZulueta, E. Salience as a condition for various social consequences of religious commitment. *Journal for the Scientific Study of Religion*, 1985, *24*, 21-38.

Hoge, D. R., & Petrillo, G. H. Determinants of church participation and attitudes among high school youth. *Journal for the Scientific Study of Religion*, 1978, *17*, 359-379.

Hoge, D. R., Petrillo, G. H., & Smith, E. I. Transmission of religious and social values from parents to teenage children. *Journal of Marriage and the Family*, 1982, *44*, 569-580.

Hoge, D. R., & Smith, E. I. Normative and non-normative religious experience among high school youth. *Sociological Analysis*, 1982, *43*, 69-82.

Hower, J. T., & Edwards, K. J. The relationship between moral character and adolescents' perception of parental behavior. *Journal of Genetic Psychology*, 1979, *135*, 23-32.

Hunsberger, B., & Brown, L. B. Religious socialization, apostasy, and the impact of family background. *Journal for the Scientific Study of Religion*, 1984, *23*, 239-251.

Hunt, R. A., & King, M. B. Religiosity and marriage. *Journal for the Scientific Study of Religion*, 1978, *17*, 399-406.

Jacob, T. Patterns of family conflict and dominance as a function of child age and social class. *Developmental Psychology*, 1974, *10*, 1-12.

Jennings, M. K., & Niemi, R. G. The political character of families and schools. Princeton, NJ: Princeton University Press, 1974.

Jernigan, J. D., & Nock, S. L. *Religiosity and family stability: Do families that pray together stay together?* Paper presented at the meeting of the Society for the Scientific Study of Religion, Knoxville, Tennessee, October, 1983.

Johnson, M. A. Family life and religious commitment. *Review of Religious Research*, 1973, *14*, 144-150.

Kleiman, J. I. Optimal and normal family functioning. *American Journal of Family Therapy*, 1981, *9*(1), 37-44.

Landis, J. T. Religiousness, family relationships, and family values in Protestant, Catholic, and Jewish families. *Marriage and Family Living*, 1960, *22*, 341-347.

Leary, T. Interpersonal Diagnosis of Personality. New York: Ronald Press, 1957.

Lerner, R. M., Schroeder, C., Rewitzer, M., & Weinstock, A. Attitudes of high school students and their parents toward contemporary issues. *Psychological Reports*, 1972, *31*, 255-258.

Lewis, C. C. The effect of parental firm control: A reinterpretation of findings. *Psychological Bulletin*, 1981, *88*, 547-563.

LoSciuto, L. A., & Karlin, R. M. Correlates of the generation gap. *The Journal of Psychology*, 1972, *81*, 253-262.

Luft, G. A., & Sorell, G. T. *Parenting style and parent-adolescent value consensus*. Paper presented at the meeting of the American Psychological Association, Washington, D.C., 1986.

Montemayor, R. Parents and adolescents in conflict: All families some of the time and some families most of the time. *Journal of Early Adolescence*, 1983, *3*, 83-103.

Mosher, W. D., & Hendershot, G. E. Religious affiliation and the fertility of married couples. *Journal of Marriage and the Family*, 1984, *46*, 671-677.

Nelsen, H. M. Gender differences in the effects of parental discord on preadolescent religiousness. *Journal for the Scientific Study of Religion*, 1981, *20*, 351-360.

Olson, D. H., McCubbin, H. I., Barnes, H., Larsen, A., Muxen, M., & Wilson, M. Families: What makes them work. Beverly Hills, CA: Sage, 1983.

Peck, R. F., & Havighurst, R. J. *The psychology of development*. New York: Wiley, 1960.

Peterson, G. W., Rollins, B. C., & Thomas, D. L. Parental influence and adolescent conformity: Compliance and internalization. *Youth and Society*, 1985, *16*, 397-420.

Potvin, R. H. Adolescent God images. *Review of Religious Research*, 1977, *19*, 43-53.

Putney, S., & Middleton, R. Rebellion, conformity, and parental religious ideologies. *Sociometry*, 1961, *24*, 125-135.

Rosik, C. H., & Gorsuch, R. L. Adolescent religiosity in relation to parental religiosity in interpersonal style. Paper presented at the meeting of the American Psychological Association, Los Angeles, 1985.

Sampson, R. Transmission of values within a traditional family structure. *Family Therapy*, 1977, *4*, 163-170.

Sherif, M. The psychology of social norms. New York: Harper, 1936.

Shrumm, W. Religious and marital instability: Change in the 1970s? *Review of Religious Research*, 1980, *21*, 135-147.

Smith, T. E. Adolescent agreement with perceived maternal and paternal educational goals. *Journal of Marriage and the Family*, 1981, *43*, 85-93.

Smith, T. E. The case for parental transmission of educational goals: The importance of accurate offspring perceptions. *Journal of Marriage and the Family*, 1982, *44*, 661-674.

Steinberg, L. D., & Hill, J. P. Patterns of family interaction as a function of age, the onset of puberty, and formal thinking. *Developmental Psychology*, 1978, *14*, 683-684.

Tedin, K. L. The influence of parents on the political attitudes of adolescents. *American Political Science*, 1974, *68*, 1579-1592.

Thomas, L. E. Political attitude congruence between politically active parents and college-age children: An inquiry into family political socialization. *Journal of Marriage and the Family*, 1971, *33*, 375-386.

Weigert, A. J., & Thomas, D. L. Socialization and religiosity: A cross-national analysis of Catholic adolescents. *Sociometry*, 1970, *30*, 305-326.

Weigert, A. J., & Thomas, D. L. Parental support, control, and adolescent religiosity: An extension of previous research. *Journal for the Scientific Study of Religion*, 1972, *11*, 389-393.

Wilkinson, M. L., & Tanner, W. C. The influence of family size, interaction, and religiosity on family affection in a Mormon sample. *Journal of Marriage and the Family*, 1980, *42*, 297-303.

Supplementary Table for Conflict, Intimacy, and Religious Values

The Relationship Between Five Family Variables and the Transmission of Religious Values from Parent to Adolescent

STUDY	SUBJECTS	TYPE OF MEASURES	MEASURE OF FAMILY VARIABLES	MEASURE OF AGREEMENT ON RELIGION	PERTINENT FINDINGS
			Parent-Adolescent Conflict		
Dudley (1978)[a]	400 9th–12th-grade Seventh-Day Adventist students	Adolescent self-report via questionnaire	Quality of parent-adolescent relations, family harmony	Adolescent alienation from religion (attitude)	1. Alienation was positively correlated with unhappy parent-adolescent relationships. 2. Alienation was positively correlated with family disharmony.
Hoge, Perrillo, and Smith (1982)[b]	254 parent-adolescent triads; middle class; predominantly white, 16-year-old adolescents; Catholic, Baptist, and Methodist	Questionnaire to parents and adolescents	Family factors	Religious value transmission (belief and practice)	1. In boys, younger parental age and good parent-child relationships were positively correlated with religious value transmission (creedal assent).
Hoge and Perrillo (1978)[c]	451 upper middle-class white, 10th-grade adolescents; Catholic, Baptist, and Methodist affiliations	Adolescent self-report via questionnaire	Family factors, peer group pressures, program and leadership factors, beliefs	Church attendance, church youth group participation, attitudes toward church and toward church youth programs	1. Overall, parental church attendance and organizational participation was positively associated with adolescent church attendance and organizational participation.

LoSciuto and Karlin (1972)[d]	Probability sample of 2,362 10th–12th-grade students	Adolescent self-report via questionnaire	Adolescent dissidence, parent-adolescent disagreement	Time spent with parent, closeness to family, rejection of religious beliefs	2. Perceived relationships with parents' control, support, and disagreement (factors). 1. Overall, parent-adolescent agreement on social issues was much more common than disagreement. 2. Disagreement generally occurred on lifestyle issues rather than on basic values. 3. Males and older students were more likely to be highly dissident. 4. Highly dissident adolescents tended to spend less time with parents, felt more separated from family members, rejected religious beliefs as source of comfort and advice.

Marital Conflict of Parents

Clark, Worthington, and Danser (1986)[f]	68 firstborn sons, 9 to 12; 136 middle SES parents who agree on belief and church attendance	Questionnaires to parents and adolescents	Marital satisfaction; adolescent perceived parental control and support	Church attendance and belief measured on the LAM scale and devotional practices	1. Marriage satisfaction not related to parent-son agreement on belief, attendance, or devotional practice.
Nelsen (1981)	2,774 male and female 4th–8th-graders from intact families	Questionnaire to adolescents	Parent religiosity (no, low, high); parent marital discord (no, low, high)	Adolescent religiosity	1. For no and low marital discord, adolescents mirrored values of parents.

Supplementary Table Continued

Study	Subjects	Type of Measures	Measure of Family Variables	Measure of Agreement on Religion	Pertinent Findings
					2. For high marital discord, adolescents tended to reject values of parents. 3. Results more pronounced in homes with high religious parents.
			Similarity of Parental Beliefs		
Hoge and Perrillo (1978)[f]	451 upper middle-class white, 10th-grade adolescents; Catholic, Baptist, and Methodist affiliations	Adolescent self-report via questionnaire	Family factors, peer group pressures, program and leadership factors, beliefs	Church attendance, youth group participation, attitudes toward church and toward church programs	1. Parents had strong influence on adolescent church attendance mainly via their own attendance behaviors but almost no influences on adolescent attitude about church. 2. Parental unity of denominational memberships was positively correlated with adolescent church attendance.
Hoge, Perrillo, and Smith (1982)[h]	254 parent-adolescent triads; middle class; predominantly white, 16-year-old adolescents; Catholic, Baptist, and Methodist affiliations	Questionnaire	Family factors	Religious value transmission (belief and practice)	1. Membership in specific denomination was more predictive of children's values than were parent's values. 2. In girls, high parental scores on creedal assent and parental agreement on creedal assent were positively correlated with religious value transmission.

				Students, conformity to parental ideologies	1. Students generally conformed to parental religious ideologies when parents were in agreement. 2. When parents disagreed, students conformed to the parent closest to the modal position (modernist Christian ideology) and also to the mother.
Putney and Middleton (1961)	1,088 predominantly middle-class college students	Self-report via questionnaire	Parental agreement on religious ideologies		

Family Intimacy

				Image of what God is like and adolescent self-esteem	1. Constructive parental communication was positively related to adolescent self-esteem. 2. Adolescent self-esteem was positively related to loving God image. 3. Constructive parental communication was positively related to loving God image.
Chartier and Goelnher (1976)	84 middle- and upper middle-class 10th- and 11th-grade students	Questionnaire	Quality of family communication (positive and constructive)		
Dudley (1978)*	400 9th–12th-grade Seventh-day Adventist students	Adolescent self-report via questionnaire	Quality of parent-adolescent relations, family harmony	Adolescent alienation from religion (attitude)	1. Alienation was positively correlated with unhappy parent-adolescent relationships. 2. Alienation was positively correlated with family disharmony.
Hoge and Smith (1982)	451 youth in suburban Catholic and Baptist churches	Questionnaire	Mother or father talks to youth about religion, mother or father attends church	Presence or absence of normative and non-normative religious experience	1. Normative religious experiences related to father who talks about religion to Catholic adolescents and father who attends church with Methodist adolescents.

Supplementary Table Continued

Study	Subjects	Type of Measures	Measure of Family Variables	Measure of Agreement on Religion	Pertinent Findings
Johnson (1973)	453 college students from stable homes, middle class to upper middle class	Self-report via questionnaire	Perceptions of family relations	Religiosity of students (general religious commitment, belief, activity)	1. Religious belief and activity in the church were positively correlated with a warm, supportive family and with a religious influence in the home.
Landis (1960)	3,000 middle-class and middle-class college students; Protestant, Catholic, Jewish, and no affiliation	Questionnaire	Children's reported feelings of closeness to parents	Religiosity of parents (very devout to antagonistic)	1. Parental religiosity and children's feelings of closeness were positively associated. 2. Females reported closer relationships with parent than did males. 3. For both males and females, feelings of closeness to father were more positively associated with parental religiosity than feelings of closeness to mother.
LoSciuto and Karlin (1972)[d]	Probability sample of 2,362 10th-grade students	Adolescent report via questionnaire	Adolescent dissidence—parent-adolescent disagreement	Time spent with parents, closeness to family, rejection of religious beliefs	1. Highly dissident students tended to spend little time with parents, felt more separated from family members, and rejected religious beliefs as source of comfort and advice.
Porvin (1977)[e]	National probability sample of 1,121	Adolescent self-report via questionnaire	Parental affection and control, parental education	Image of what God is like	1. Overall, parental religious practice and years adolescent attended religion classes consistently discriminated

Parental Control and Support

Study	Sample	Method	Variables measured	Findings
	adolescents ages 13 to 18			between belief and nonbelief in a personal God. 2. Parental affection discriminated between belief and nonbelief in a personal God among younger females and between belief in a loving/punishing God and nonbelief among older males. (Nonbelievers scored lower than believers on parental affection.)
Clark, Worthington, and Danser (1986)	68 firstborn sons, 9 to 12; 136 middle SES parents who agree on belief and church attendance	Questionnaires to parents and adolescents	Marital satisfaction, adolescent perceived parental control and support; Church attendance and belief measured on the LAM scale and devotional practices	1. Marriage satisfaction not related to parent-son agreement on belief, attendance, or devotional practice.
Dudley (1978)	400 9th–12th-grade Seventh-Day Adventist students	Adolescent self-report via questionnaire	Parental authoritarianism; Adolescent alienation from religion (attitude)	1. Perceived parental authoritarianism was positively correlated with adolescent alienation from religion.
Luft and Sorrell (1986)	195 college-aged adolescent-parent family units	Questionnaires to parents and adolescents	Swedish EMBU to assess perceptions of parental childrearing practices: control, nurturance, communication; Religious values inventory: creedal assent, religious relativism scale, religious individualism scale	1. For fathers, control and nurturance influenced agreement on belief and devotional practice. 2. For mothers, control and communication influenced agreement on belief and devotional practice.

Supplementary Table Continued

Study	Subjects	Type of Measures	Measure of Family Variables	Measure of Agreement on Religion	Pertinent Findings
Potvin (1977)[f]	National probability sample; 1,121 adolescents, ages 13 to 18	Adolescent self-report via questionnaire	Parental affection and control, parental education	God image	1. Parental control and/or parental education were the most important predictors of belief in a loving/punishing God and nonbelief among males. (Nonbelievers scored lower than believers on parental affection.)
Rosik and Gorsuch (1985)	41 Sunday School youth, 11–13, and parents	Questionnaires to parents and adolescents	Leary's Interpersonal Checklist: love and dominance	Age universal, religious orientation scale	1. Fathers had less impact than mothers on sons' beliefs. 2. For daughters, mothers who spent time with them and disciplined them had influence. 3. Dominant fathers weaken maternal influence.
Weigert and Thomas (1970)	Cross-national sample of 740 11th-grade Catholic adolescents in urban setting	Adolescent self-report via questionnaire	Parental control and support	Adolescent religiosity (belief, experience, knowledge, and practice)	1. Highest scores on religiosity were obtained by adolescents reporting high control and support from mother or father or both parents. 2. Lower scores on religiosity were obtained by adolescents reporting low parental control and support.

Weigert and Thomas (1972)	44 middle-class Mormon adolescents	Adolescent self-report via questionnaire	Parental control and support	Adolescent religiosity (attitude toward church attendance)	3. Maternal, paternal, and parental support accounted for an amount of variance in global religiosity, practice, and belief in both of the Anglo samples.
					1. Highest scores on religiosity were adolescents who reported high parental control and support. 2. Lowest scores on religiosity were adolescents who reported low parental control and support. 3. Low support/high control yielded a higher adolescent religiosity than high support/low control.
Wilkinson and Tanner (1980)	223 lower-class, middle-class, upper-class Mormon parent-adolescent triads; ages of adolescents unspecified	Questionnaires	Family affection	Religiosity of parents (temple attendance), family size, family activity and interaction	1. Path analysis: parental temple attendance, especially maternal attendance, had a direct effect on family affectional relationships independent of family activities.

a.b.c.d.e.f Studies with the same superscript are included in more than one section as appropriate; the results pertinent to each section differ.

Parent-adolescent relationships have been thought to be characterized by more conflict than parent-child relationships when children are younger. A dialectical view of the family when children enter adolescence would indicate that developmental changes during adolescence make it necessary for adolescents and parents to redefine their relationship. This study was designed to examine the relations between cognitive ability of adolescents and (a) perceptions of the family environment and (b) observed affect in parent-adolescent interaction in families with early pubertal and late pubertal adolescents. Data are from 24 families. A measure of perceptions of the quality of family environment and a measure of cognitive ability were obtained from each family member. Mothers, fathers, and adolescents were videotaped as they engaged in three discussions. Although the results are tentative, it may be inferred from the data that pubertal and cognitive development of adolescents is associated with adolescents' and mothers' perceptions of families. The association between the two indicators of development and observed affect in parent-adolescent interaction is less clear.

9

Pubertal Status, Cognitive Development, and Parent/Adolescent Relationships

LYNDA HENLEY WALTERS AND J. ELIZABETH NORRELL

INTRODUCTION

Because of their belief that formal operations influence adolescent social relationships, Hill and Palmquist (1978) suggested that

we might profit from studies of the inter-relations of formal operations and parent-child interaction in the family with the notion that the newly developing cognitive capacities may facilitate or impede interactions depending on parental capacity to tolerate the products of higher order reasoning. (p. 22)

Lynda Henley Walters • Department of Child and Family Development, University of Georgia, Athens, GA 30601. J. Elizabeth Norrel • Erskine College, Due West, SC 29639.

Ten years earlier Baumrind (1968) suggested that the onset of formal operational thought changes the way adolescents relate to their parents and that parents need to change the way parental authority is legitimated as their adolescents become more skillful at questioning parental reasoning.

By the time their children reach adolescence, a pattern of interaction has been established between parents and children. Still, there is a general expectation that parents and children will experience discord in their relationship during adolescence. Indeed, in a thorough review of the literature on parent and adolescent conflicts, Montemayer (1983) concluded that parents and adolescents do experience conflict in their relationships.

If it is assumed that the appearance of conflict represents a change in the relationship, then it is logical to look for a change in the environment or a change within one or more individuals that would cause the change in relationship. Because the way we organize and use information affects the way we perceive the environment, it is reasonable to suspect that cognitive change in the adolescent is at least partially responsible for the change in parent-adolescent relationships.

Such a possibility was investigated by Steinberg and Hill (1978), who, in examining the influence of adolescent development on parent-adolescent relationships, concluded that difficulty in interaction increases between mothers and sons during the early part of the pubertal period until the son reaches peak rate of growth. Once sons passed their peak rate of growth--an external indicator of the physiological changes of puberty, thus they may have been mature enough to have gained some experience with formal operational thought--difficulty in interaction with mothers subsided. However, the improvement in interaction was found to be independent of reasoning ability. Apparently, interaction improved because mothers deferred to sons, perhaps because their son's physical appearance more nearly approximated that of a man. These results supported the earlier findings of Jacob (1974) that increased influence of sons during adolescence is associated with a decrease in the influence of mothers. Steinberg reconfirmed this finding in 1981.

In another study of cognitive development and parent/adolescent relationships, and building on the work of Elkind (1967), Adams and Jones (1982) studied the predictive relation between parental behaviors and adolescent imaginary audience behavior (the belief that others are as admiring or as critical as the adolescent is of him- or herself). Imaginary audience has been considered to be an expression of egocentrism, which emerges as adolescents become capable of formal thought. The behavioral outcome of imaginary audience is acute self-consciousness. Adams and Jones postulated that perceived rejection and control by parents would be associated with increased self-consciousness, perceived supportive parental behaviors would be associated with decreased self-consciousness, and perceived withdrawal behaviors would be associated with increased self-consciousness. Although some of their expectations were supported, results were different for males and females. However, in this study, Adams and Jones (1982) were not postulating that an intra-individual cognitive change would predict parent-adolescent relationship scores; rather, they thought that a change in parent behaviors toward adolescents would result in an increase in their adolescent's self-consciousness behaviors (i.e., imaginary audience behaviors).

There is some question as to whether or not imaginary audience behavior is a function of the transition to formal thought (cf. Lapsley et al., 1986). Riley et al. (1984) investigated the question of the association between imaginary audience behavior and transition to formal thought and found a relation between self-consciousness and formal operations, but not what had been expected. With increased ability to use formal operations, self-consciousness decreased. They also confirmed their earlier finding of the predicted relation between parent behaviors and self-consciousness, i.e., increased perceptions of parental support were associated with decreased self-consciousness.

It appears that the findings of Adams and colleagues reflect an association between perceptions of parent behaviors and some sort of change that occurs during early adolescence, but the change is not unquestionably a cognitive change. In addition, the direction of influence is not certain.

The importance of a family environment characterized by positive relationships as a support for adolescent development and as a deterrent to deviance behavior of an adolescent is well supported in the literature (Grotevant and Cooper, 1983; Montemayer, 1986; Papini and Sebby, 1987). According to Yourglich (1964), the climate in the home is more pleasant as a result of interaction, even if interaction involves differences of opinion. Others, however, believe that it is positive, understanding responses from parents that lead to more communication and positive relationships within the home (Elder, 1963; Patterson, 1982; Rallings, 1969; Steiner, 1970; Stone, 1963).

The purpose of this study was to examine the relations between maturity and cognitive ability of adolescents and (a) perceptions of the family environment and (b) observed affect in parent-adolescent interaction in families with early pubertal and late pubertal adolescents. Two sets of questions and one final question guided the analyses of these data.

Maturity and Gender

1. Do adolescents', fathers', or mothers' perceptions of the family differ according to maturity or gender of adolescent?

2. Is there an association between affective quality of family interaction and maturity or gender of adolescent?

Cognitive Development

1. Is there an association between adolescents' cognitive ability and mothers', fathers', and adolescents' perceptions of the family?

2. Is there an association between adolescent cognitive ability and the affective quality of observed interaction of adolescents, mothers, and fathers?

Final Question

What is the relative importance of maturity, gender, and cognitive ability of adolescents for family members' perceptions of the family and affective quality of observed interaction?

Subjects

Twenty-four white, middle-income families consisting of father, mother, and adolescent served as subjects. Subjects were solicited through local ads. In addition, families who responded to ads were asked if they knew of other families with adolescent children who might meet our criteria. Finally, if we heard about families through any source who might meet our criteria, we got names and contacted them. Mean age for fathers was 43 and most had completed several years of graduate study. Mean age for mothers was 42; some had completed some graduate education but most had no schooling beyond high school.

Adolescents were categorized by gender and developmental maturity. Because the focus was on adolescents who were average in their developmental timing, categorization for developmental maturity was partially a function of age and partially a function of development. The indicator of development was peak rate of growth. Growth rate is easily observed by parents and adolescents, especially for boys. Therefore, both parents and adolescents were asked if a period had been experienced when growth was so rapid that it was difficult to have clothes that fit properly. In every case, parents and adolescents agreed in their answers to this question. If the response was "yes" and the age was 14-16 (girls) or 16-18 (boys), the adolescent was placed in the mature group. For girls to be placed in the mature group, the additional indicator of menarche was required because it is such a clear indicator of developmental status. If the growth spurt had not been noticed and the age was 11-13 (girls) or 13-15 (boys), the adolescent was placed in the young group. Families of adolescents who had (a) experienced a growth spurt (and, in the case of girls, menarche) and were in the younger age group or (b) had not experienced a growth spurt (and/or menarche, girls) and were in the older group were not included in the analysis. It is recognized that using only the growth spurt for categorization could easily lead to inappropriate categorization (parents and/or adolescent not observant enough, growth spurt not a part of individual developmental pattern). By controlling for age, categorization is likely to be correct and to be reflective of the "average" adolescent (see Katchadourian, 1977, and Marshall and Tanner, 1969, 1970, for excellent discussions of physiological indicators of pubertal development).

Data were collected from every family we contacted who met our criteria. Because we required that parents be in a first, intact marriage and that adolescents clearly fit our developmental categories, it was difficult to find families. Funding was the primary limitation on sample size. The first two families served as pilot subjects; incomplete data were obtained from two families. The sample reported here contained 24 families, 6 in each cell (female adolescents: early puberty, late puberty; male adolescents: early puberty, late puberty).

Instruments

Cognitive development. Level of cognitive development was assessed with the Group Assessment of Logical Thinking (GALT) developed by Roadrangka et al. (1982) (see also Yeany et al., 1986). This is one of several tests based on Piaget's theory of cognitive development that have been developed to avoid such problems as (a) too much time required for testing, (b) necessity of trained interviewers, and (c) under-standardized methodology of the clinical interview (cf. Bart, 1972,; Burney, 1974; Lawson, 1978; Longeot, 1965; Raven, 1973; Rowell and Hoffman, 1975; Tobin and Capie, 1980). The authors have determined that this paper-and-pen test possesses the following characteristics (Roadrangka et al., 1983):

1. The test measures six logical operations: conservation, proportional reasoning, controlling variables, combinatorial reasoning, probabilistic reasoning, and correlational reasoning.

2. The test uses a multiple-choice format for presenting options for answers as well as the justification or reason for that answer.

3. Pictorial presentations of real objects are employed in all test items.

4. The test is suitable for students reading at the sixth grade level or higher.

5. The test has sufficient reliability and validity to distinguish between groups of students at concrete, transitional, and formal stages of development.

6. The test can be administered in one class period to a large group by individuals who serve simply as proctors (pp. 3-4).

Reliability of the test was estimated by the test authors for the total test and for the subtests. Using 628 students (including elementary through high school grades), the Cronbach alpha estimate for the total test was .85; subtest estimates ranged from .37 to .83 with only two subtests below .58.

Using a subsample of 43 subjects, validity was examined by correlating GALT scores with scores obtained from the same students using the traditional Piagetian interview test. The estimate for the total test was .71.

The test authors developed a short form, taking into account sub-test structure, reliability, and validity. The short form contains the two items from each subset comprising the best-functioning items in the pool. Because this study includes adults and the data from which the short form was developed did not include adults, an additional item was added to the short form in the subset measuring combinatorial ability. Thus, the test used in this study contains 13 items: 2 conservation, 2 proportion, 2 control variables, 2 probability, 2 correlation, and 3 combination. Reliability was estimated to be .84 for adolescents.

Family Life Questionnaire (FLQ). This instrument was designed by Guerney (1977) to measure harmony and satisfaction with family life. Variables include amount of fighting, concern for other members, degree of family happiness, understanding, and communication. The 24 items contain response choices of Yes, strongly agree (Y); Yes, mildly agree or yes, but not so sure (y); No, mildly disagree or no, not so sure (n); and No, strongly disagree (N). The FLQ is scored as follows: $Y = 4$, $y = 3$, $n = 2$, and $N = 1$ for items 1, 4, 5, 11, 14, 15, 16, 20, 23, and 24. For the remaining items, $Y = 1$, $y = 2$, $n = 3$, and $N = 4$. High scores indicated positive perceptions of family.

Test-retest reliability was estimated in three separate studies. Ely (1970) obtained a reliability estimate of .61 after eight weeks. Rappaport (1976) estimated reliability at .86 after a similar time span. Ginsberg (1971) retested after a 10-week interval and obtained a reliability estimate of .77. Alpha estimates ranging from .84 to .91 have been reported for the various forms of the FLQ. In this sample, the alpha estimate was .94.

Construct validity was assessed by Collins (1971), who correlated the FLQ for couples with the Marital Adjustment Test (.78, $p < .001$), the Marital Communication Inventory (.78, $p < .001$), and the Primary Communication Inventory (.69, $p < .001$). Concurrent validity was estimated by Ginsberg (1971), who reported significant correlation coefficients for the FLQ and Parent Adolescent Communication Checklist (.62, $p < .001$), Parent-Adolescent Communication Inventory (.73, $p < .001$), the Semantic Differential-Self (.40, $p < .01$), and the Semantic Differential-Other (.38, $p < .01$). Ginsberg (1971) also correlated the FLQ with two measures of observed behavior: Acceptance of Others (.39, $p < .01$) and Unobtrusively Observed Acceptance of Others (.26, $p < .05$).

Measure of Observed Interaction

Stimulus for interaction. Interactions were elicited through discussions of dilemmas. Two of the dilemmas chosen were from Kohlberg's (1958) Moral Development studies. Families were asked to discuss what the people in the dilemmas should do and why. No effort was made to create differences among family members; however, some differences were expected due to the nature of the dilemmas--the dilemmas had no easy solutions. Several of the dilemmas were piloted, and the two that elicited the most discussions were used: "Escaped Prisoner" and "Heinz and the Drug" (Heinz was changed to John). The third dilemma was a hypothetical situation involving the adolescent:

Imagine that (adolescent's name) is in a public place with a good friend and the friend begins to smoke marijuana and offers (adolescent's name) a smoke too. Since they are in a public place, (adolescent's name) knows there is a good chance that they might be caught. How would you, (adolescent's name), handle this situation? As parent, how would you suggest that (adolescent's name) handle this situation?

The Couple Interaction Scoring System (CISS) developed by Gottman (1979) and associates was the system used to code the above categories. The CISS has been used to identify structure and pattern of interaction. It is based on two well-known older coding formats, the Marriage and Family Interaction Coding System (Olson and Ryder, 1970) and the Marital Interaction Coding System (Weiss et al., 1973). It contains only 11 major categories (8 content and 3 nonverbal affect), thus avoiding the two extremes of coding categories, too numerous categories that must be lumped together to be meaningful (Olson and Ryder, 1970; Rausch et al., 1974) and so few categories that many meaningful categories are ignored (Wampler and Sprenkle, 1980). Additionally, the codes are not limited to a particular theoretical orientation, verbal and nonverbal behavior are scored separately, and categories are similar to descriptions of interaction used by clinicians. CISS has been extensively studied for reliability and validity of the coding system (Gottman, 1979). Only the nonverbal portion of the data are included in this report. Nonverbal behavior was coded into three categories: positive, negative, and neutral, based on facial, voice tone, and body cues.

Coding procedures. The audio-video tapes of each family's discussions were transcribed and divided into thought units. As described by Gottman (1979), the thought unit is a relatively small variable unit representing a single thought. It may be a phrase, a sentence, or even a word. Because thought units are most often broken at pauses in speech, the transcripts were unitized while listening to the soundtrack of the videotapes. Each observation was coded twice, once for content and once for nonverbal behavior. Nonverbal behavior was coded for each thought unit; only nonverbal codes are reported here. All codes were recorded on the transcripts that had been formatted for entry of codes. Reliability was calculated as a percentage of agreement for each thought unit and was estimated for each of the three nonverbal affect categories separately. Reliability checks were conducted throughout the coding procedure, with each rater independently coding one page (selected randomly) of a transcript coded by another rater. This method of random checking was used to avoid reliability decay (Johnson and Bolstad, 1973). The trainer of the student raters also periodically coded entire transcripts to check for observer drift. All reliabilities were .85 or above. Overall level of observer agreement for combined nonverbal categories was estimated to be .92 (Cohen's, 1977 Kappa).

Scores for affective quality of family interaction were obtained from the nonverbal categories and were calculated as number of positives/number of positives + number of negatives. Arc sine transformations were used for analyses.

Laboratory Procedure

Upon arrival, families were told that they were participating in a study of family interaction and that they would be asked to discuss three topics, each for 10 minutes. The procedure was explained to them, including the fact that they would be asked to complete several questionnaires. Confidentiality was assured, and, if willing to participate, each family member was asked to sign a consent form. After the consent form was signed, payment for participation was made and families were assured they could withdraw at any time.

Families were taken to a comfortable room resembling a living room with a one-way mirror on one wall and a microphone on a coffee table. They were asked to complete the questionnaires

without discussing them. The experimenters left the room, but
could see the participants through the mirror.

When the questionnaires were completed by all members, the
family was given its first topic. The dilemma was read aloud.
Families were told that they should not worry about solving the
dilemma. Instead, they should discuss what the people in the story
should do and why. They were informed that they should continue
discussing until notified that 10 minutes had elapsed. Location of
the camera and the microphone was explained.

While the families were being taped, questionnaires were
reviewed for any missing or unclear data. When necessary, family
members were asked separately for clarification of questionnaire
data after the taping was completed.

RESULTS

Before analyzing the data to answer the questions under investigation, an analysis was conducted to determine whether gender
or the interaction of gender and maturity had an effect on cognitive ability. The purpose of this analysis was to identify sources of
variability that might provide alternative explanations for results.

It was found, using a 2(gender) x 2(maturity) ANOVA, that mature adolescents scored significantly higher on the test of cognitive
ability (GALT) than did younger adolescents, $F(1,20) = 16.57, p <$
.001. This effect of age was, of course, expected. The difference
between means of males ($M = 5.00$) and females ($M = 4.67$) in the
young group was slight. The difference in means in the mature
group was greater, but no effect of gender and no interaction effect
was obtained (mature males $M = 10.67$, mature females $M = 7.67$).

Are Adolescents', Fathers', or Mothers' Perceptions of the Family Affected by Either Maturity or Gender of Adolescent?

As can be seen in table 1, adolescents reported less positive feelings about the family environment than did fathers and mothers.
Males were generally less positive than females, and mature males
were the least positive group. The presence of a mature male
seemed to adversely affect mothers' scores; otherwise it seemed
that the presence of a young female was associated with less positive perceptions of both fathers and mothers. It should be noted

Table 1

Family Life Questionnaire Mean Scores of Adolescents,
Fathers, and Mothers Grouped by Gender
and Maturity of Adolescent

GROUP	ADOLESCENT	FATHER	MOTHER*
Young Female	73.00	70.33	70.83
Mature Female	70.67	77.50	77.33
Young Male	70.00	72.67	77.33
Mature Male	65.83	72.33	68.67

*Gender X Maturity, $F(1, 20) = 4.93, p < .04$.

that the only significant difference found in means was in mothers'
scores when gender and maturity both were considered.

The possible range of scores on the FLQ is 24 to 96. Mean
scores ranging from 65.83 to 77.50 would indicate that most perceptions of families were mildly positive.

Is the Observed Affective Quality of Family Interaction Affected by Either Gender or Maturity of Adolescent?

The effect of gender of adolescent was statistically significant,
$F(1,20) = 3.09, p < .05$, but maturity of adolescent had no effect.
Families with male adolescents exhibited more positive interaction
whereas families with females (particularly young females) exhibited the least positive interaction (see table 2).

Table 2

Mean Scores on Observed Affective Quality When Families
Are Grouped by Gender and Maturity of Adolescents

GROUP	OBSERVED POSITIVENESS*
Young Female	.91
Mature Female	1.18
Young Male	1.32
Mature Male	1.54

*There was an effect of gender that was significant at .05, $F(1, 20) = 3.09, p < .0504$.

Is There An Association Between Adolescents' Cognitive Ability and (a) Adolescent's, Mother's, or Father's Perceptions of the Family or (b) the Observed Quality of Family Interaction?

Examining correlations between adolescents' GALT scores and
perceptions of the family, it was found that although the relation

was small and was not statistically significant, an increase in
adolescent cognitive ability appeared to be associated with a
decrease in the adolescent's and the mother's perceptions of family harmony (see table 3). Fathers' perceptions of families were es-
sentially not related to adolescent cognitive ability. Likewise,
there was no relation between adolescent GALT scores and scores
derived from observations of family interactions. With a larger
sample, two of these correlations would have been statistically significant (see note at the end of table 3). As is, these data are only
suggestive of a factor that may influence perceptions of families.

Table 3

Correlations of Adolescent GALT Scores with Scores
on Perceptions of Families and Observed Effect in Families

QUALITY SCORES	ADOLESCENT GALT SCORES
Perceptions of Adolescents FLQ (n = 24)	−.385
Perceptions of Fathers FLQ (n = 24)	−.166
Perceptions of Mothers FLQ (n = 24)	−.385
Observed Effect	.185

Note: None of these correlations were statistically significant. Power was 61%; in order to have an
acceptable level of power (approximately 80%), a sample size of 40 would be required (Cohen, 1977);
however, if the n were increased by 3 in this sample, the correlations of .385 would be significant. The
lack of power is a problem in all of these analyses as it is in many observational studies.

*What Is the Relative Importance of Maturity, Gender, and Cog-
nitive Ability of Adolescents on Family Members' Perceptions of
the Family and Affective Quality of Observed Interaction?*
Stepwise multiple regression was used to examine the relative
importance of maturity, gender, and cognitive ability for understanding variability in perception of the family and observed interaction. Although it is recognized that multiple regression does not
provide an adequate test of relative importance, it is an acceptable
first step. One regression equation was calculated for each of four
criterion variables: adolescents' perceptions of family, fathers' perceptions of families, mothers' perceptions of families, and affective quality of observed interaction. In two of the four analyses
(fathers' perceptions and observed interaction), no predictor met
the criteria for inclusion in an equation. In the other two analyses
(adolescents' perceptions and mothers' perceptions), only one variable was selected for entry: adolescent cognitive ability. In the
analysis of adolescents' perceptions, the results approached sig-

nificance, $R^2 = .148, p < .06$. The analysis of mothers' perceptions yielded less significant results, $R^2 = .122, p < .10$. Even though these results were not significant, they support the suggestion that cognitive ability may be an important contributor to our understanding of adolescents' and mothers' perceptions of families.

DISCUSSION

The purpose of this study was to investigate the relation between maturity and cognitive abilities of adolescents and both perceptions of families and observed affective quality of family interaction. Results are discussed in broad categories of findings.

Perceptions of Families

Perceptions of families were quite variable across family types and family members. Male adolescents were less positive than female adolescents; mature male adolescents were the least positive of any group. However, parents in families with a young female were least positive in their perceptions except for mothers in families with an older male adolescent.

Steinberg and Hill (1978) and Steinberg (1981) found a change from difficult interaction to easier, more positive interaction with mothers as adolescent males matured. The present results support Steinberg's finding in that interaction was most positive in families with older male adolescents. However, mothers in this study *perceived* their families less positively when their sons were older. Likewise, older sons had the lowest scores on perceptions of positive qualities in families.

Cognitive ability of adolescents was associated with both adolescents' and mothers' perceptions of families, with an increase in the cognitive ability of these adolescents associated with a decrease in positive perceptions of families. Fathers' perceptions were unrelated to cognitive ability of adolescents. Steinberg and Hill (1978) and Steinberg (1981) had reported that there was no change in father-son interaction as sons progressed through adolescence; sons simply did not challenge fathers as they interacted with them. If sons are suppressing a desire to challenge fathers, this may be a source of decreased positive perceptions of families on the part of adolescent males as they mature.

Observations of Families

In observations of families, frequency of positive nonverbal affective cues was associated with both gender and maturity of adolescents; younger females were most responsible for the gender effect. It should be noted that a low score on affective quality does not necessarily mean that interaction in a family was negative. Instead, because so little negative affect was found in these families, a low score should be interpreted as neutral affect. Papini and Datan (1983) also found that a decrease in positive affect did not mean that affect was negative.

Although there was no significant effect of adolescent maturity on observed family interaction, the trend as seen in the means is supportive of Steinberg's (1981) finding that interaction becomes less difficult as sons get older. Positive nonverbal cues were most frequent in families with older sons.

Relative Importance of Gender, Age, and Cognitive Ability

When the relative importance of gender, age, and cognitive ability were examined, results were only suggestive. The finding, albeit not statistically significant, that only adolescent cognitive ability was selected for entry into equations associated with mothers' and adolescents' perceptions is of interest. In previous studies, it has appeared that maturity (age) was more responsible than cognitive ability for the quality of interaction between parents and adolescents. This may be true for observed interactions, but it is suggested in these results that perceptions may be another matter.

SUMMARY AND CONCLUSIONS

It has been predicted that the transition to formal operations would be associated with less positive perceptions of families and would contribute to overall less positive behaviors in interaction. The findings of this study indicate that there may very well be an association between maturity and cognitive ability and perceptions of families, but not between cognitive ability and interaction behaviors in families when interaction is measured as observed quality of affect.

Except for mothers with mature male adolescents, both parents' perceptions of families were least positive when the target child was a young female. Also, although the effect was not great, when affect was scored from observations of families, more positive nonverbal cues were found in families with male adolescents. Families with female adolescents were more neutral than positive in their affective cues.

The results of this study support the findings of a growing number of researchers (Adams and Jones, 1982; Hill and Palmquist, 1978; Jacob, 1974; Riley et al., 1984; Steinberg, 1981; Steinberg and Hill, 1978) that parent/adolescent relationships change during the years that adolescents experience puberty. The cause of the change is unknown. Adams and Jones (1982) and Riley et al. (1984) have argued that when parental expectations are not met when a child reaches adolescence, parents increase rejection behaviors, which in turn cause a change in adolescent self-consciousness behaviors. Others (Baumrind, 1968; Hill and Palmquist, 1978) have suggested that cognitive change in the adolescent creates a difference in parent/adolescent interaction that can result in conflict. Investigating such a possibility, Steinberg and Hill (1978) and Steinberg (1981) found that it was pubertal change and not cognitive change that was associated with change in the parent/adolescent relationship. In contrast, there is the suggestion in the results of this study that cognitive change may be an important contributor to change in parent/adolescent relationships.

Additional investigation of these developmental changes appears warranted. However, to adequately test the relative effects of cognitive ability and maturity, greater variability in combinations of maturity and cognitive ability would be required; perhaps most importantly, one would need to include cognitively precocious early puberty adolescents and cognitively delayed late puberty adolescents. Also, the inclusion of a variety of indicators of parent/adolescent relationships would be desirable.

The findings of this study indicate that the methodology used to study parent/adolescent relationships may affect the outcome. For example, adolescent perceptions of families became less positive as they matured with the least positive perceptions of families being those of older males. Also, parents in families with older adolescent males were some of the least positive in their perceptions of families. Yet, observed affect in these families was the most positive. It may be that perceptions and nonverbal, affective behaviors respond to change agents at different rates so that this result of most positive interaction could be found in families with less positive perceptions. Or it may be that this result is a methodological artifact. In either case, it is a finding that warrants additional investigation.

Finally, one finding that has implications for practitioners is that mothers and adolescents were more affected by each other than were fathers and adolescents. Indeed, fathers seemed to affect their families but not be affected by them. More investigation of this result is needed because of its significant implications for family-life educators and for family therapists.

REFERENCES

Adams, G. R., & Jones, R. M. Adolescent egocentrism: Exploration into possible contributions of parent-child relations. *Journal of Youth and Adolescence*, 1982, *11*, 25-31.

Bart, W. Construction and validation of formal reasoning instruments. *Psychology Reports*, 1972, *30*, 663-670.

Baumrind, D. Authoritarian vs. authoritative parental control. *Adolescence*, 1968, *3*, 255-272.

Burney, G. M. *The construction and validation of an objective formal reasoning instrument.* Doctoral dissertation, University of Northern Colorado, 1974.

Cohen, J. *Statistical power analysis for the behavioral sciences* (Rev. ed.). New York: Academic, 1977.

Collins, J. D. *The effects of the conjugal relationship modification method on marital communication and adjustment.* Doctoral dissertation, The Pennsylvania State University, 1971.

Elder, G. H., Jr. Parental power legitimation and its effects on the adolescent. *Sociometry*, 1963, *25*, 50-65.

Elkind, D. Egocentrism in adolescence. *Child Development*, 1967, *38*, 1025-1034.

Ely, A. L. *Efficacy of training in conjugal therapy.* Doctoral dissertation, Rutgers University, 1970.

Ginsberg, B. G. *Parent-adolescent relationship development: A therapeutic and preventive mental health program.* Doctoral dissertation, The Pennsylvania State University, 1971.

Gottman, J. M. *Marital interaction: Experimental investigations.* New York: Academic, 1979.

Grotevant, H. D., & Cooper, C. R. (Eds.). *Adolescent development in the family: New directions for child development 22.* San Francisco: Jossey-Bass, 1983.

Guerney, B. G. *Relationship enhancement.* San Francisco: Jossey-Bass, 1977.

Hill, J. P., & Palmquist, W. J. Social cognition and social relations in early adolescence. *International Journal of Behavioral Development*, 1978, *1*, 1-36.

Jacob, T. Patterns of family conflict and dominance as a function of age and social class. *Developmental Psychology*, 1974, *10*, 1-12.

Johnson, S. M., & Bolstad, O. D. 1973 Methodological issues in naturalistic observation: Some problems and solutions for field research. In L. A. Hamolyni, L. C. Handy & E. J. Mask (Eds.), *Behavior change*. Champaign, IL: Research Press.

Katchadourian, H. *The biology of adolescence*. San Francisco: W. H. Freeman, 1977.

Kohlberg, L. *The development of modes of moral thinking and choice in the years 10 to 16*. Doctoral dissertation, University of Chicago, 1958.

Lapsley, D. K., Milstead, M., & Quintana, S. M. Adolescent egocentrism and formal operations: Tests of a theoretical assumption. *Developmental Psychology*, 1986, *22*, 800-807.

Lawson, A. E. The development and validation of a classroom test of formal reasoning. *Journal of Research in Science Teaching*, 1978, *15*, 11-24.

Longeot, F. Analyse statistique do trois test genetiques collectits. *Bulletin de l'Institut National D'Etude*, 1965, *20*(4), 219-237.

Marshall, W. A., & Tanner, J. M. 1969 Variations in the pattern of pubertal changes in girls. *Archives of Disease in Childhood*, 1969, *44*, 291-303.

Marshall, W. A., & Tanner, J. M. Variations in the pattern of pubertal changes in boys. *Archives of Disease in Childhood*, 1970, *45*, 13-23.

Montemayer, R. Parents and adolescents in conflict: All families some of the time, some families most of the time. *Journal of Early Adolescence*, 1983, 3, 83-103.

Montemayer, R. Family variation in parent-adolescent storm and stress. *Journal of Adolescent Research*, 1986, 1, 15-31.

Olson, D. H., & Ryder, R. G. Inventory of marital conflicts. *Journal of Marriage and the Family*, 1970, *32*, 443-448.

Papini, D. R., & Datan, N. *The transitions into adolescence: An interactional perspective*. Paper presented at the biennial meetings of the Society for Research in Child Development, Detroit, MI, 1983.

Papini, D. R., & Sebby, R. A. Adolescent pubertal status and affective family relationships: A multivariate assessment. *Journal of Youth and Adolescence*, 1987, 16, 1-15.

Patterson, G. R. *Coercive family process*. Eugene, OR: Castalia Publishing, 1982.

Rallings, E. M. Problems of communication in family living. *The Family Coordinator*, 1969, *18*, 289-291.

Rappaport, A. F. Conjugal relationship enhancement program. In D. H. Olson (Ed.), *Treating relationships*. Lake Mills, IA: Graphic, 1976.

Rausch, H. L., Barry, W. A., Hertel, R. K., & Swain, M. A. *Communication, conflict, and marriage*. San Francisco: Jossey-Bass, 1974.

Raven, R. J. The development of a test of Piaget's logical operations. *Science Education*, 1973, *57*, 33-40.

Riley, T., Adams, G. R., & Nielsen, E. Adolescent egocentrism: The association among imaginary audience behavior, cognitive development, and parental support and rejection. *Journal of Youth and Adolescence*, 1984, *13*, 401-417.

Roadrangka, V., Yeany, R. H., & Padilla, M. J. *Group test of logical thinking.* Unpublished manuscript, University of Georgia, Department of Science Education, 1982.

Roadrangka, V., Yeany, R. H., & Padilla, M. J. *The construction and validation of group assessment of logical thinking (GALT).* Paper presented at the annual meeting of the National Association for Research in Science Teaching, Dallas, TX, 1983.

Rowell, J. A., & Hoffman, P. J. Group test for distinguishing formal from concrete thinkers. *Journal of Research in Science Teaching*, 1975, *12*, 157-164.

Steinberg, L. D. Transformations in family relations at puberty. *Developmental Psychology*, 1981, *47*, 833-840.

Steinberg, L. D., & Hill, J. P. Patterns of family interaction as a function of age, the onset of puberty, and formal thinking. *Developmental Psychology*, 1978, *14*, 683-684.

Steiner, G. J. Parent-teen education: An exercise in communication. *The Family Coordinator*, 1970, *19*, 213-218.

Stone, C. L. Family recreation: A parental dilemma. *Family Life Coordinator*, 1963, *12*, 85-87.

Tobin, K. G., & Capie, W. *The development and validation of a group test of logical thinking.* A paper presented at the annual meeting of the American Educational Research Association, Boston, MA, 1980.

Wampler, K. S., & Sprenkle, D. H. The minnesota couple communication program: A follow-up study. *Journal of Marriage and the Family*, 1980, *42*, 577-584.

Weiss, R. L., Hops, H., & Patterson, G. R. A framework for conceptualizing marital conflict: A technology for altering it, some data for evaluating it. In L. A. Hamerlynck, L. C. Handy & E. J. Mash (Eds.), *Behavior change.* Champaign, IL: Research Press, 1973.

Yeany, R. H., Yap, K. C., & Padilla, M. J. Analyzing hierarchical relationships among modes of cognitive reasoning and integrated science process skills. *Journal of Research in Science Teaching*, 1986, *3*, 277-291.

Yourglich, A. Explorations in sociological study of sibling systems. Family *Life Coordinator*, 1964, *13*, 91-94.

In recent years parent-child research has begun to reflect the impact of family systems theory. This paper describes a family assessment device that attempts to address and incorporate some of the complexities of systems-oriented family research. The series of self-report instruments are administered to several family members and include multidimension measurement of various family relational processes. A contrasting family case study analysis is used to illustrate the utility of such a design in better understanding individual and family functioning.

10

The Analysis of Family and Parent-Child Relations in a Systems-Oriented Perspective

KLAUS A. SCHNEEWIND

INTRODUCTION

There has been a remarkable shift in the analysis of parent-child relations in recent years, stemming from a changed perspective on theoretical, methodological, and applied aspects in the field of psychological family research. Concerning *theory*, a family systems approach has become a major conceptual tool emphasizing the wholeness, organization, and relationships of the family, seen as a unity of codeveloping persons in context (e.g., Schneewind, 1987a; Steinglass, 1987; Thomas and Wilcox, 1987). In *methodology* as well, systems thinking has become rather influential as can be seen, for instance, in Cromwell and Peterson's (1983) multisystem-multimethod framework that permits the distinction between different *systems levels* (i.e., individual, dyadic, and family system) and different *assessment methods* (i.e., self-reports, behavior observations, and therapist ratings). Regarding the professional *application* of family

Klaus A. Schneewind • Department of Psychology, University of Munich, West Germany.

related knowledge, a host of methods and techniques for intervention in clinical and psychoeducational contexts using a systems approach has also been developed in recent years (e.g., Piercy, Sprenkle et al., 1986; Sherman and Fredman, 1986).

When conceiving of the family as a unity of codeveloping persons in context, the term *context* may take on different meanings. First, this term may designate the *intrafamilial context*, comprising the material and social conditions that directly influence the ongoing transactions within the family. Thus, the term *intrafamilial context* largely parallels what Bronfenbrenner (1979) has called a microsystem. Second, one can also speak of *extrafamilial context*, which puts the family in a larger socioecological framework. The family's ecology can be broken down into different systems levels. This has been proposed in Bronfenbrenner's (1979, 1986) ecosystem approach to human development and family life, leading to such concepts as meso-, exo-, and macrosystem. The *extrafamilial context* can thus be seen as the *opportunity structure* existing outside of the family that can exert a direct or indirect influence on the quality of family life. Although much conceptual and empirical progress in linking together extra- and intrafamilial aspects of the family's life space has been made, research results, though generally supporting the hypothesis of an interrelation of extra-and intrafamilial factors, are not as convincing as one would have expected in the beginning (e.g., Bronfenbrenner, 1986; Schneewind, in press).

In this paper, focus will not be placed on the interplay of extra- and intrafamilial influences on the family, but, rather, a closer look at a certain aspect of the intrafamilial context, namely the interpersonal relationships within the family system, will be made. First, an assessment device for measuring family relations on different systems levels will be briefly outlined. Second, based on a contrasting family case study approach, the usefulness of some of the assessment tools will be illustrated. Third, the strengths and weaknesses of this approach will be discussed along with some guidelines for further research.

THE FAMILY-DIAGNOSTIC-TEST-SYSTEM (FDTS)

Assessment of the various relationship constellations within the family can be accomplished by using different data sources. In a frequently cited article, Cromwell et al. (1976) suggested distinguishing between an insider and an outsider perspective. Insiders are all members of the family, who experience how they themselves and others relate to the various persons making up the family system. In contrast, outsiders are all persons (friends, colleagues, clergymen, professionals, etc.) who more or less know the family, which allows them to form an impression of the family and its members. Another important distinction provided by Cromwell et al. (1976) concerns the quality of data that can be gathered when studying family units. The data are either subjective in nature (i.e., self-reports, ratings) or they refer to objective aspects of family life (e.g., behavioral observations).

Beyond this twofold classification scheme, there are several other dimensions that can serve the purpose of cataloging instruments of family diagnosis. We shall only name two that are of immediate importance in the present context. First, family diagnosis can be further distinguished according to different family system levels (i.e., the entire family system, various family subsystems like the marital, parent-child, and sibling subsystems, the intrapsychic system) (Cromwell and Peterson, 1983). Second, family diagnosis can be based on either a uni- or multidimensional approach in measuring family relations.

With reference to the above fourfold classification scheme, the family assessment device to be described in this paper utilizes (a) an insider perspective using (b) subjective self-report data that refer to (c) various family systems levels and allow for a (d) multidimensional measurement of family relations constructs. The instrument has been given the name *Family-Diagnostic-Test-System* (FDTS) and has been described elsewhere in more detail (cf. Schneewind, 1987b; Schneewind et al., 1985).

The FDTS consists of a set of a total of 29 questionnaires, measuring between 4 and 13 relationship constructs depending on the relationship constellation that is the focus of a particular test. Special attention has been given to the parent-child *subsystem* that was broken down into four parent-child configurations (namely, the mother-son, mother-daughter, father-son, and father-daughter dyads). In each dyad the parent-child relationship was assessed from the perspective of the parent and the corresponding perspective of the child, thus yielding eight different subjective views of those involved in a dyadic parent-child relationship. Furthermore, we distinguished between three different relational aspects of the parent-child subsystem. These are: (a) *parent-child attitudes*, i.e., cognitions held by a particular parent or child concerning the quality of their specific relationship (permissiveness, rejection, openness, etc.); (b) *parent-child goals*, i.e., cognitions held by a particular parent or child concerning the goals that parents set for their children (achievement orientation, conformity, self-responsibility, etc.); (c) *parent-child behavior*, i.e., cognitions by a particular parent or child with respect to concrete verbal and nonverbal behaviors of the parent toward the child (reward, punishment, expression of anger, etc.). Given the three relational aspects, the four parent-child configurations, and the two perspectives within each of these configurations--all tests devised for the parent-child subsystem add up to a total of 24.

In addition to the four dyadic constellations of the parent-child subsystem, the *marital subsystem* was also considered as a relationship dyad. The corresponding questionnaires measure four constructs of perceived marital interaction (i.e., "tenderness," "conflict," "resignation," and "suppression") from both the wife's and the husband's point of view.

Finally, on the *family system* level, the Family Environment Scale (FES), developed by Moos and his associates (cf. Moos, 1974; Moos and Moos, 1986), was adapted for use in German-speaking countries (cf. Schneewind, 1987c; Schneewind et al., 1985). The FES consists of 10 subscales measuring various aspects of relationship, personal growth, and system maintenance dimensions (e.g., "cohesion," "independence," "control"). Again, the German FES was devised to assess the perceived family climate from the perspective of both parents and the child, which resulted in three conceptually equivalent instruments. The various subsets of tests that constitute the total FDTS were carefully analyzed according to usual psychometric standards, and they yield sufficient reliabilities and factorially valid scales. Normative data as well as information on additional validity checks are available based on a representative sample of 570 German families with children and adolescents aged 9 to 14 (cf. Schneewind et al., 1985).

The FDTS is designed as a modular test system, which means the subtests can be used separately according to the user's special interests, thus providing the opportunity of gradually expanding diagnostic information when additional data seems to be desirable. Additionally, in family research studies the FDTS can be and is being used as a diagnostic tool in various settings where family counseling and therapy is practiced (e.g., child guidance clinics, institutions of child psychiatry) and in evaluation studies on preventive and interventive programs for the family (e.g., parent-child training programs, divorce counseling programs).

INTRAFAMILIAL RELATIONSHIP SYSTEMS: A CONTRASTING FAMILY CASE STUDY

In the following, a subset of the various FDTS modules will be described along with additional data to illustrate its applicability for a systems-oriented analysis of parent-child relations. For the purpose of illustration, a contrasting family case study approach will be used. In this approach, two otherwise comparable families, but showing marked differences concerning their intrafamilial relationships on the family systems level, will be analyzed with respect to more detailed aspects on dyadic and intrapsychic subsystems. The main hypothesis of this approach is that differences in the structure of relationships manifest themselves on the various levels of the family system and its subsystems. Furthermore, it is hypothesized that the particular pattern of relationship constructs within a given family can be meaningfully linked across systems levels and, at the same time, aid in a more valid differential family diagnosis.

The analysis includes two families, Family B and Family R, who at first glance appear to be quite similar in many ways. Both families have a single son, age 9 in the 4th grade, and both sons appear to be physically and mentally healthy. Both families live in comparable southwest German cities of about 30,000 inhabitants with appropriate infrastructural facilities. They both own their own homes and belong to the upper middle class. The fathers work in middle management positions while the mothers do not work outside of the house. In all, Family B and R appear to be highly comparable regarding objective criteria of family structure, material living conditions, and the extrafamilial ecology.

Perceived Relationships on the Family Systems Level

Despite the socioecological similarities of both families, there are equally striking differences in the pattern of intrafamilial relationships on the family systems level. This is seen by looking at the perceived family climate data of both families as measured by the German FES. Figure 1 shows the family climate profile for Family B (unbroken line) and Family R (broken line) in sten-scale units (mean and standard deviation of the sten-scale: $X = 5,5$ and $s = 2,0$). The profiles are based on aggregated data, i.e., the individual scores were averaged across all three family members (mother, father, and son).

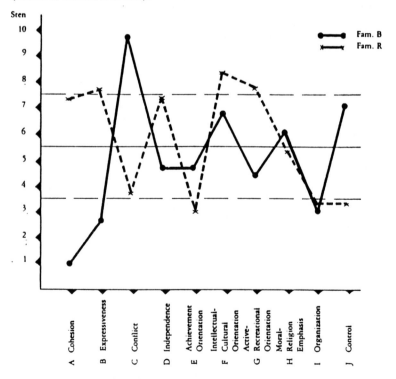

Figure 1. Family Climate Profiles of Two Contrasting Families (Aggregated Data).

On inspection of figure 1 it can easily be seen that the two family profiles are quite dissimilar in shape. When using the more objective measure of profile pattern similarity (cf. Cattell, 1949; Cattell et al., 1966), this visual impression is substantiated with a highly significant $r_p = -.74$. Thus there is a strong indication that Family B and R perceive their family climate quite differently.

Family B's profile is characterized especially by its salient values on the relationship dimensions. There is an extremely low level of cohesion (scale A) along with a high amount of conflict (scale C) and, simultaneously, a low degree of expressiveness (scale B) and low family organization (scale I). In addition, the amount of mutual control (scale J) is rather high, whereas the two scales that are the main indicators of a stimulating family climate (scale F and G) are on a medium level. Seen as a whole, Family B's FES profile gives the impression of a highly conflict-laden and emotionally negative family atmosphere, coupled with a high degree of intrafamilial control and sanctions.

In contrast, Family R shows a pattern of relationship dimensions that seems to signify a rather satisfactory family life. There is a high degree of family solidarity (scale A), spontaneity and expressiveness of feelings (scale B), and a low conflict-proneness (scale C). The corresponding scale value on family organization (scale I) is rather low. But, unlike Family B, this appears to be less a sign of disturbed intrafamilial communication than an expression of Family R's flexible and undogmatic handling of family rules (cf. scale J). Furthermore, Family R seems to foster personal independence (scale D) as a major value, whereas achievement orientation (scale E) plays a minor role. This again can be interpreted as a rather person-oriented and adaptable family lifestyle. Finally, scores on the intellectual-cultural and active-recreational dimension (scale F and G) are well above average and thus indicative of an active, open, and stimulating family life. In sum, from Family R's profile a high level of positive emotionality, activity, and liveliness can be inferred, along with flexible enforcement of family rules that give the individual family member a high degree of freedom of movement.

Perceived Relationships on the Marital Subsystems Level

So far the aggregated family climate data has been used to ar-
rive at an overall picture of both families' relationship structure.
Next, the marital subsystem will be explored in more detail to see
how the husbands and wives of both families perceive their
relationship. The marital relationship questionnaire (MRQ)
module from the FDTS will be used. This instrument consists of
48 items measuring four factorially derived aspects of the marital
relationship from both the husband's and the wife's perspective.
The four scales are (a) *tenderness*: "In our marriage I enjoy being
alone with my partner"; (b) *conflict*: "There are lots of fights and
arguments in our marriage"; (c) *dissatisfaction*: "In our marriage I
miss any stimulation and change"; (d) *suppression*: "In our marriage I give in just for the sake of peace." The scale reliabilities
range between $r_{tt} = .88$ and $r_{tt} = .98$.

In figure 2 the MRQ data are presented for Mr. and Mrs. B and
for Mr. and Mrs. R, respectively. As with the FES data, the raw
scores were transformed to a sten-scale. In addition, the individual profiles were compared using Cattell's r_p coefficient (cf.
Cattell, 1949).

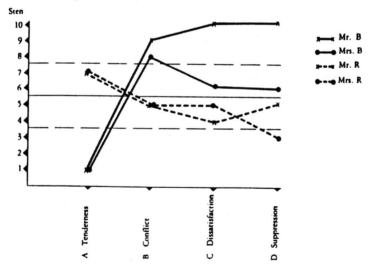

Figure 2. Marital Relationship Profiles for Two Contrasting Families.

The profile pattern of Mr. and Mrs. R shows a similarity of $r_p =$ .67 ($p < .05$), whereas Mr. and Mrs. B achieve a nonsignificant r_p = -.10, mostly due to differences on the dissatisfaction (scale C) and suppression (scale D) scales. Concerning the pattern similarity across the two families, Mr. B's profile is more dissimilar to Mr. and Mrs. R's profile (r_p = -.62 and -.65, $p < .01$) than is Mrs. B's profile to both spouses of Family R (r_p = -.30 and - .34, $p < .05$).

Comparing the profiles of figure 2 on a subscale level, it can be seen that Mr. and Mrs. R both have an elevated score on the tenderness scale (scale A), whereas the scores on the remaining subscales tend to be in the medium range. The exception is Mrs. R, who has a somewhat lower score on the suppression scale (scale D). Both marital partners in Family R seem to experience an emotionally stable and satisfying relationship without much exaggeration in either direction of the four relationship constructs measured by the MRQ.

In contrast, Mr. and Mrs. B perceive their relationship as extremely strained. Their tenderness score (scale A) is down to a minimum, and both experience a rather high level of conflict (scale B) in their relationship. On the dissatisfaction and suppression subscales (scales C and D), Mr. B has an extremely high score on both scales, whereas the corresponding scores of his wife remain on a medium level. This indicates that Mr. B is in an even more distressed situation than Mrs. B.

Further confirmation of these rather drastic family differences on the marital subsystems level comes from diagnostic data that have been gathered in addition to the MRQ scales. Using a 12-item personality rating system (PRS), described elsewhere in greater detail (cf. Schneewind, 1982), a personality dissatisfaction score was developed.

Both partners of the marital dyad judge their spouse's personality on the PRS according to two instructions. First, they are asked to rate their partner's personality as they think it really is (real partner personality). Second, both partners use the same procedure to rate the personality of their spouses as they would like it to be (ideal partner personality). It can be assumed that the higher the discrepancies between the real and ideal personality ratings, the higher the amount of dissatisfaction with the corresponding partner.

Figure 3 illustrates the personality dissatisfaction scores for both marital partners of Family B and Family R. The data refer to four factorially derived personality dimensions, each of which was measured by three bipolar graphic rating scales using 7-point intervals. The three ratings of each personality dimension were averaged, yielding a score within the range of 0 (low personality dissatisfaction) and 6 (high personality dissatisfaction). In figure 3, w→h signifies the wife-husband relationship as seen from the wife's perspective, and hw refers to the corresponding personality dissatisfaction score from the husband's perspective.

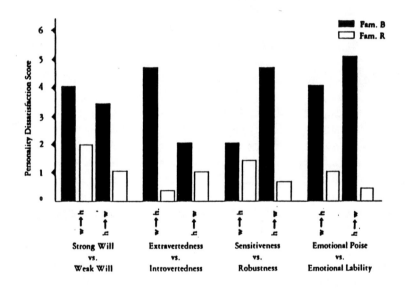

Figure 3. Personality Dissatisfaction Scores in Marital Relationship of Two Contrasting Families.

Although normative data are not available for the personality dissatisfaction score, it can easily be seen that marked differences exist between Family B (dark bars) and Family R (light bars). Across all four personality dimensions, Mr. B has an average personality dissatisfaction score of 3.75, with his wife being only slightly lower (3.67). In contrast, for Family R the amount of mutual personality dissatisfaction scores seems to be rather low, with an average score of .75 for Mr. B's dissatisfaction with his wife and a corresponding mean score of 1.17 for Mrs. R.

Thus, the data provide further support for the heavily distressed marital relationship of Mr. and Mrs. B. Moreover, while the picture appears to be quite balanced for Family R, some interesting differences for Family B on the four personality dimensions can be seen. Besides the fact that both partners seem to be especially annoyed by their spouse's emotional lability and strong will, Mrs. B complains more about her husband's withdrawn and closed attitude. This manifests itself in a personality dissatisfaction score of 4.67 on the extravertedness vs. intravertedness dimension, as opposed to her husband's corresponding score of 2.0. On the other hand, Mr. B is especially concerned about his wife's lack of sensitivity and understanding, as can be seen in his dissatisfaction score of 4.67 on the sensitiveness vs. robustness dimension. Mrs. B, on the other hand, has a much lower score of 2.0. These differences could be used as valuable diagnostic information by a marital counselor in case of an eventual intervention in the marital relationship system.

In any case, from the data obtained by the marital relationship questionnaire and the personality dissatisfaction analysis, it becomes quite evident that the marriage of Mr. and Mrs. B is experienced by both partners as a highly unrewarding, emotionally upsetting, and conflict-ridden relationship with a high degree of personal disrespect. Quite the opposite appears true for Mr. and Mrs. R. Although they do not view their marriage as being perfect, they both experience their relationship as predominantly rewarding and display a high degree of mutual personal acceptance.

Perceived Relationships on the Parent-Child Subsystems Level

Since space does not permit presentation of all the data on the parent-child subsystem, two sets of data will be presented to illustrate the parent-child relation from the parent's point of view.

As will be recalled, Family B and R both have 9-year-old sons. Theo B and Karl R are the target persons in the relationship analysis that follows. Data obtained from a parental attitude questionnaire (PAQ), which is part of the FDTS, will be presented first. The PAQ consists of 11 factor-analyzed scales to assess various attitudinal aspects that the parents hold with respect to a particular child. The PAQ contains up to 117 items, depending on which version of the parent-child constellation (e.g., mother-son, father-son, etc.) is used.

The descriptive levels and sample items for the PAQ scales for the mother-son and father-son version are (a) *permissiveness*: "It's all right with me if my son does not follow my directions"; (b) *self-criticism*: "I sometimes doubt whether I can handle my son the way I should"; (c) *authoritarian rigidity*: "What my son is allowed to do and not do depends solely on me"; (d) *overprotection*: "I protect my son from all adversities of life"; (e) *calm detachment*: "I avoid exploiting my son's weaknesses"; (f) *experimenting*: "In bringing up my son I often try something new"; (g) *parental disagreement*: "My husband/wife and I often differ on how to raise our son"; (h) *similarity*: "My son and I have much in common"; (i) *reliance on own parents' parenting style*: "I raise my son exactly the same way I was brought up"; (j) *inconsistency*: "After rewarding my son for something special he did, it may be that I do not mention it when he does it again"; (k) *intentional decision for the child*: "We deliberately decided when to have our son."

The scale reliabilities for the PAQ range between $r_{tt} = .81$ and $r_{tt} = .98$. (For further information concerning the validity of the PAQ see Schneewind et al., 1985).

Figure 4 shows the parent-child relationship data for both parents of Family B and R. Again, the raw scores were transformed in stens, which allow quantification of parental profiles within and between families via Cattell's (1949) pattern similarity coefficient, r_p.

When looking at the profile similarities within and between the families, it appears that when compared to completely unrelated profile patterns, Mr. and Mrs. B are only somewhat dissimilar in their profiles ($r_p = -.19$). Mr. and Mrs. R tend to be somewhat similar ($r_p = .12$), although both coefficients do not reach conventional levels of significance according to the tables provided by Horn (1961). When using parent-child relationship data it may be argued, however, that for the purpose of analyzing contrasting parenting styles it is more important to look at the profile similarities between families, especially with respect to same-sex comparisons. Here we find that both fathers, Mr. B and Mr. R, are quite dissimilar in their attitudes toward their sons ($r_p = -.43, p <$

.01), as are both mothers, whose profile patterns are only slightly less dissimilar ($r_p = -.38, p < .05$) than those of the fathers.

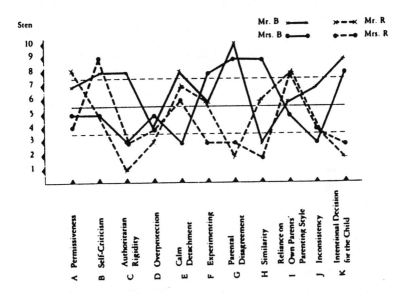

Figure 4. Parental Attitudes in Mother-Son and Father-Son Relationships of Two Contrasting Families.

It should be kept in mind, however, that pattern similarity coefficients provide only a summary statement of how close or how distant two profiles are. This necessitates a closer look at the various PAQ scales. Besides the fact that Theo B apparently was a "planned child" while Karl R was not (scale K), it can be seen that Theo B's parents have a lot of disagreement and conflict concerning their son's upbringing (scale G). This, in fact, is another indicator of Mr. and Mrs. B's strained relationship, which seemingly is not confined to their marital interaction but also generalized to an impaired coordination of their parental roles. Furthermore, it becomes apparent that Theo B's mother has a much less problematic relationship with her son than her husband. This can be inferred from Mr. B's elevated scores on the self-criticism (scale B), authoritarian rigidity (scale C), and inconsistency (scale J) scales. At the same time, Mr. B feels that his son does not have much in common with him (scale H), which can be interpreted as an indicator of emotional distance. Considering this scale configuration, it seems that the rather high scores on the calm detachment (scale E) and permissiveness (scale A) scales may be further cues of Mr. B's rather distant and uninterested attitude toward his son.

Contrary to her husband, Mrs. B appears to be more lenient (scale C) and consistent (scale J) in relation to her son. She also perceives him to be more like herself (scale H). Finally, Mrs. B seems to be more involved in issues concerning the upbringing of her son. This can be inferred from her rather salient scores on the calm detachment (scale E) and experimenting (scale F) scales.

In conclusion, two aspects become evident from a more detailed analysis of Mr. and Mrs. B's parental attitude profile. First, both parents show a high degree of discord regarding their son's upbringing. Second, in Mr. B's view there is a rather high amount of emotional distance while Mrs. B experiences an equally marked emotional closeness to their son.

The parental attitudes expressed by Karl R's parents are quite different. Here, both parents show a high degree of commonness and cooperation with respect to their son's upbringing (scale G). They also share the opinion that the way they are raising their son is rooted in their own upbringing (scale I). Furthermore, both parents agree in a basic unauthoritarian attitude toward their son (scale C), and they are also in accord concerning a below-average score on the overprotection (scale D) and an above-average score on the calm detachment (scale E) scales.

Despite these similarities there are also some remarkable attitudinal differences between Mr. and Mrs. R. Thus we find that in comparison to Mr. R, Mrs. R's relationship with her son is somewhat more troubled. She experiences more problems with her childrearing competence (scale B), and she describes herself as being less permissive toward her son (scale A). Finally, she reports fewer similarities with her son than Mr. B does (scale H).

In sum, both parents in Family R apparently have no problems synchronizing their parental roles. At the same time, they show a low degree of parental control and restrictiveness. Concerning emotional closeness, Mrs. R seems to perceive her relationship with her son as being somewhat more distant than does Mr. R.

In order to get some additional evidence on the quality of parent-child relations from the parents' point of view, an analysis of perceived personality dissatisfaction was carried out, similar to the marital subsystems level. The computational procedure was the same as described in the preceding section except that this time the personality dissatisfaction scores were obtained from both parents regarding their respective son. Figure 5 provides an impression of the results of this analysis. The ms and fs terms in figure 5 refer to the mothers' and fathers' personality dissatisfaction scores regarding their sons. The dark bars represent the data for Family B and the light bars those of Family R.

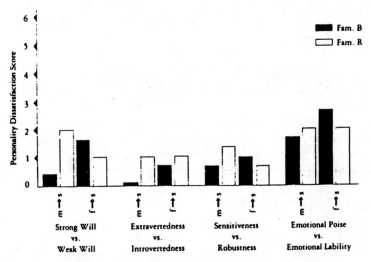

Figure 5. Personality Dissatisfaction Scores in Mother-Son and Father-Son Relationships of Two Contrasting Families.

Although normative data again is not available concerning the perceived personality dissatisfaction scores, it becomes quite evident that, on an average, the magnitude of the scores is rather small. Besides the fact that both sets of parents seem to be most challenged by their sons' uneven temper, it should also be noted that there are consistent differences within and between families. While in Family B Mrs. B is clearly less critical of her son than her husband (Mrs. B's mean personality dissatisfaction score is 0.75 as opposed to Mr. B's corresponding score of 1.50), the reverse is true for Family R (Mrs. R's score is 1.58, Mr. R's score

is 1.00). This is in accordance with the data stemming from the
PAQ analysis. It will be recalled that Mrs. B reported more closeness to her son than Mr. B, whereas in Family R it was Mr. R who
felt closer to his son than did his wife.

Although these differences should not be overstated, the data
nevertheless seem to indicate that in view of Mr. and Mrs. B's
highly strained marital relationship, Mrs. B and her son Theo form
a coalition against Mr. B. Presuming that this coalition reflects a
"rigid triangle" (cf. Minuchin et al., 1978), this may have adverse
effects on Theo's personality development. In this context it
might be of special importance that Theo's father, although
nominally present, appears to be psychologically absent. According to Lamb (1977), this situation might be especially damaging
for sons who are in need of a positive male model.

For Karl R, one would not expect similar problems. His parents
live in a seemingly untroubled marital relationship, and the data
suggest that Karl's father is psychologically more available than
his mother. This might even facilitate Mr. R's accessibility as a
male model. We shall not explore this in greater detail, but it
should be mentioned that these hypotheses receive additional support from data that due to space limits cannot be reported in the
present context.

The Intrapsychic Systems Level

Starting from the family systems level we have seen that a more
fine-grained analysis of perceived intrafamilial relationships on
the marital and parent-child subsystems level has led us to a better
understanding of the two contrasting families. If the data
presented thus far is sufficiently consistent and stable, it might be
argued that the kind of relationships experienced in a particular
family will be reflected in the personality level as well. This
should be especially true for the personality structure of the two
boys coming from different family relationship backgrounds, since
it may be assumed that they are still in their formative period of
personality development. Thus the psychological functioning of
Theo B and Karl R on the intrapsychic or personality level will be
briefly explored.

For the purpose of personality assessment, a German multidimensional personality questionnaire, especially designed for
children and adolescents ages 9 to 14 was administered to both

boys (cf. Seitz and Rausche, 1976). The questionnaire consists of
15 factor-analytically confirmed scales that are subdivided in three
categories, i.e., *behavioral styles* (e.g., emotional irritability), *motives* (e.g., aggressive self-assertiveness), and *self-concept components* (e.g., self-confidence). For information concerning the
psychometric properties, see the test manual (cf. Seitz and Rausche, 1976).

Figure 6 depicts the results of the personality analysis for Theo
B and Karl R. Again, the raw scores of the 15 scales were transformed to sten-scale units and then connected to form a personality profile.

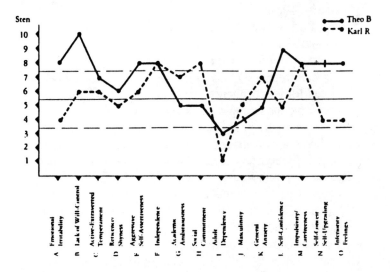

Figure 6. Personality Profiles of Sons Coming from Two Contrasting Families.

In order to gain an overall quantitative term of Theo's and
Karl's profile similarity, Cattell's (1949) r_p coefficient was used
again. The similarity of the two profiles turned out to be $r_p=.01$,
suggesting that they are virtually unrelated. On closer inspection
of figure 6, it can be seen that Theo B has a set of salient scores
that are remarkable in three respects. First, there are marked signs
of low ego-control as can be inferred from scales B ("lack of will-control"), F ("aggressive self-assertiveness"), and M ("impulsivity/carefreeness"). Second, he has rather extreme scores
indicative of a high degree of emotional lability and insecurity,

i.e., scale A ("emotional irritability") and scale O ("inferiority feelings"). Third, there are elevated scores on two self-concept components and one motive: scale L ("self-confidence"), N ("self-conceit/self-upgrading"), and F ("independence"). In light of the other two salient aspects of Theo's personality structure, this might be interpreted as a strategy of compensatory and offensive self-enhancement. At least the two personality aspects mentioned first, undercontrol and emotional lability, are consistent with empirical evidence from other studies showing that boys, in particular, suffer from marital discord or predivorce familial stress that often occurs a long time before family disruption (cf. Block et al., 1986; Emery, 1982).

In contrast, Karl R's personality profile does not show any extreme scores on the scales that are characteristics of Theo B's personality pattern except for scale F ("independence") and scale M ("impulsivity/carefreeness"). Concerning scale F it can be argued that Karl's need for independence is probably a cue to his active striving to preserve his freedom of movement (which is further substantiated by an extremely low score on the "adult dependency" scale) and not a means for upgrading his self. Furthermore, his need for independence does not appear to be asocial in nature as seen from Karl's high score on scale I ("social commitment"). With respect to scale M, where Karl also shares a high score with Theo, it should be noted that this score is not accompanied by high scores on scale B ("lack of will-control") and F ("aggressive self-assertiveness") as is the case with Theo. Thus it seems that Karl's impulsive and carefree behavior is less a sign of what Seitz and Rausche (1976:34) have called a "crude, go-getting way of self-assertion" but is rather an expression of a lighthearted and causal behavioral attitude.

In conclusion, we find signs of a far more problematic personality structure in the data for Theo B than for Karl R. It is also noteworthy that the personality differences between the two boys seem to be quite plausible in view of the differences that exist between both families regarding perceived family, marital, and parent-child relationships. A synopsis of all the data referring to the different systems levels reveals that Theo comes from a family background that is characterized by a high degree of negative emotionality, conflict, and mutual control. This is mainly due to a severely distressed marital relationship that also affects his parents' dysfunctional and antagonistic parenting style, leading to disputes, inconsistencies, and presumably to Theo's triangulation against his father. Although on theoretical grounds much needs to be done to explain in greater detail how the interplay of relationships at the different family systems levels concur in personality development, it might be speculated, from a social learning perspective, that Theo adopted his undercontrolled, emotionally insecure, and self-upgrading behavior from similar behaviors of his feuding parents.

In contrast, Karl R experiences an atmosphere of positive emotionality, openness, stimulation, and flexibility in his family that fits with the psychologically untroubled relationships on the marital and parent-child level. Here again it might be argued that Karl's intrafamilial social learning experiences have greatly contributed to his emotionally expressive, autonomous, and socially responsible behavior.

CONCLUSIONS

The quintessence of the present paper is that it seems worthwhile to analyze intrafamilial relationship contexts in greater detail if one is interested in a better understanding of individual functioning within the family. A contrasting family case study approach was used to illustrate this point, and it has been shown that it is possible to apply quite "traditional" methods of personality and relationship assessment within a family systems paradigm, although some may argue that the "new epistemology" stemming from systems thinking calls for a new and different methodology in studying family relations (cf. Gurman, 1983, who critically examines this argument). Within the present context it was seen that using self-report data, based on different data sources and on multidimensional personality and relationship constructs, can be helpful in analyzing the interrelatedness of the persons making up a family system. It was also demonstrated that the meaning of particular constructs will only become evident if consideration is given to how these constructs are embedded in the larger context of the perceived relationships being studied. This clearly calls for a configural analysis of relationship and personality data as it has been applied in the present contrasting family case study approach.

Although a contrasting family case study design appears to be suitable for illustrating the usefulness of a contextual analysis of intrafamilial relations, it should also be noted that, as with all case studies, the results can hardly be generalized to other families. Nevertheless, it is assumed that a contrasting family case study approach could be used to generate hypotheses that may lead to a typology of familial relationship constellations, including the various subsystems of the family. This typology might then be empirically tested on a sufficiently large sample of families. Even then, however, it might be difficult to generalize the results obtained from such typological studies, considering the number of parameters (e.g., phase of the family life cycle, transgenerational and subcultural norms, etc.) that might moderate the structure and meaning of relationships that are characteristic of a given family.

With respect to the present study it should be noted that the analysis was based on a cross-sectional design using self-reported relationship and personality data. This leaves quite a few questions unanswered. Among these, the following are especially pertinent. First, to what degree are the relationship structures transitory or stable in nature? This is an empirical question that can only be answered by studying the families over a longer period of time. Second, should the data that are exclusively based on self-report measures be validated using different data sources, e.g., behavioral data from independent observers? The additional use of data of this type is strongly advocated, particularly since there are quite a few instruments that seem to be suitable for this purpose (cf. Filsinger, 1983; Markman and Notarius, 1987). Nevertheless, it should be kept in mind that the use of self-report data will remain a special and indispensable route to the analysis of family systems aiming at the experiential level of those engaged in family interaction.

This leads to a final point concerning the interplay of experiential and behavioral assessments in the analysis of family transactions. It is quite apparent that this can only be done using real time process analyses based on sound theoretical and methodological reasoning (cf. Kaye, 1985). Recognizing this, it becomes even more evident that much needs to be done in the field of family systems research.

REFERENCES

Block, J. H., Block, J., & Gjerde, P. F. The personality of children prior to divorce: A prospective study. *Child Development*, 1986, *57*, 827-840.

Bronfenbrenner, J. *The ecology of human development*. Cambridge: Harvard University Press, 1979.

Bronfenbrenner, J. Ecology of the family as a context for human development. Research perspectives. *Developmental Psychology*, 1986, *22*, 723-742.

Cattell, R. B. Rp and other coefficients of pattern similarity. *Psychometrika*, 1949, *14*, 279-298.

Cattell, R. B., Coulter, M. A., & Tsujioka, B. The taxonometric recognition of types and functional emergents. In R. B. Cattell (Ed.), *Handbook of multivariate experimental psychology*. Chicago: Rand McNally, 1966.

Cromwell, R. E., Olson, H. D., & Fournier, D. G. Tolls and techniques for diagnosis and evaluation in marriage and family therapy. *Family Process*, 1976, *15*, 1-49.

Cromwell, R. E., & Peterson, G. W. Multisystem-multimethod family assessment in clinical contexts. *Family Process*, 1983, *22*, 147-163.

Emery, R. E. Interparental conflict and the children of discord and divorce. *Psychological Bulletin*, 1982, *92*, 310-330.

Filsinger, E. E., (Ed.). *Marriage and family assessment: A source book for family therapy*. Beverly Hills, CA: Sage, 1983.

Gurman, A. Family therapy research and the 'new epistemology'. *Journal of Marital and Family Therapy*, 1983, *9*, 227-234.

Horn, J. L. Significance tests for use with rp and related profile statistics. *Journal of Educational and Psychological Measurement*, 1961, *21*, 363-370.

Kaye, K. Toward a developmental psychology of the family. In L. L'Abate (Ed.), *The handbook of family psychology and therapy* Vol. 1. Homewood: Dorsey, 1985.

Lamb, M. E. The effects of divorce on children's personality development. *Journal of Divorce*, 1977, *2*, 163-174.

Markman, H. J., & Notarius, C. I. Coding marital and family interaction: current status. In T. Jacob (Ed.), *Family interaction and psychopathology: Theories, methods, and findings*. New York: Plenum, 1987.

Minuchin, S., Rosman, R. L., & Baker, L. *Psychosomatic families*. Cambridge: University of Cambridge Press, 1978.

Moos, R. H. Family Environment Scale (FES). Preliminary Manual (Social Ecology Laboratory, Department of Psychiatry). Palo Alto: Stanford University, 1974.

Moos, R. H., & Moos, B. S. *Family environment scale*. Manual (2nd ed.). Palo Alto: Consulting Psychologists Press, 1986.

Piercy, F. P., Sprenkle, D. H., & Associates *Family therapy sourcebook*. New York: Guilford, 1986.

Schneewind, K. A. *Persönlichkeitstheorien I (Personality Theories I)*. Darmstadt: Wissenschaftliche Buchgesellschaft, 1982.

Schneewind, K. A. Familienentwicklung (Family development). In R. Oerter & L. Montada (Eds.), *Entwicklungspsychologie (Developmental Psychology)*. München-Weinheim: Psychologie Verlags Union, 1987.

Schneewind, K. A. Das familiendiagnostische Testsystem (FDTS): Ein fragebogeninventar zur erfassung familiärer beziehungsaspekte auf unterschiedlichen systemebenen (The family-diagnostic test-system (FDTS): An inventory for assessing familial relationships on different systems levels). In M. Cierpka (Ed.), *Familiendiagnostik (Family Diagnosis)*. Heidelberg: Springer, 1987.

Schneewind, K. A. Die familienklimaskalen (The family climate scales). In M. Cierpka (Ed.), *Familiendiagnostik (Family Diagnosis)*. Heidelberg: Springer, 1987.

Schneewind, K. A. Contextual approaches to family systems research: the macro-micro puzzle. In K. Keppner & R. M. Lerner (Eds.), *Family systems and life span development*. Hillsdale: Erlbaum, in press.

Schneewind, K. A., Beckmann, M., & Hecht-Jackl, A. 1985 Familiendiagnostisches Testsystem (FDTS) (Family Diagnostic Test System (FDTS)"). Berichte 1/1985 bis 9.2 1985. Forschungsberichte aus dem Institutsbereich Persönlichkeitspsychologie und Psychodiagnostik (Reports 1/1985 to 9.2/1985. Research reports from the Department of Personality Psychology and Psychodiagnostics). München.

Seitz, W., and Rausche, A. 1976 Persönlichkeitsfragebogen für Kinder (PFK 9-14) [Personality Questionnaire for Children (PQC 9-14)]. Braunschweig: Westermann.

Sherman, R., and Fredman, N. 1986 Handbook of Structured Techniques in Marriage and Family Therapy. New York: Brunner/Mazel.

Steinglass, P. A systems view of family interaction and psychopathology. In T. Jacob (Ed.), *Family interaction and psychopathology: Theories, methods, and findings*. New York: Plenum, 1987.

Thomas, D. L., & Wilcox, J. E. The rise of family theory: A historical and critical analysis. In M. B. Sussman & S. Steinmetz (Eds.), *Handbook of marriage and the family*. New York: Plenum, 1987.

Author Index

Subject Index